Literary Studies and Human Flourishing

THE HUMANITIES AND HUMAN FLOURISHING

Series editor: James O. Pawelski, *University of Pennsylvania*

Other volumes in the series

Philosophy and Human Flourishing
Edited by John J. Stuhr

History and Human Flourishing
Edited by Darrin M. McMahon

Literary Studies and Human Flourishing
Edited by James F. English and Heather Love

Religious Studies, Theology, and Human Flourishing
Edited by Justin Thomas McDaniel and Hector Kilgoe

Theater and Human Flourishing
Edited by Harvey Young

Cinema, Media, and Human Flourishing
Edited by Timothy Corrigan

Music and Human Flourishing
Edited by Anna Harwell Celenza

Visual Arts and Human Flourishing
Edited by Selma Holo

The Humanities and Human Flourishing
Edited by James O. Pawelski

Literary Studies and Human Flourishing

Edited by

JAMES F. ENGLISH AND HEATHER LOVE

OXFORD
UNIVERSITY PRESS

OXFORD
UNIVERSITY PRESS

Oxford University Press is a department of the University of Oxford. It furthers
the University's objective of excellence in research, scholarship, and education
by publishing worldwide. Oxford is a registered trade mark of Oxford University
Press in the UK and certain other countries.

Published in the United States of America by Oxford University Press
198 Madison Avenue, New York, NY 10016, United States of America.

Library of Congress Cataloging-in-Publication Data
Names: English, James F., 1958– editor. | Love, Heather, editor.
Title: Literary studies and human flourishing /
[edited by] James F. English and Heather Love.
Description: New York, NY : Oxford University Press, [2023] |
Series: The humanities and human flourishing |
Includes bibliographical references and index.
Identifiers: LCCN 2022029587 (print) | LCCN 2022029588 (ebook) |
ISBN 9780197637234 (paperback) | ISBN 9780197637227 (hardback) |
ISBN 9780197637258 (epub)
Subjects: LCSH: Literature—Philosophy. | Conduct of life. | Happiness. |
Well-being. | Positive psychology.
Classification: LCC PN45 .L4896 2023 (print) | LCC PN45 (ebook) |
DDC 801/.3—dc23/eng/20220822
LC record available at https://lccn.loc.gov/2022029587
LC ebook record available at https://lccn.loc.gov/2022029588

DOI: 10.1093/oso/9780197637227.001.0001

Contents

List of Illustrations   vii

Series Editor's Foreword   ix

List of Contributors   xxv

Introduction: Literary Studies and Human Flourishing   1
James F. English and Heather Love

PART I: HAPPY READING: LITERATURE WITHOUT THE ACADEMY

1. Bibliotherapy and Human Flourishing   25
Leah Price

2. Bad Habits on Goodreads? Eclecticism vs. Genre-Intolerance among Online Readers   35
James F. English, Scott Enderle, and Rahul Dhakecha

PART II: FLOURISHING BEYOND REASON: LITERATURE'S AUGMENTED REALITIES

3. Flourishing Spirits   65
Christopher Castiglia

4. Sage Writing: Facing Reality in Literature   80
David Russell

PART III: FLOURISHING IN CRISIS: THE POETICS OF DISASTER

5. Literature of Uplift   99
David James

6. Black Ecological Optimism and the Problem of Human Flourishing   123
Sonya Posmentier

PART IV: NON-NORMATIVE FLOURISHING: DISABILITY AND AGING

7. Literary Study, the Hermeneutics of Disability, and
the Eudaimonic Turn   143
Janet Lyon

8. Wise Old Fools: Positive Geropsychology and
the Poetics of Later-Life Floundering   164
Scott Herring

PART V: POSITIVE AFFECT: REDESCRIPTION AND REPAIR

9. Therapeutic Redescription   185
Beth Blum

10. Merely Ameliorative: Reading, Critical Affect, and
the Project of Repair   207
Heather Love

Index   219

List of Illustrations

2.1 Analysis of a corpus containing all the 4- and 5-star Goodreads reviews of 500 top-10 annual bestsellers and 1,300 prize-listed novels published between 1960 and 2016.   41

2.2 The Linguistic Inquiry and Word Count 2015 tool (LIWC).   43

2.3 Most distinguishing words in reviews of bestsellers (left) and prize-listed novels (right).   44

2.4 Most distinguishing words for reviews of bestsellers (left) and prize-listed novels (right), 4- or 5-star reviews only.   45

2.5 Taste profiles by genre of 1,672 highly active Goodreads fiction readers.   51

2.6 Distribution by genre of books reviewed by readers primarily of romance and science fiction.   54

2.7 Taste profiles of 1,672 readers with slide bar from Genre map to Reader Network map at 96 percent.   55

2.8 Two readers who favor historical fiction.   56

2.9 Reading by the numbers: stats tracking on Goodreads.   58

8.1 Christopher Peterson, "Table 2.2. Classification of Psychological Disorders."   169

9.1 From Joseph V. Ciarrochi and Ann Bailey, *A CBT Practitioner's Guide to ACT* .   190

Series Editor's Foreword

Imagine being invited to a weekend meeting to discuss connections between the humanities and human flourishing. You talk about ways in which the humanities can help us understand what human flourishing is—and is not. You explore how the humanities can help increase human flourishing. And you consider whether human flourishing is an absolute good, or whether it comes with certain limits and even potential dangers. How do you imagine the conversation playing out? What contributions might you make to the discussion?

The volumes in this series were borne out of just such a meeting. Or rather a series of such meetings, each gathering including some dozen scholars in a particular discipline in the humanities (understood to be inclusive of the arts). These disciplines include philosophy, history, literary studies, religious studies and theology, theater, cinema and media, music, and the visual arts. Participants were asked to consider how their work in their discipline intersects with well-being (taken to be roughly synonymous with human flourishing), along with a series of specific questions:

- How does your discipline conceptualize, understand, and define well-being?
- What does your discipline say about the cultivation of well-being? How does it encourage the implementation of well-being?
- In what ways does your discipline support flourishing? Do some approaches within your discipline advance human flourishing more effectively than others? Are there ways in which certain aspects of your discipline could more effectively promote well-being?
- Does your discipline contribute to well-being in any unique ways in which other endeavors do not?
- Are there ways in which your discipline can obstruct human flourishing?

As might be expected, the conversations in these meetings were rich and wide-ranging. Some of them headed in expected directions; others were more surprising. Each of them yielded opportunities to question assumptions and deepen perspectives. The conversations were rooted in disciplinary contexts and questions but yielded many generalizable insights on how to conceptualize human flourishing more clearly, how to cultivate it more effectively, and how to avoid negative consequences of understanding it in incomplete or overblown ways. I cannot properly describe or even summarize the richness of the discussions here, but I would like to point out a few of the highlights included in each of the resulting volumes.

Philosophy and Human Flourishing, edited by John J. Stuhr, addresses a number of fundamental questions. What is the value of discussing human flourishing in a world that in so many ways is decidedly not flourishing? In what ways is flourishing similar to and different from happiness? What is the role of morality in human flourishing? How does it relate to systemic privilege and oppression? To what degree is flourishing properly the concern of individuals, and to what degree is it a function of communities and societies? What are key factors in the fostering of flourishing? In addressing these questions, philosophers explore concepts such as mattering, homeostasis, pluralism, responsibility, and values, and consider the roles of individuals, educational institutions, and governments.

History and Human Flourishing, edited by Darrin M. McMahon, centers on the question, What is the value of history for life? This core question leads to a number of further inquiries. Is history only about the past, or does it have important implications for the present and the future? If the latter, then how can historical inquiry most effectively contribute to well-being? Does such inquiry currently focus in an imbalanced way on ill-being—on prejudices, class struggles, and wars? Such work is doubtless of great importance, not least by investigating how claims about happiness can serve as propaganda for continued oppression. But would hope for the future be more effectively kindled and concrete steps toward its realization more adeptly guided by increased attention to what has actually gone well in the past and what we can learn from it, or by more focus on how human beings have responded positively to adversity?

Literary Studies and Human Flourishing, edited by James F. English and Heather Love, focuses on the transformative power of literature. Scholars examine a range of topics, including the reparative possibilities of a literary encounter, the value of bibliotherapy and of therapeutic redescription, the genre of "uplit," and evolving methods for studying the activities and experiences of actual readers. A central question of this volume concerns the limits on transformations effected through literature. Several contributors worry that harnessing literary studies to the enterprise of human flourishing might lead readers merely to conform rather than to transform. To what extent might human flourishing serve as a palliative, enabling and encouraging readers to adapt to individual lives that lack moral depth and to social conditions that are rife with injustice, and thus obstruct the difficult and unsettling work of disruptive transformation needed for lasting individual and collective betterment?

Religious Studies, Theology, and Human Flourishing, edited by Justin Thomas McDaniel and Hector Kilgoe, explores ways in which individual and collective well-being can be increased through various religious perspectives and practices, including the Hindu concept of *sanmati* ("goodwill, wisdom, and noble-mindedness"), Buddhist meditation, and the cultivation of spiritual joy even while facing adversity. Scholars consider challenging questions concerning the proper contexts for learning *about* religion and for learning *from* religion, the right balance between the acknowledgment of suffering and the fostering of well-being, and the relationship between human flourishing and nonhuman worlds (including both natural and supernatural domains). A concern of some of these scholars is whether human flourishing entails a false universalism, one that seeks to reduce cultural diversities to one particular notion of what is desirable or even acceptable, and whether such a notion could be used to rate the value of different religions, or even ban religious practices (e.g., fasting, celibacy, or other ascetic austerities) that might be deemed misaligned with well-being.

Theater and Human Flourishing, edited by Harvey Young, considers the unique resources of theater and performance for imagining and enhancing well-being. Because theater involves both performers and audience members, it is inherently communal in ways many humanities disciplines and art forms are not. Theater allows groups of people—often strangers—to come together and experience the world in new ways. More than just an escape from ordinary life or a simple mirroring of reality, theater can provide opportunities for communal reimagining of the world, exploring new ways of thinking, feeling, and relating that can be experienced and then enacted to bring about a more flourishing future. Scholars examine connections between theater and human flourishing in more and less traditional spheres, looking at ways performance practices can be used to critique inadequate notions of human flourishing and to increase well-being in a wide variety of contexts, ranging from community theater to organizations serving soldiers with post-traumatic stress disorder (PTSD), and from oppressed groups to politically divided societies.

Cinema, Media, and Human Flourishing, edited by Timothy Corrigan, looks to film and a whole range of contemporary forms of digital media for what they can teach us about the nature of human flourishing and how it can be cultivated. These forms of communication have vast audiences and thus great power to support or subvert well-being. Contributors to this volume observe that human flourishing often seems to come piecemeal and as a hard-won result of conflict and struggle, and they explore ways in which well-being can be supported by collaborative practices for creating content, by the particular ways narratives are crafted, by certain genres, and by the various values that are embraced and transmitted. Contributors also consider how these popular forms can support individuals and groups on the margins of society by making more visible and sympathetic their struggles toward flourishing.

Music and Human Flourishing, edited by Anna Harwell Celenza, complements the commonly accepted and scientifically supported view that participating in music—as a listener, performer, or composer—can increase individual well-being. Instead of focusing on music as a performing art, this volume examines music as a humanities discipline, emphasizing the importance and value of music scholarship for fostering individual and collective human flourishing. How can music scholars (musicologists, ethnomusicologists, and music theorists) strengthen the effects of music on flourishing through a consideration of broader cultural, social, and political contexts? Contributors explore how processes of contemplation, critique, and communication within music scholarship can deepen the experience of music, resulting not just in the enhancement of individual well-being but in the more effective cultivation of wisdom and the greater realization of social justice.

Visual Arts and Human Flourishing, edited by Selma Holo, begins with the experience of artists themselves and the function of art in our society. If well-being is thought of as the happiness of self-satisfied complacency, then it would seem to be the antithesis of art, which is often disruptive, unnerving, and unsettling, asking viewers to question their assumptions and inviting them to see the world in new ways. But if well-being is understood more deeply as the flourishing that can arise from the full range of human experience, including the discomfort of contending forms of meaning and contested visions of reality, then it is difficult to think of it without art. Contributors to this volume consider the overwhelming personal necessity artists have to create, the role of well-being in art history, the increasing emphasis on human flourishing in architecture and public art, and salient questions of ethics, accessibility, and social justice in the context of art museums.

The Humanities and Human Flourishing, for which I serve as editor, is an interdisciplinary, capstone volume that contains contributions from the editors of the eight disciplinary volumes. After the disciplinary meetings were concluded, we gathered together to discuss what we had learned through the process. We considered both similarities and differences across the disciplinary discussions on human flourishing, identifying social justice and pedagogy as two common themes that emerged in the meetings. Like the other volumes in the series, this volume does not pretend to provide simple solutions or even unified answers to questions of how the humanities are or should be connected to the conceptualization and cultivation of human flourishing. Rather, it provides thoughtful questions and perspectives, distilled as it is from a deliberate process of extended engagement from diverse groups of scholars across eight different arts and humanities disciplines.

I would like to welcome you, the reader, to this book series. I hope you find it stimulating and even inspiring in its explorations into the complexities of the relationship between the humanities and human flourishing. And I hope you read across the volumes, as they are written in an accessible style that will yield valuable insights whether or not you have particular expertise in the discipline of the author whose work you are reading. To whatever degree you immerse yourself in this book series, though, I am sure of one thing: You will find it incomplete. As deep and as broad ranging as we tried to be in our explorations, none of the participants are under the illusion that the discussions and volumes brought it to a conclusion. We are keenly aware that a group of a dozen scholars, no matter how diverse, cannot speak for an entire discipline, and we realize that a focus on eight disciplines does not cover the entire domain of the humanities. Furthermore, our discussions and most of the writing were completed before the COVID-19 pandemic, which has made the nature and importance of flourishing all the more salient and has raised a host of new questions about well-being. Instead, we think of our work as an important beginning, and we would like to invite you to join the conversation. We hope a greater number and diversity of scholars, researchers, creators, practitioners, students, leaders in cultural organizations and creative industries, office holders in government, philanthropists, and members of the general public will bring their interests and expertise to the conversation, perhaps leading to new volumes in this series in the future. Investigations into human flourishing contribute to our knowledge and understanding of the human condition, and they have practical implications for the well-being of scholars, students, and societies. We hope our ongoing work together will enable the humanities to play a greater role in these investigations, effecting changes in scholarship, research, pedagogy, policy, and practice that will make them more supportive of human flourishing in academia and in the world at large.

Background and Rationale

For readers interested in more information on the background and rationale of this book series, I am happy to share further details on the perspectives, aims, and hopes that motivated it. A key catalyst for the development of this series was the dual observation that a growing number of individuals and organizations are focusing on human flourishing and that most of the headlines in this domain seem to be coming from the social sciences. Yale psychology professor Laurie Santos, for example, made the news when she developed a course on "Psychology and the Good Life"—and some 1200 students (nearly a quarter of Yale's undergraduate population) signed up for it.[1] As of this writing, her subsequent podcast, "The Happiness Lab," has reached 65 million downloads.[2] On an international scale, dozens of countries around the world have adopted psychological measures of subjective well-being as a complement to economic indicators, and a growing number of nations have embraced well-being, happiness, or flourishing as an explicit governmental goal.[3] The Organization for Economic Co-operation and Development (OECD), founded in 1961 to stimulate economic progress and world trade, has acknowledged the insufficiency of economic indicators

---

[1] David Shimer, "Yale's Most Popular Class Ever: Happiness." *The New York Times*, January 26, 2018. https://www.nytimes.com/2018/01/26/nyregion/at-yale-class-on-happiness-draws-huge-crowd-laurie-santos.html

[2] Lucy Hodgman, and Evan Gorelick, "Silliman Head of College Laurie Santos to Take One-Year Leave to Address Burnout." *Yale News*, February 8, 2022. https://yaledailynews.com/blog/2022/02/08/silliman-head-of-college-laurie-santos-to-take-one-year-leave-to-address-burnout/

[3] https://weall.org/; https://www.ons.gov.uk/peoplepopulationandcommunity/wellbeing/articles/measuresofnationalwellbeingdashboard/2018-04-25; https://www.gnhcentrebhutan.org/history-of-gnh/; https://www.worldbank.org/en/news/feature/2013/10/24/Bolivia-quiere-replicar-el-indice-de-felicidad-de-Butan; https://u.ae/en/about-the-uae/the-uae-government/government-of-future/happiness/;

alone for tracking progress. It launched its Better Life Initiative in 2011 to measure what drives the well-being of individuals and nations and to determine how countries can best support greater progress for all.[4] The United Nations publishes the World Happiness Report every year, releasing it on March 20, the UN International Day of Happiness.[5]

These are examples in the social sciences of what I have elsewhere called a "eudaimonic turn," an explicit commitment to human flourishing as a core theoretical and research interest and a desired practical outcome.[6] Over the last several decades, there has been a growing interest in human flourishing in economics, political science, psychology, and sociology, and in fields influenced by them, such as education, organizational studies, medicine, and public health. Perhaps the most well-known example of this eudaimonic turn in the social sciences occurred in psychology with the advent of positive psychology. Reflecting perspectives developed in humanistic psychology in the mid-twentieth century and building on increasing empirical work in self-efficacy, self-determination theory, subjective and psychological well-being, optimism, flow, passion, hope theory, positive emotions, and related areas, Martin Seligman and his colleagues launched the field of positive psychology. During a 1998 presidential address to the American Psychological Association, Seligman pointed out that mainstream psychology had become fixated on understanding and treating psychopathology. He argued that, although extremely important, healing mental illness is only part of psychology's mission. More broadly, he claimed, psychology should be about making the lives of all people better. He noted that this requires the careful empirical study of what makes life most worth living, including a deep understanding of flourishing individuals and thriving communities. Such study, he believed, would both increase well-being and decrease ill-being, since human strengths are both important in their own right and effective as buffers against mental illness. Known as "the scientific study of what enables individuals and societies to thrive,"[7] positive psychology has had a

---

[4] https://www.oecd.org/sdd/OECD-Better-Life-Initiative.pdf
[5] https://worldhappiness.report/
[6] James O. Pawelski, "What Is the Eudaimonic Turn?," in *The Eudaimonic Turn: Well-Being in Literary Studies*, ed. James O. Pawelski and D. J. Moores (Madison, NJ: Fairleigh Dickinson University Press, 2013), 3; and James O. Pawelski, "The Positive Humanities: Culture and Human Flourishing," in *The Oxford Handbook of the Positive Humanities*, ed. Louis Tay and James O. Pawelski (New York: Oxford University Press, 2022), 26.
[7] Constitution of the International Positive Psychology Association, Article 1, Section 2.

transformative effect on psychology and has deeply influenced many other fields of research and practice.

What role do the humanities play in all of this? What role could and should they play? How can the humanities help us conceptualize human flourishing more deeply, cultivate it more effectively, and critique it more insightfully? As a philosopher working in the field of positive psychology for more than twenty years, I have been concerned that there are not more voices from the humanities centrally involved in contemporary work in human flourishing. One of the core aims of this project and book series is to make a way for humanities scholars to play a larger role in this domain by inviting them to consider explicitly what contributions their work and their disciplines can make to the theory, research, and practice of human flourishing.

Historically, of course, human flourishing is at the root of the humanities.[8] The humanities were first defined and developed as a program of study by Renaissance scholars dissatisfied with scholasticism, which they perceived as leading to an overly technical university curriculum removed from the concerns of everyday life and unable to guide students toward human flourishing. They advocated, instead, a return to the Greek and Roman classics, reading them for insights and perspectives on how to live life well. Indeed, the Greeks and Romans had developed comprehensive programs of study (*paideia* and *artes liberales*, respectively) designed to teach students how to flourish individually and how to contribute to collective flourishing by participating effectively and wisely in civic life.

This emphasis on the understanding and cultivation of human flourishing that was so important to the Greeks and Romans was also of central concern to other philosophical and religious traditions that developed in the ancient world during what Karl Jaspers called the Axial Age.[9] Hinduism, Buddhism, Confucianism, Daoism, and Judaism, for example, along with the later Christianity and Islam, addressed the problem of human suffering and offered ways of promoting individual and collective flourishing. Although different in their cultural context and specific details, each of these traditions counseled against lives exclusively devoted to pleasure, wealth, power, or fame. They held that such lives only magnify suffering and that flourishing is actually fostered through a cultivation of virtue that allows

---

[8] Pawelski, "The Positive Humanities," 20–21; and Darrin M. McMahon, "The History of the Humanities and Human Flourishing," in *The Oxford Handbook of the Positive Humanities*, ed. Louis Tay and James O. Pawelski (New York: Oxford University Press, 2022), 45–50.

[9] Karl Jaspers, *The Origin and Goal of History* (Abingdon, UK: Routledge, 2011), 2.

for the transcendence of narrow, individual concerns in favor of a connection with the larger social world, the broader universe, or even the divine. Cultural forms such as literature, music, visual art, architecture, theater, history, and philosophical reflection were employed in the cultivation of virtue and the establishment of the broader and deeper connections valued for human flourishing.

Today, the humanities tend to be thought of less as a comprehensive program of study or means to cultivate virtue and more as a collection of academic disciplines. These disciplines are located largely within colleges and universities and are thus shaped by the values of these institutions. Much of higher education is driven more by the aim of creating knowledge than the goal of applying wisdom. To succeed in such an environment, scholars are required to become highly specialized professionals, spending most of their time publishing books and articles for other highly specialized professionals in their discipline. The courses they teach often focus more on the flourishing of their discipline than on the flourishing of their students, requiring students to learn *about* course content but not necessarily to learn *from* it. When human flourishing is addressed in the classroom, it is all too often done in a way that makes it difficult for students to apply it to their lives, and in many cases, it focuses more on obstacles to flourishing than on the nature and cultivation of well-being. It is important, of course, to understand and resist alienation, injustice, and malfeasance in the world and to expose corrosive ideologies that can permeate texts and other forms of culture. But it is also important to understand that flourishing is more than just the absence of languishing. And the argument has been made that "suspicious" approaches in the humanities need to be balanced by reparative approaches[10] and that critique needs to be complemented by a "positive aesthetics"[11] and a "hermeneutics of affirmation."[12] Meanwhile, students in the United States, at least, are reporting astonishingly high levels of anxiety, depression, and suicidality,[13] while at the same time coming under increasing economic

[10] Eve K. Sedgwick, "Paranoid Reading and Reparative Reading: Or, You're So Paranoid, You Probably Think This Introduction Is About You," in *Novel Gazing: Queer Readings in Fiction*, ed. Eve K. Sedgwick (Durham, NC: Duke University Press, 1997), 1–37.

[11] Rita Felski, *Uses of Literature* (Malden, MA: Blackwell, 2008), 22.

[12] D. J. Moores, "*The Eudaimonic Turn in Literary Studies*," in The Eudaimonic Turn: Well-Being in Literary Studies, ed. James O. Pawelski and D. J. Moores (Madison, NJ: Fairleigh Dickinson University Press, 2013), 27.

[13] Publications and Reports, National College Health Assessment, American College Health Association, accessed December 11, 2021, https://www.acha.org/NCHA/ACHA-NCHA_Data/Publications_and_Reports/NCHA/Data/Publications_and_Reports.aspx?hkey=d5fb767c-d15d-4efc-8c41-3546d92032c5

pressure to select courses of study that will directly help them find employment. Students who in the past might have followed their interests in the humanities are now more likely to major in STEM fields or to enroll in preprofessional tracks. Consequently, the number of students earning bachelor's degrees in the humanities is decreasing significantly.[14]

Would a eudaimonic turn in the humanities be helpful in addressing these obstacles of narrow professionalism, imbalanced focus, and student pressure? Would it help with what Louis Menand has called a "crisis of rationale" in the humanities, with scholars unable to agree on the fundamental nature and purpose of the humanities and thus unable to communicate their value clearly to students, parents, philanthropists, policymakers, and the general public?[15]Could the eudaimonic turn provide a unifying rationale in the humanities? Of course, there is a sense in which such a turn would actually be a eudaimonic *return*. This return would not be a nostalgic attempt to recover some imagined glorious past. The human flourishing historically supported by the humanities was significant, as mentioned above, but it was also very far from perfect, often embracing perspectives that supported unjust power structures that excluded many people—including laborers, women, and enslaved persons—from participating in flourishing and that enabled the exploitation of these individuals to the advantage of those in power. Tragically, our society suffers from some of these same injustices today. Instead of a glorification of a problematic past, which could well reinforce these injustices, a eudaimonic re/turn would invite us to focus our attention on perennial questions about human flourishing, building on wisdom from the past, but committing ourselves to a search for more inclusive answers that are fitting for our contemporary world.[16]

Not surprisingly, there is disagreement among scholars in these volumes, with some contributors endorsing the eudaimonic turn in the humanities and working to advance it and others putting forward a variety of concerns about the limitations and potential dangers of such an approach—and some even doing both. Scholars supporting a eudaimonic turn believe it could

---

[14] Jill Barshay, "PROOF POINTS: The Number of College Graduates in the Humanities Drops for the Eighth Consecutive Year," *The Hechinger Report*, November 22, 2021, https://hechingerreport.org/proof-points-the-number-of-college-graduates-in-the-humanities-drops-for-the-eighth-consecutive-year.

[15] Louis Menand, "The Marketplace of Ideas," American Council of Learned Societies Occasional Paper No. 49 (2001) http://archives.acls.org/op/49_Marketplace_of_Ideas.htm.

[16] Pawelski, "What Is the Eudaimonic Turn?" 17; Pawelski, "The Positive Humanities," 26; and McMahon, "The History of the Humanities and Human Flourishing," 45, 54.

revitalize the humanities by encouraging deeper investigations into the eudaimonic hopes that initially gave rise to their disciplines and the various ways in which contemporary work can support and develop these hopes. They believe these investigations could bring together scholars across the various humanities disciplines to create a common understanding and language for an examination of questions of human flourishing appropriate for our times. To be successful, such a project would not require complete agreement among scholars on the answers to these questions. On the contrary, diverse perspectives would enrich the inquiry, opening up new possibilities for human flourishing that are more equitable and widespread and that support the flourishing of the nonhuman world as well. Some contributors see significant potential in collaborating with the social sciences in their eudaimonic turn, a process that can be facilitated through the Positive Humanities, a new, interdisciplinary field of inquiry and practice focused on the relationship between culture and human flourishing.[17]

Scholars endorsing a eudaimonic turn in the humanities believe it could also inform, inspire, and support the work of museums, libraries, performing arts centers, and even creative industries (in music, movies, publishing, and other domains) to advance human flourishing more broadly in our society. They see a eudaimonic turn as also being of potential value to the millions of students who study the humanities each year. Without expecting humanities teachers and professors to take on therapeutic roles, they see considerable possible benefits in a pedagogical focus on how human flourishing can be understood and cultivated, with resulting courses intentionally designed to promote and preserve students' well-being and mitigate and prevent their ill-being.[18] Indeed, these scholars believe the volumes in this series might serve as useful texts for some of these courses.

Scholars with misgivings about a eudaimonic turn, on the other hand, raise a number of important concerns. Some contributors wonder whether human flourishing is a proper ideal in a world with so much suffering. Would such an ideal raise false hopes that would actually contribute to that suffering? Furthermore, are there more valuable things than human flourishing

---

[17] For more information on the Positive Humanities, see Louis Tay and James O. Pawelski, eds., *The Oxford Handbook of the Positive Humanities* (New York: Oxford University Press, 2022), especially the first three foundational chapters. Also, visit www.humanitiesandhumanflourishing.org.

[18] Furthermore, would students who perceive real life value in humanities courses be more likely to make room for them in their schedules, as suggested by the students who enrolled in Laurie Santos's course on "Psychology and the Good Life" in such large numbers? If so, could a side benefit of the eudaimonic turn be greater numbers of students signing up for courses in the humanities?

(e.g., ethics, the environment), and should flourishing be limited in favor of these greater goods? Is human flourishing inextricably linked to problematic ideological perspectives, perhaps ones that place too much emphasis on the individual and downplay or ignore issues of systemic injustice, or perhaps ones that serve the interests of a small number of persons in power and encourage everyone else to conform to the status quo? Is human flourishing a false universalism that might result in a failure to see and acknowledge deep cultural differences—or worse, that might see these differences as deviances that need to be suppressed and punished? Could an emphasis on well-being be employed to exploit individuals or groups of people, as notions of happiness have sometimes been used in the past? Are there other unexpected harms that might arise from a eudaimonic turn?

The unresolved tensions among the various chapters are part of what makes these volumes compelling reading. Are there ways to overcome concerns about the eudaimonic turn by clarifying its nature and aims, avoiding the dangers raised? Or will these concerns always persist alongside efforts to achieve individual and communal betterment through a theoretical and practical emphasis on flourishing? I welcome you, the reader, to join this discussion. What are your views on the perspectives expressed in these volumes? What points might you contribute to the ongoing conversation?

Process and People

I would like to conclude with a fuller account of the process by which the various volumes were created and an acknowledgment of the individuals and institutions who have made this book series possible. With the desire to give contributors ample time to reflect on how their work and their discipline relate to human flourishing, as well as to create opportunities to discuss these ideas with colleagues, we put into place an extended process for the creation of these volumes. After deciding on the eight disciplines in the arts and humanities we would be able to include in the project, we invited a leading scholar to chair the work in each of these disciplines and asked them to bring together a diverse group of some dozen noted scholars in their discipline.[19] For each group, we provided participants with some background

---

[19] For a full list of project participants, visit www.humanitiesandhumanflourishing.org.

reading[20] and asked them to prepare a draft essay on how their scholarly work informs the conceptualization and cultivation of human flourishing. Many participants chose to address the background reading—appreciatively, critically, or both—in their papers, although none were required to address it at all. We then circulated these drafts to the entire group in preparation for a three-day, face-to-face meeting, during which the disciplinary chair led a discussion and workshopping of the drafts. These disciplinary consultations, held in 2018 and 2019, were also joined by a junior scholar (usually a graduate student) in the field, one or two social scientists with work on relevant topics, and the Core Team.

Following these meetings, participants were asked to revise their drafts in light of our discussion, with the chairs serving as editors for the resulting disciplinary volumes. Given the nature of the project, I also read each of the contributions, providing comments along the way. From beginning to end, the process for creating and editing each of the volume manuscripts took well over a year and allowed for deep engagement with the subject matter and with other scholars. The disciplinary chairs and I were careful to emphasize that these discussions were intended to be robust and the writing authentic, with no foregone conclusions about the nature of human flourishing or the value of exploring it, and we were pleased by the range and depth of thinking undertaken by each group.

As mentioned above, after we held the eight disciplinary consultations, we held a ninth meeting where we invited the chairs of each of the disciplinary groups to present and discuss drafts of essays for a ninth, interdisciplinary volume sharing what they and their colleagues had learned through the process. We also invited a few humanities policy leaders, including past National Endowment for the Humanities Chairman William Adams, to join us and help think about the broader implications of this work.

---

[20] Martin E. P. Seligman and Mihaly Csikszentmihalyi, "Positive Psychology: An Introduction," *American Psychologist* 55 (1) (2000): 5–14; Darrin M. McMahon, "From the Paleolithic to the Present: Three Revolutions in the Global History of Happiness," in *e-Handbook of Subjective Well-being*, ed. Ed Diener, Shigehiro Oishi, and Louis Tay (Champaign, IL: DEF Publishers, 2018); James O. Pawelski, "Defining the 'Positive' in Positive Psychology: Part I. A Descriptive Analysis," *The Journal of Positive Psychology* 11 (4) (2016): 339–356; James O. Pawelski, "Defining the 'Positive' in Positive Psychology: Part II. A Normative Analysis," The Journal of Positive Psychology 11 (4) (2016): 357–365; James O. Pawelski, "Bringing Together the Humanities and the Science of Well-Being to Advance Human Flourishing," in *Well-Being and Higher Education: A Strategy for Change and the Realization of Education's Greater Purposes*, ed. Donald W. Harward (Washington, D.C.: Bringing Theory to Practice, 207–216); and Louis Tay, James O. Pawelski, and Melissa G. Keith, "The Role of the Arts and Humanities in Human Flourishing: A Conceptual Model," *The Journal of Positive Psychology* 13 (3) (2018): 215–225.

The compiling of the volumes was organized and overseen by the Humanities and Human Flourishing (HHF) Project at the University of Pennsylvania. HHF was founded in 2014 to support the interdisciplinary investigation and advancement of the relationship between the humanities and human flourishing. As the founding director of HHF, I am pleased that it has developed into a growing international and multidisciplinary network of more than 150 humanities scholars, scientific researchers, creative practitioners, college and university educators, wellness officers, policy experts, members of government, and leaders of cultural organizations. In addition to the disciplinary consultations described above and the resulting book series, we have published a number of conceptual papers and systematic reviews, developed conceptual models to guide empirical research, and created and validated a toolkit of measures. Designated a National Endowment for the Arts Research Lab, HHF has developed ongoing programs of research (including on art museums and human flourishing and on narrative technologies and well-being) to understand, assess, and advance the effects of engagement in the arts and humanities on human flourishing. We have published *The Oxford Handbook of the Positive Humanities* to help establish the Positive Humanities as a robust field of inquiry and practice at the intersection of culture, science, and human flourishing. For more information on HHF, including each of these endeavors as well as its current undertakings, please visit www.humanitiesandhumanflourishing.org.

I am deeply grateful to all the individuals and institutions whose collaboration has made this book series possible. I would like to begin by thanking Chris Stewart and Templeton Religion Trust for the generous grants that have underwritten this work. Thanks also go to the University of Pennsylvania for their robust institutional and financial support. (Of course, the views expressed in these volumes are those of the authors and do not necessarily reflect the views of Templeton Religion Trust or of the University of Pennsylvania.) I am grateful to the more than 80 contributors to these volumes for accepting our invitation to be a part of this work and bringing more depth and richness to it than I could have imagined. I am especially grateful to the chairs of each of the disciplinary groups for their belief in the importance of this work and their long-term dedication to making it a success. I also wish to express my appreciation for the hard work of the entire HHF Core Team, including Research Director Louis Tay, postdoctoral fellows Yerin Shim and Hoda Vaziri, Research Manager Michaela Ward, and especially Assistant Director Sarah Sidoti, who meticulously planned and oversaw each of the disciplinary consultations and used her expertise in academic publishing to help shape this book series in countless crucial ways. Most of the disciplinary consultations took place on the beautiful grounds of the Shawnee Inn & Golf Resort along the banks of the Delaware River. I am grateful to Charlie and Ginny Kirkwood, John Kirkwood, and all the folks at Shawnee for their gracious support and hospitality. Additionally, I am grateful to Jonathan Coopersmith and the Curtis Institute for donating space for the music group to meet, and to Bill Perthes and the Barnes Foundation for similarly donating space for the visual arts group. Thanks to the Penn Museum for a beautiful setting for the first day of our Chairs consultation and to Marty Seligman and Peter Schulman for donating further space at the Positive Psychology Center. Finally, I am grateful to Peter Ohlin and all the staff and reviewers at Oxford University Press for their partnership in publishing the volumes in this book series. I hope these volumes inspire further conversation, welcoming more people from a larger number of disciplines and a greater range of nationalities and cultural and ethnic backgrounds to inquire into what human flourishing is, how its potential harms can be avoided, and how its benefits can be more deeply experienced and more broadly extended.

James O. Pawelski
February 19, 2022

List of Contributors

Beth Blum is the Harris K. Weston Associate Professor of Humanities at Harvard University. She teaches works from all periods with an emphasis on modernist and contemporary literature. Her monograph *The Self-Help Compulsion: Searching for Advice in Modern Literature* was published in 2020. Other writing has appeared in *PMLA, Modern Language Quarterly, Modernism/modernity, The NewYorker.com, The Chronicle of Higher Education*, and *Aeon Magazine*.

Christopher Castiglia is Distinguished Professor of English at the Pennsylvania State University. He is the author of *Bound and Determined: Captivity, Culture-Crossing, and White Womanhood from Mary Rowlandson to Patty Hearst, Interior States: Institutional Consciousness and the Inner Life of Democracy in the Antebellum United States, The Practices of Hope: Literary Criticism in Disenchanted Times*, and, with Christopher Reed, *If Memory Serves: Gay Men, AIDS, and the Promise of the Queer Past*. He is cofounder of C19: the Society of Nineteenth-Century Americanists and founding coeditor of *J19: the Journal of Nineteenth-Century Americanists*.

Rahul Dhakecha is a professional programmer. He received a Masters degree in Computer and Information Sciences from Penn Engineering in 2018.

Scott Enderle was Digital Humanities Specialist and Lecturer in English at Penn Libraries. He earned his PhD in Penn's English department and was an assistant professor of English at Skidmore College. His research on copyright law, a portion of which appeared in *PMLA*, investigated the joint development of literary and legal forms that struggled to theorize the communication of ideas in the context of the market-driven literary sphere of eighteenth-century Britain. His subsequent work focused on creating and analyzing textual datasets at medium and large scales. He was an active software developer, creating new technologies for textual analysis using methods from statistics and machine learning.

James F. English is John Welsh Centennial Professor of English at the University of Pennsylvania and founding Faculty Director of the Price Lab for Digital Humanities. His main fields of research are the sociology and economics of culture; the history of literary studies as a discipline; and contemporary British fiction, film, and television. His books include *Comic Transactions: Literature, Humor, and the Politics of Community in Twentieth-Century Britain* (1994), *The Economy of Prestige: Prizes, Awards, and the Circulation of Cultural Value* (2005), and *The Global Future of English Studies* (2012). He is currently studying the history of rating and ranking systems in the arts.

Scott Herring is Professor of American Studies and Women's, Gender, and Sexuality Studies at Yale University. He has published four books, including *The Hoarders: Material Deviance in Modern American Culture* (2014) and *Aging Moderns: Art, Literature, and the Experiment of Later Life* (2022).

David James is Professor of English at the University of Birmingham, before which he was Reader in Modern and Contemporary Literature at Queen Mary, University of London. His recent books include *Modernist Futures* (2012) and *Discrepant Solace* (2019), along with edited volumes such as *The Legacies of Modernism* (2012), *The Cambridge Companion to British Fiction since 1945* (2015), and *Modernism and Close Reading* (2020). He is an Editor for British and World Anglophone Writing at *Contemporary Literature* and coedits the Columbia University Press book series Literature Now. He is currently completing *Sentimental Activism*.

Heather Love teaches English and Gender Studies at the University of Pennsylvania. She is the author of *Feeling Backward: Loss and the Politics of Queer History*, the editor of a special issue of *GLQ* on Gayle Rubin ("Rethinking Sex"), and the coeditor of a special issue of *Representations* ("Description across Disciplines"). Love has written on topics including comparative social stigma, compulsory happiness, transgender fiction, the ethics of observation, spinster aesthetics, reading methods in literary studies, and the figure of the tragic lesbian. Her most recent book, *Underdogs: Social Deviance and Queer Theory*, was published in October 2021.

Janet Lyon teaches in the English department at Penn State, where she is also a faculty affiliate of the Department of Women's, Gender, and Sexuality Studies. She founded and directs Penn State's Disability Studies minor. She coedits the *Journal of Modern Literature*. She publishes in the area of modernist studies and she teaches courses in experimental literature, critical theory, Irish literature, and disability/embodiment. She is completing a monograph, *Idiot Child on a Fire Escape: Disability and Modernism*, for the Modernist Latitudes series.

Sonya Posmentier is associate professor of English at New York University. Her first book, *Cultivation and Catastrophe: The Lyric Ecology of Modern Black Literature*, was published in 2017. This book argues that extreme environmental experiences such as hurricanes, floods, and earthquakes as well as the slower social disaster of enforced agricultural enslavement have shaped Black modern literature and culture, and in particular poetic forms. She is at work on *Black Reading*, a book about the intersecting histories of Black cultural studies and modern lyric theory. Her essays and articles have appeared in *The New York Times Book Review*, *American Literature*, *American Literary History*, *Public Books*, and elsewhere, and she has published poems in *Grey*, *The Seneca Review*, and *Perihelion*. Prof. Posmentier teaches classes on Black diasporic literature and culture and is part of the NYU Sanctuary Campus Coalition.

Leah Price's books include *What We Talk about When We Talk about Books* (2019; Christian Gauss Prize), *How to Do Things with Books in Victorian Britain* (2012;

Patten Prize, Channing Prize), and *The Anthology and the Rise of the Novel* (2000). She edited *Further Reading* (with Matthew Rubery, 2020), *Unpacking My Library*, and (with Pam Thurschwell) *Literary Secretaries/Secretarial Culture*. She writes for the *New York Times Book Review*, *London Review of Books*, *Times Literary Supplement*, *Public Books*, and *New York Review of Books*, and is a section editor for *Public Books*. She teaches at Rutgers University, where she is the founding director of the Initiative for the Book.

David Russell is Associate Professor of English at Oxford University, and a tutorial fellow of Corpus Christi College. He is the author of *Tact: Aesthetic Liberalism and the Essay Form in Nineteenth-Century Britain* (2018). He is currently writing books on John Ruskin and Marion Milner.

Introduction

Literary Studies and Human Flourishing

James F. English and Heather Love

Uneasy Relations

To an outside observer, the study of literature and the study of human flourishing might seem natural partners. What, after all, is the function of great literature if not to enhance the human endeavor and raise its potential beyond what is otherwise conceivable? As Toni Morrison said in her acceptance speech at the Nobel Prize banquet, literary artists mine the resources of language to produce "illuminations none of us has dreamed of." The moral and ethical force of those illuminations has long been recognized, installing literature as an important object of study for philosophers from Plato and Aristotle to Richard Rorty, Cornel West, and Judith Butler. The idea that literature provides imaginative access to the inner lives of others, widening our capacity for empathy and mutual understanding, has become a virtual truism. Parents take pains to instill a love of reading in their young children. Busy professionals commit to monthly book club gatherings or make New Year's resolutions to read more books and watch less television. Practically everyone believes that, one way or another, reading is good for them, and good for us all, collectively. As the academic discipline most responsible for teaching literature, defending its place in the curriculum, and producing future schoolteachers and public librarians, literary studies plays a major role in maintaining this positive view of books, reading, and literary art. And as the academic field that has emerged in recent decades to focus rigorous research on the determinants of human flourishing, the traits, habits, conditions, and attainments that "make life most worth living" (Peterson et al. 19), positive psychology has staked out literature as an important area for its scientific inquiries. What could be easier (our outside observer might think) than to

James F. English and Heather Love, *Introduction* In: *Literary Studies and Human Flourishing*. Edited by: James F. English and Heather Love, Oxford University Press. © Oxford University Press 2023.
DOI: 10.1093/oso/9780197637227.003.0001

assemble a volume of essays in which literary scholars explore their common ground with scholars of human flourishing?

To an academic insider, on the other hand, this alliance looks a whole lot harder to arrange. Of all humanities disciplines, probably none is more resistant to the program of positive psychology or more hostile to the prevailing discourse of human flourishing than literary studies. The rise of literary studies in the twentieth century, to its still unchallenged position as the largest of the humanities disciplines, depended on a foundational antagonism toward modern technocratic, business-oriented society and toward that society's undergirding by scientific, technical, and professional fields of higher education. To literary scholars of practically every stripe, those other fields appear to lack moral compass and higher seriousness of purpose; they are content to produce complacent, integrated citizens of a society that cries out for critical scrutiny and dissent. Positive psychology, a field devoted to fostering such "virtues of . . . better citizenship" as "civility," "moderation," and "work ethic" (Seligman and Csikszentmihalyi 5), can seem all too amenable to the social status quo. Especially poisonous to literary studies is the language of "improved performance and productivity" in the neoliberal workplace, which positive psychology at times willingly shares with the field of business management and which is woven through much of the literature on human flourishing.[1] From the standpoint of literary studies, positive psychology can look like little more than an academic offshoot of the late-capitalist self-help racket. Meanwhile, from the standpoint of positive psychology, literary studies can look like the academy's designated safe space for expressions of social maladjustment and congenital crankiness.

As literary scholars, then, the contributors to this volume have come together not out of any sense of natural affinity with the "positive" science of

[1] An example of the way positive psychology tends to shade over into business management literature and workplace coaching is the work of Shawn Achor, founder of GoodThink Inc. and the Institute for Applied Positive Research, and author of, among other books, *The Happiness Advantage: The Seven Principles of Positive Psychology That Fuel Success and Performance at Work*. At this point Achor is regarded as more of a happiness guru than a serious researcher of positive psychology, but he is a direct product of that field. Parts of his 2013 book *Before Happiness: The 5 Hidden Keys to Achieving Success, Spreading Happiness, and Sustaining Positive Change* are rooted in research he conducted at Yale with Alia Crum (now a professor of psychology at Stanford) and Peter Salovey (now president of Yale University) and published in a leading academic journal, the *Journal of Personality and Social Psychology*. Even in the kind of academic research that seems very distant from Achor's well-branded, profit-seeking version of positive psychology, one finds a convergence with business interests, as when in their careful empirical study of reading, fictional narrative, and empathic response, Bal and Veltkamp explain that "empathy study is important because high empathic persons are more prosocial, which is associated . . . in the workplace [with] higher performance, productivity, and creativity" (2).

well-being, but fully aware of the chasm of institutional, philosophical, and methodological differences that separates us from that field. We aim to do more, though, than simply to launch a series of blasts against the "happiness industry" (Cabanas and Illouz 2019). Our essays are attempts to reflect on how the kinds of literary research we ourselves are doing, the kinds of work to which we are personally committed, might become part of an interdisciplinary conversation about human flourishing. All of us appreciate the high stakes involved. There is a real question here of who has the authority to judge matters of literary value or to guide students toward an appreciation of the transformative potential of literary experiences and literary ways of thinking. Specialists in the science of well-being are already making claims about what literature can do for whom. Metrics of human flourishing are already being used to assess the value and determine the future funding of literary and arts festivals and of public-facing literary research projects around the world. With the further advance of positive psychology through the curricula of "positive education," this encroachment will reach our classrooms.[2] Literature departments will be expected to develop courses that may be counted toward a minor in Well-Being Studies, for example, or a certificate in Humanities and Human Flourishing. Such classes will need to meet external criteria for program approval while also aligning with our own pedagogical aims and standards of rigor and focusing on matters of genuine concern to us as literary scholars. Of course, the basis of any interdisciplinary enterprise is shared authority, pooled expertise. But the nature of the sharing in this case has yet to be worked out, and literary scholars fear that their authority is susceptible to eclipse by that of the sciences. There is understandable distrust of collaborations in which we figure merely as "domain experts" with knowledge of literary history and literary forms, while the methodological expertise, the authoritative understanding of tools and outputs, is ceded to social scientists. The contributors to this volume take different views on the limits of interdisciplinarity, but all agree there are good reasons for getting started now on this complex task of extending our discipline—its theories and methods as well as its objects—into the space of research on literature and human flourishing.

---

[2] Influential works in the field of positive education (or "happiness education") include Noddings 2003, Cohen 2006, and Seligman et al. 2009. Seligman and Adler (2019) provide a recent survey of the field's international impact. On applications of positive education philosophy at university level, see Oades et al. 2011.

A Literary History of Happiness

Our way of approaching this interdisciplinary terrain may strike some readers as sidelong and piecemeal. Happiness is one of the great themes of literature: why not simply trace its history from the ancient classics through the major works of modern times? It would not be difficult to identify a set of key texts and a suitable group of scholars for a canonical survey of that kind. We would begin with Aristotle's *Nicomachean Ethics*, the foundational text for Western discourse on human flourishing. For Aristotle, the concept of happiness, or *eudaimonia*, presents itself as a problem of moral philosophy; true happiness consists in living a full and purposeful life "in accordance with the highest virtue" (X.vii). The achievement of happiness in this eudaimonic sense—true flourishing—is not one good thing among others but the "good life" itself, the very meaning and purpose of human existence, "something final and self-sufficient, . . . the end of action" (I.vii). Hence such standard expressions as "I only want you to be happy" or "all that matters is your happiness"; we invoke the term comprehensively, as containing in itself everything truly good and important in life.

As Julia Annas showed in *The Morality of Happiness* (1993), virtually every school of thought in ancient Greece—including Stoicism, Skepticism, and even Epicureanism—adopted Aristotle's conception of happiness as the achievement of a life well led. Indeed, the Aristotelian perspective on happiness has loomed so large for so long over the field of classical studies that classical scholars rarely consider positive states of being through any other lens. They have produced detailed studies of negative emotions in classical literature—including anger (Harris 2001), jealousy (Sanders 2014), spite (Konstan and Rutter 2003), and remorse (Fulkerson 2013)—but when it comes to the classical treatment of positive affects, few studies look beyond *eudaimonia* and its framework of virtue ethics. Only quite recently have scholars begun to focus attention on the importance of other, non-eudaimonic varieties of good and positive feeling in ancient literature, exploring phenomena like "joy, contentment, elation, hope, goodwill, and mercy" as they arise in Homer, Seneca, Virgil, Juvenal, and other great poets of Greece and Rome (Caston and Kaster 2).

The Aristotelian tradition has been central to most of the scholarship on happiness in medieval and early modern literature, as well. Jessica Rosenfeld's *Ethics and Enjoyment in Late Medieval Poetry* (2010) argues that the medieval poetics of enjoyment only took coherent form after the appearance of the first full translation of the *Nicomachean Ethics* in the mid-thirteenth century. The "reception of Aristotelian ethics in a Christian world" (9), she writes, prompted a reorientation of vernacular literature that merged conceptions of pleasure, love, and joy into a single project at once Aristotelian and Christian. This involved a reconciliation of Aristotle's ethics of the "good life," achieved here and now, with a Christian ethics directed toward communion with God in the afterlife. As Rosenfeld describes it, the vernacular literature of this period sought to demonstrate that the eudaimonistic and Christian paths were directed toward the same ultimate goal: the *summum bonum* or "sovereign good" (2). Rosenfeld shows, for example, how Chaucer's handling of erotic pleasure and friendship in *Troilus and Criseyde* depended on an ethical framework emerging from the mutual illumination of Aristotle and Boethius around the question of "how to pursue the good in the context of lived experience" (145).

Chaucer and other medieval writers had to develop this way of thinking about happiness without recourse to the actual word *happiness*. As Tim Withington has discussed, the word was unknown to Chaucer and was still rare a century and a half after his death in 1400. Even when it did appear at that later time, its meaning was largely confined to the concept of fortune. To possess *happiness* in the first half of the sixteenth century was to have good luck, to enjoy a state of good fortune. But over the course of the early modern period the term accrued a wider range of meanings and became central to the project Rosenfeld sees first arising in the middle ages. "Happiness" comes to serve as the primary "conduit of classical and patristic ideas into the vernacular," being increasingly used by translators as the English equivalent both of the Greek *eudaimonia*, the good life of Aristotelian ethics, and the Latin *summum bonum*, the sovereign or divine good of Augustinian theology: the good afterlife (Withington 30–31). By the time Milton writes in book 12 of *Paradise Lost* of the "paradise within thee, happier far," the word has been loaded up with this complicated freight. Further, on top of the admixture of classical and Christian meanings, the term seems by this time to have accrued something of its modern sense, having to do with individual psychology, personal feelings of well-being.

Precisely when this modern, psychological sense of the term takes hold is difficult to say. Kevin Laam sees the process already underway in Shakespeare. Attempting to read *Troilus and Cressida* and *Richard III* in light of the ongoing integration of classical eudaimonism into Christian thought, Laam finds in these plays a "messy" variety of attitudes toward happiness and "no clean separation" between its ethical dimensions (concerned with right actions) and its psychological ones (concerned with positive affects) (Laam 441, 449). It can be tempting to say that, with the rise of the novel in the eighteenth century, this conceptual messiness gets cleared away and happiness becomes a definitively psychological category, aligned with both the interest in individual feelings that animates the novel form and the broader "affective revolution" in Enlightenment thought and culture: the rise of a secular discourse on emotion. It is certainly the case that, as Brian Michael Norton observes, the eighteenth century witnessed an "explosion of interest in happiness" (1), and that alongside the many philosophical treatises on the subject, which sought to "theorize the conditions that make happiness possible in general," novels were written—by Sterne, Diderot, Mary Hays, and others—to examine the problem of happiness "one case at a time, delving into the specifics of a character's unique psychology and temperament" (134). Charles Taylor influentially argued that a culture's "notions of the good" are "interwoven with its modes of narrative" (396), and there is no doubt that in the eighteenth century, writers found a good fit between a secular conception of the good as personal happiness and the increasingly popular narrative mode of the novel. What is less certain is whether in making this turn toward its inward, psychological dimensions, the novel ever fully disarticulated the concept of happiness from ethics, virtue, and the *summum bonum* or highest good. Like Adam Potkay (2000), who has written extensively on the literary history of happiness, Norton sees much continued complexity not only in the evolving relationship between fiction and philosophy in the eighteenth century but also within the works of fiction themselves. The novel may indeed be the key form for exploring and extending Enlightenment discourse on happiness, but that discourse remains "rich and heterogeneous . . . drawing on a variety of sources, religious and secular, ancient and modern, Stoic and Epicurean" (Norton 2). For Alasdair MacIntyre, the English novel remains deeply entwined with classical and Christian conceptions of happiness as virtue right through into the nineteenth century. In his account, Jane Austen remains a "great representative of the classical tradition of virtues" (243); "when she speaks of 'happiness' she does so as an Aristotelian" (240). The whole importance of her marriage-plot comedies, he argues, lies in their "uniting of Christian and Aristotelian themes in a determinate social context" (240). Even Henry James, writing a century later, appears to MacIntyre as participating in a struggle (albeit a losing one) to maintain the novel's investments in the idea of happiness as the ethical life.

These scholars do agree, though, that whatever the exact timetable, the novel must be seen as hastening a shift in the broader culture onto the tracks of a modern ideology of happiness. Augustine and Aristotle may continue to reverberate in fiction, but more and more faintly. Between the eighteenth century and the twentieth, the notion that every individual has a right to pursue their personal happiness becomes a kind of narrative law, and literary attempts to reconcile that self-interested pursuit with the good and the true come to seem forced. If a novel is to tell the truth, it is no good pretending that bad people can't be happy, or that they can't get even happier as they act even more badly. It is for this reason that Vivasvan Soni, in his study of happiness and the politics of narrative, *Mourning Happiness*, writes that the grand enlightenment project to "confer respectability on secular happiness" ultimately narrows and weakens the concept, undermining the seemingly radical insistence on human flourishing as a universal franchise (an "unalienable right" as it is expressed in the *Declaration of Independence*). "The eighteenth century's very obsession with happiness," Soni argues, "culminates in the political obsolescence of the idea" (3). And the rise of the novel bears much of the blame for this short-circuiting of human happiness as a project of political and social reform. Through the ministrations of the mainstream novel, happiness is effectively reoriented toward bourgeois complacency, designating "a purely narcissistic interest in one's private well-being, devoid of political content" (3). This is not to say that literature after the eighteenth century gives up on politics, only that its political energies veer away from the theme of happiness. Once the concept of happiness has been thoroughly banalized and politically neutered, argues Soni, the most radical writers—beginning with the Romantics and continuing with the modernists—abandon it in favor of "negative affects such as anxiety, despair, boredom, suffering, and melancholy" (4). Or, to put this differently, the works of modern and contemporary literature that are most committed to human flourishing as a project of social and moral reform are the ones in which happiness is hardest to come by and suffering is most pronounced.

This line of argument implies that a literary history of happiness would need, especially over the last hundred years or so, to include not just texts in which happiness is directly thematized and celebrated but also those in which it is in some sense rejected, "mourned," or invoked through negation. In *Against Happiness*, Eric Wilson conducts a survey of literary works whose

power to move and inspire is inseparable from their authors' entanglement with depression and despair. For writers like Franz Kafka, Hart Crane,
Virginia Woolf, Dylan Thomas, and Rita Dove, Wilson argues, the end of
melancholia would be the end of beauty and invention, and the end of any
happiness worth pursuing. The "desire to purge sadness from our lives" is
actually a kind of death drive, leading not to greater flourishing but toward
a dystopia of vacant smiles (4). Sara Ahmed likewise traces a line through
recent literary history that, while concerned with human flourishing and its
obstacles, runs counter to the ideal of personal happiness. She centers her
2010 study *The Promise of Happiness* on what she calls "unhappy archives,"
consisting of works by feminist, queer, and migrant writers more inclined
toward anger or melancholy than to joy. Ahmed reads novels like Woolf's
Mrs. Dalloway, Radcliffe Hall's *Well of Loneliness*, Ama Ata Aidoo's *Sister
Killjoy*, Toni Morrison's *The Bluest Eye*, and Andrea Levy's *Fruit of the Lemon*
as works that mount a concerted "struggle against happiness" (12). They are
not simply "supplements" to the large body of literature in which happiness
is embraced, but works that challenge the very premise of that embrace,
"unraveling happiness, and the threads of its appeal" (18).

Many of the most canonical texts of modernism and the subsequent
literary avant-gardes could be said to fit this description. Adam Potkay
(2014) wonders if Lionel Trilling wasn't right to say that the serious literature of our time is less devoted to the pursuit of happiness than to "the
fantasy of death." Reading T. S. Eliot's *The Waste Land*, Potkay observes that
in this most canonical of modernist poems, "the words 'die,' 'dying,' 'death,'
or 'dead' appear eighteen times (in several languages) and 'joy' (or 'bliss' or
'happiness') not at all" (251). Of course, when we speak of *serious* or *canonical* literature we are isolating a small fraction of a very large field. Viewed
in a wider context, works that belong in the unhappy archives represent
small countercurrents against a steady powerful flow of positive affects
and happy endings. In most of the literature that most people read—not
to mention the films and TV we watch—the narrative of the pursuit of individual happiness is more preeminent than ever. It is just that the works
of dark and resistant tendency have attracted most of the scholarly attention and critical esteem. We could even say that the discipline of literary
studies in its modern form, which developed concurrently with the rise of
modernism, is premised on the same commitment to resist the customary
paths toward happiness and fulfillment in favor of a more obscure and difficult *telos*.

The Negative Capability of Literary Studies

Indeed, its refusals of happiness, or at least of many forms of happiness and happiness-promotion, are so widespread that literary criticism has earned a reputation as a killjoy profession. We are all familiar with the image of a cynical and dour critic who, reading suspiciously between the lines, sees through the ruses of ideology to encounter—heroically, wreathed in cigarette smoke and possibly wearing a cape—the workings of a more fundamental violence. In recent years, such satiric characterizations have emerged even within literary criticism itself, as the field has cultivated new methods explicitly geared toward generosity and joy.[3] But this turn to reparative or just methods of literary study has relied too much on ungenerous accounts of the discipline's traditional procedures and commitments, overemphasizing the most ponderously critical aspects of our work and failing to grapple with the deep entanglements of the study of literature and the search for the good life.

To many people, the fact that studying literature is bound up with the quest for meaning and fulfillment is evident in memories of a beloved English teacher—a teacher whose marked passion or idealism or even their appealing hokeyness made clear that this class was not like the others. This difference—in tone, rules of engagement, and forms of address—has a long history, which, as Ian Hunter has shown, trades in charisma but is not merely personal. Literary pedagogy derives from rhetorical instruction and Romantic aesthetics, as well as from traditions of pastoral care, and extends its techniques of surveillance, correction, and self-improvement, embedding them in institutional forms with great longevity.

This long view of the institution of literary pedagogy can be refined with reference to key moments in the development of literary criticism. Hunter focuses on the influence of Matthew Arnold, whose role as a purveyor of culture was bolstered by his appointment as Inspector of Schools for England in 1851. The codification of literary studies as a university-level academic discipline in the late nineteenth and early twentieth centuries depended on its role in cultivating citizenship, training young people to a life of moral rectitude and civic duty. After World War II, the demographics of university education changed rapidly, moving the field of literary criticism from a genteel pursuit undertaken by the children of the wealthy to a more diverse (if still far from

---

[3] For a critical account of the self-indictments of literary critics in the recent "method wars," see Kurnick 2020.

universal) discipline. This period marked the rise of the New Criticism in the United States, with its seminar-style teaching focused on the specialized skill of close reading. The small-classroom format and the intensive discussions centered on individual texts set a pattern for the teaching of literature in US universities that has outlived the New Criticism itself by several decades. While such intimately dialogic teaching has become more and more aspirational in the current era of austerity, it remains an ideal for literary pedagogy.

A similar if less rapid postwar expansion of the British university system gave rise there to progressive forms of literary and cultural education. The critic F. R. Leavis had argued influentially in the 1930s on behalf of a pedagogy tightly focused on individual texts. The aim for Leavis and his followers was to rigorously train elite students, the nation's future leaders, in the exercise of critical judgment. By learning the difference between great and lesser literature, students would not merely cultivate superior taste but also resist the degrading influences of modernity and mass culture, in particular its incursions on sensibility. But with the influx of working-class students into the university and the rise of adult education after the war, Leavisite pedagogy found itself addressing a new constituency that compelled a rethinking of mass culture. With consumers of popular fiction, film, and music now taking seats in university classrooms, sweeping indictments of their poor judgment and blunted sensibilities no longer served.

Rather than dismiss the Leavisite program altogether, however, a younger generation of progressive and often working-class literary scholars adapted it to their own needs. As Christopher Hilliard details in *English as a Vocation*, figures including Raymond Williams and Richard Hoggart took up many of the principles of Leavisism in order to launch a social critique of modernity. In the work of these sociological and Marxist thinkers, the root problem with modern life was not the dissociation of sensibility, or a disordered aesthetic. Such dissociation had to be understood as an effect of a profoundly unequal, violent, and reified social world. Retooling early twentieth-century forms of holist criticism toward a class critique and a vision of social totality, these critics inaugurated a mode of analysis that would come to be known as cultural studies.

British cultural studies exerted a powerful influence on the field of literary criticism in the second half of the twentieth century. It is most readily identified, through the work of Hoggart and Williams, as well as that of Stuart Hall, Angela McRobbie, Paul Gilroy, and Richard Dyer, with the critique of ideology and its opposition to state violence. But tracing the roots of cultural studies reminds us as well of the frankly ameliorative aims of work in this field. The striving after what Williams called "a whole way of life" is as palpable in this work as is its indictment of capitalist hegemony or state racism.

The energy of British cultural studies made its way into political criticism and identity-based subfields such as feminist and African American criticism in the United States in the 1980s. The confluence of British cultural studies and European poststructuralism gave rise to a specifically American form of cultural studies, in which the focus on social class was softened in favor of a critical form of identity politics. Yet the ambivalence of British cultural studies was retained. This work, most closely identified with the critical analysis of race, class, and gender, was also deeply invested in forms of empowerment and progress. The persisting ties to early twentieth-century literary pedagogy were evident in the focus on highly prized texts and the elevation of a new canon, but also in the special importance attaching to the figure of the teacher as the literary professoriat underwent dramatic changes. As the faculty became more diverse, women faculty and faculty of color served as crucial and charismatic role models to their students, who were themselves increasingly diverse as well. The new interdisciplinary fields of cultural studies became known, and rightly, for their powerful critiques of racism and sexism, colonialism and patriarchy, nationalism and xenophobia. But it is clear that such critiques were undertaken in the service of collective uplift, in order to make flourishing a possibility open to all. The aim was ultimately to deliver on the broken promise of the Enlightenment embrace of happiness: to promote flourishing as a fundamental human right.

The authors in this volume are in their various ways inheritors of this tradition: addressing forms of inequality by using the tools of critique, but in a spirit that is broadly ameliorative and aimed toward the individual and collective potential. In their work, as in the field at large, attention to transformation exists in tension with recognition of social injustice. There is no sound approach to flourishing without addressing the stubborn material and ideological obstacles to flourishing. For this reason, critique remains a primary, indispensable mode of analysis. And among the concepts subject to critical reframing and scrutiny must be flourishing itself, which, as Janet Lyon shows in her analysis in this volume of the relation between positive psychology and eugenics, can be used not only to promote growth but also to exclude those deemed incapable of it. It is a basic principle of this kind of work that concepts—and especially positive concepts—must be exposed to what they exclude. The eudaimonistic idea of happiness as human flourishing must be tested again and again in relation to the concomitant realities of poverty, violence, and mortality.

This form of thought, which doubles back on itself, is what gives the field of literary studies its misleading appearance of joylessness. Literary critics are not by nature melancholic or morose, or dismissive of the value of happiness. But they do believe that happiness must be pursued in full view and awareness of its opposite. They embrace positive feelings, but they reject positivist thought, the epistemology of a naïve science of happiness that would install flourishing as a shining ideal, undimmed by the shades of contingency and contradiction. The discipline's commitment to dwell with the darkness might be called, after John Keats, its negative capability. It is what unites the heterogeneous essays in this volume, which pursue through literature the goals of fulfillment, recognition, and community in all their entanglement with dissension and deprivation.

Angles of Approach

The ten essays gathered here were presented and discussed in early draft form at a three-day workshop, "Literary Studies and Well-Being," in September 2018. Participating in that workshop alongside the literary scholars were the lead organizers of the Humanities and Human Flourishing Project, the philosopher James Pawelski and the psychologist Louis Tay, and two social psychologists who work on well-being, Norman Bradburn and Melanie Green.[4] Their involvement helped us keep our discussions open to the perspectives of other disciplines, an essential goal of the project and, for the volume editors, one of its principle attractions. But we also took care to assemble a group of literary scholars who represent a wide range of subfields and orientations, and come to the question of literature and human flourishing from quite different angles of approach. Of particular importance to us was the participation of literary scholars working in the "interdisciplines" of gender and sexuality studies, disability studies, and black studies, where issues of stigma and exclusion are paramount, and which have critiqued the discourse of human flourishing for its failure to grapple with structural

---

[4] For more information about the Humanities and Human Flourishing Project at the University of Pennsylvania, visit www.humanitiesandhumanflourishing.org.

inequality and human difference. Even some of the participants working in more traditional fields approached the project via the relation of literature to illness, aging, and social stratification. These emphases put pressure on the group to tackle hard questions and avoid anodyne formulations, and to respect the positive value of critique, complaint, and conflict.

Because these essays were workshopped together and then shared again at various points in the revision process, they speak to each other in multiple ways. Scott Herring, Janet Lyon, and Sonya Posmentier all consider human flourishing in relation to questions of normativity and stigma, for example. Beth Blum, David James, Heather Love, and Leah Price all consider claims for the therapeutic or ameliorative effects of literature. Chris Castiglia, James English, and David Russell all treat literature and reading as they pertain to the injuries of class. The relationship between literary studies and the "happiness industry" comes up at least glancingly in most of the pieces, and most express deep reservations about the promotion of reading as a practice of self-improvement. Given these many points of convergence and overlap, the five pairings into which we have organized the essays might easily be otherwise. But our scheme should draw attention to some especially salient points of emphasis, and of tension, in the project as a whole.

The first pairing, under the heading "Happy Reading: Literature without the Academy," brings together Leah Price's "Bibliotherapy and Human Flourishing" with "Bad Habits on Goodreads?" by the team of Jim English, Scott Enderle, and Rahul Dhakecha. These are the only chapters in the volume that serve primarily to advance the field of *reader studies*, i.e., the study of habits, practices, and effects of reading among "ordinary readers" in the wider society. Studies of this kind are often concerned with the cultural institutions that direct or mediate the activities of readers and their relationships to books. As we have already discussed, the university itself is clearly one of the most important of these institutions, and Ian Hunter's work is only the most prominent in a sizable body of scholarship in critical sociology that addresses the way institutions of higher learning deploy literature as a mechanism of cultural policy and social governance (Baldick 1987, Hunter 1988). But inasmuch as ordinary readers are understood to engage with books elsewhere and differently than scholars in the academy do, work in reader studies tends to bring other institutions to the fore. Price's focus is on the interactions between readers and the "bibliotherapy" industry, and English's team studies readers' behavior on Amazon's Goodreads social media platform.

In "Bibliotherapy and Human Flourishing," Price describes both the longer history of bibliotherapy, which emerged in the nineteenth century, and its more recent rise. As she sees it, the movement's success has been aided by a widespread view that the experience of reading literature is an emotionally nourishing one which the academic discipline of literary studies transmutes into something needlessly unpleasant and cold-blooded. Price is critical of the self-appointed reading-for-well-being coaches, but she argues that it is not enough simply to sneer at the inanities (or denounce the profit motives) of these rivals to our pedagogical authority. We need also, she says, to recalibrate our discipline, reconnect it to the joy and wonder of everyday reading—a reorientation that she sees as already in fact underway.

Like Price, English, Enderle, and Dhakecha find that ordinary readers are encouraged to take joy and solace from ways of reading that are sharply at odds with what is positively valued—deemed to be "good for you"—in academic literary studies. The team's study of many thousands of ratings and reviews on the Goodreads social reading site suggests that the vast majority of readers turn to literature to enjoy the repeatable satisfactions of a single favored genre such as romance, mystery, or science fiction. Even Goodreads users who describe their attachment to reading in the academically approved terms of an eclectic openness to new kinds of literary encounter appear actually to seek the comforts of belonging to a narrow community of shared tastes. In this respect, the traditional divide between academically legitimate reading and disesteemed popular consumption appears to be more durably entrenched than prevailing narratives about cultural democratization have assumed. Literature continues to serve as an effective instrument of social division.

For both Price and English's team, the broader point of method is that no account of the relationship between literature and human flourishing can be adequate if it ignores the social and institutional terrain of popular reading, where the majority of encounters between books and readers occur. Several other essays in the volume do concern themselves with the activities and orientations of nonacademic readers. But they work less from historical and empirical evidence about such readers than from what may be inferred about them by literary scholars and philosophers paying close attention to certain literary works or forms of literary language. This still affords scope for a wide range of thinking about literature and human flourishing. In the second pairing, "Flourishing beyond Reason: Literature's Augmented Realities," Christopher Castiglia and David Russell draw on their research into nineteenth-century spiritualism and aesthetics, respectively, to suggest ways that literature figures the positive as an excess or supplement to the versions of reality supported by empirical evidence and scientific rationality. Castiglia's aim in "Flourishing Spirits" is to set aside the usual dismissive skepticism toward the spiritualist movement in nineteenth-century America, and take seriously the forms of belief at work in the literature arising from séances and involving supposed messages from the dead. Drawing on the work of William James, he reads the proliferation of such literature as a testament to the *will to believe*. Spiritualist practices were embraced less as a means of communication with the dead than as a way to refresh and strengthen the belief in belief itself, the capacity to seize passionate hold of possibilities—what Bruno Latour has called "invisibles" (183)—on the other side of factual evidence. To embrace these possibilities, Castiglia argues, can be a kind of principled utopianism and a form of political engagement. By exercising their capacity to choose belief over reason, spiritualists strengthened their will to "act on behalf of belief." Many advocated for the abolition of slavery and the rights of women, or for other radical and seemingly impossible transformations of the social order. However empirically unsound, the spiritualist way of reading—the willingness to read certain texts as authentic transcriptions of the utterances of the dead—produced a relation to belief that, says Castiglia, "enabled the 'real fight' to make the world otherwise than it was."

In "Sage Writing: Facing Reality in Literature," David Russell makes a related argument about how a serious engagement with certain forms of writing can reorient one's relationship to the realities of the world. He reads the work of John Ruskin as exemplifying a tradition of philosophical criticism that seeks from art and literature a kind of aesthetic supplement or "addition" to what may be otherwise known and felt about the world. This extra or excess can never be accessed by the tools of social or cognitive science. It is "something so distinct as to be inassimilable to established scales of measurement" such as might be grasped through data or assigned a quantity of value, a specified degree of utility. It does not consist in new or more accurate information about reality, but in a different *affective* relationship to things that may already be known perfectly well at the level of cognition. For those who find their way to it through literature or art, this aesthetic supplement, this intensified way of feeling, is essential for leading a good and meaningful life. That does not mean a life of pure joy and happiness. Just as for spiritualists the will to believe in literature's "impossible" figments could support a stance of determined opposition to the realities of slavery and social subjugation, for this mode of critical aesthetics, the transformation that is achieved can move people "towards a radical sense of their interpenetration with others," prompting outrage at exploitative social and economic arrangements that they would otherwise merely acknowledge as cold facts of the world.

In the third pair of essays, "Flourishing in Crisis: The Poetics of Disaster," David James and Sonya Posmentier consider forms of literature that can uphold an ethically optimistic perspective in the face of catastrophic circumstances. James's essay, "Literature of Uplift," takes as its starting point a volume of twenty-four "stories of hope" published in response to the Grenfell Tower catastrophe in 2017. Just as the Grenfell fire is emblematic of systemic social failings in the United Kingdom—increasingly disastrous disparities of income, access, health, safety, and security—the anthology of uplifting stories exemplifies an increasingly common form of literary response to such failings: "ameliorative acts" of writing that set "narratives of fugitive hope" against the cruelties of racist and capitalist social structures. Such narratives are the most widespread and visible form of uplifting literature; they constitute a recognized trend in the book world that publishers have labeled "Up Lit." Literary studies is programmed to disparage this literature and the traditions of literary sentimentalism from which it derives. But James sees its rise as offering "an occasion for us to reassess these customary misgivings about literature that holds out the promise of amelioration." He focuses in particular on the more austere strains of uplifting literature, which probe ambivalently at the "intersection of well-being and ill-being, elevation and desperation." An example is *Skybound*, a 2018 memoir by Rebecca Loncraine that documents her efforts to learn to fly a glider during a time when she was suffering the effects of grueling chemo treatments for breast cancer—a disease that returned to kill her just as she was finishing the book. For all its soaring effects of language and ameliorative structures of feeling, *Skybound* keeps the reader at a certain distance, resisting sentimental identification and withholding any easy promise of happiness. Such work, James argues, captures human capacities for hope, for the possibility of mutual attachment and care, but holds them in balance with acknowledgment of forms of damage, both personal and collective, that lie beyond remedy.

In her essay "Black Ecological Optimism and the Problem of Human Flourishing," Sonya Posmentier also turns to a memoir written by a woman struggling with breast cancer: *Cancer Journals* by the Black lesbian feminist poet Audre Lorde. Posmentier places this 1980 meditation on disease, recovery, and the politics of gender in dialogue with Lorde's later writings, after she had relocated to the Caribbean island of St. Croix, about the ravages of Hurricane Hugo, which destroyed a third of the homes and many lives in the Virgin Islands. Lorde's work, says Posmentier, asks us to consider what is meant by human flourishing in the context of these disasters, one personal and one collective, and in the wider catastrophic frame that shaped all Lorde's thought and writing, the traumas of transatlantic enslavement and its aftermath. Flourishing, for Lorde, could never be a matter of individual happiness. Only a "depraved monster," she wrote, could be happy "in this disastrous time, when little girls are still being stitched shut between their legs, when victims of cancer are urged to court more cancer in order to be attractive to men, when twelve-year-old Black boys are shot down in the street at random by uniformed men who are cleared of any wrong-doing." Lorde's work, says Posmentier, develops a stringent alternative to the idea of human flourishing as a matter of positive affect, conceiving individual well-being in terms of environmental health and justice, and deploying ecological tropes (wind, hurricane, weather, cycle) as models for "speculating about what it might mean to flourish while also acknowledging the structural, economic, environmental, and political conditions of unfreedom that have long shaped Black diasporic life." If Lorde's ecological approach to well-being involves a principled rejection of happiness, it is equally a rejection of despair. Toward the possibilities of flourishing, argues Posmentier, Lorde is ultimately "optimistic, even positive." Her ecological poetics supports belief in the "transformative powers of poetry . . . as a communal resource," a "vital and relational form of human flourishing."

The fourth pair of essays, "Non-Normative Flourishing: Disability and Aging," considers what literary studies can contribute to the discourse of human flourishing as it pertains to the disabled and the elderly. In "Literary Study, the Hermeneutics of Disability, and the Eudaimonic Turn," Janet Lyon seizes on certain works of modernist and contemporary fiction in which the conventional figure of the "idiot" or the "retard" is represented in especially complex ways. What commends these texts, in her view, is not that they offer positive images of cognitively disabled people, but that, if we read them closely, they guide us into the "complex entanglements of affirmation, critique, and reparation [that are] connected to disability." In highlighting difficulty and complexity, Lyon takes up a theme that runs throughout the volume: it is not enough simply to read, or even simply to read certain relatively obscure works favored by literary scholars (works of aesthetic criticism,

Stoical rhetoric, modernist poetry, and so on). In order to derive from these works insights or experiences relevant to the pursuit of human flourishing, we need to read them against the smooth grain of plot or simple content-extraction, experiencing all the harshness of their negative aspects. As this way of reading must be learned through practice, Lyon puts special stress on literary studies as a mode of teaching and learning. Classroom discussions of literary texts, she says, can "create new forms of collaborative understanding around human character, non-human forces, complex life events, and the many varieties of embodiment and mindedness." All the more so when the works being taught foreground disability and challenge the normative language and grounding assumptions of ableism. When we read disability literature with our students in the classroom, says Lyon, we "draw on the expansive properties of literary language and form to cultivate breadth of imagination and openness to meaning." As a pedagogical practice, literary studies of disability thus "creates an interactive community in which ethics can be tested and enigmas honored."

In "Wise Old Fools: Positive Geropsychology and the Poetics of Later-Life Floundering," Scott Herring considers another set of literary works that can challenge the association of human flourishing with normative bodies and abilities: "artworks of growing older." Works that grapple with aging, he argues, can usefully complicate the emphases in positive psychology on optimality and the wisdom of the elderly with more generous considerations of "confusion . . . incoherence, fret, and ignorance." Late-style poetry such as that of A. R. Ammons teaches us to see a different kind of flourishing in the tragicomedy of floundering. What would ordinarily be viewed as a decline into senility may be perceived in this work as a kind of elevation as the aging person develops, not special wisdom, but "creative forms of ignorance and non-mastery" which can also be indispensable "forms of resilience."

In presenting this argument, Herring describes his aim as "conjuring a peaceable kingdom for the fields of literary gerontology and positive geropsychology." His essay is no more an attack on the social and medical sciences of aging than Lyon's is an attack on the social and medical sciences of disability. Both see the reading and teaching of literature as contributing something of distinct value to what is necessarily an interdisciplinary endeavor. To maintain this spirit of critical but constructive collaboration is not easy for literary scholars, whose bent for polemics against positivity surfaces, as already noted, at various points in this volume. But it is a spirit fundamental to our enterprise, and is nowhere given fuller and clearer expression than in Herring's generous meditation on the varieties of "geroresilience."

The final pair of essays, by Beth Blum and Heather Love, appears under the heading "Positive Affect: Redescription and Repair." Both pieces address the recent shift of method—or perhaps rather, as Love suggests, of disposition—in literary studies, away from a project of implacable critique toward one of close attention and care. As Blum notes in "Therapeutic Redescription," the discipline's postcritical movements have been motivated in part by a desire to escape the "charismatic master discourses of theory's golden age." In place of critical theory's grand promises of revelation and demystification, and its posture of unyielding suspicion and paranoia toward literary works, scholars such as Rita Felski, Paul Saint-Amour, and Love herself, says Blum, have embraced a turn to descriptive methods of literary study. Indeed, since their ways of describing a work detach it radically from the received perspective of critique, these are programs of *redescription*. Blum traces this strategy back to the ancient Stoics, for whom the ability to redescribe a familiar thing "developed as a form of volitional training meant to emancipate the individual from the false 'impressions' that govern their lives." As a means of liberating oneself from rigidly habitual outlooks and dispositions, redescription was understood by the Stoics as a therapeutic practice, and Blum notes its revival and promotion in recent years by self-help gurus pushing therapeutic redescription as a "life hack." But she argues that its more suitable and enduring home has been literature itself, for redescription is above all "a literary skill." Blum traces a lineage of therapeutic redescribers that extends from Proust through Doris Lessing to writers of contemporary autofiction such as Sheila Heti and Karl Ove Knausgaard. Through readings of their work, she shows that the redescriptive disposition is not at all the stance of cool detachment we might associate with Stoicism. The point of the technique is not to deny one's attachments but to become conscious of their susceptibility to rhetorical and analytical reframing: to "make them poignant by bringing their risky fragility into full view." And this, says Blum, is what recommends therapeutic redescription to postcritical literary scholars as well as to contemporary novelists. It can be a way not to discard the enterprise of critique as such, but rather to continue working to advance realism against illusion while still "preserving a space for attachment, appreciation, and . . . love."

Heather Love addresses the debates over postcritical reading and descriptive method from the direction of queer theory and affect studies. In "Merely Ameliorative: Reading, Critical Affect, and the Project of Repair," she begins with the work of Eve Kosofsky Sedgwick, one of the founding figures of both fields and an influential early proponent of the turn to positive affect in literary criticism. In place of the paranoid style of criticism that has dominated literary studies, linking literature to histories of injury and damage, Sedgwick called for critics to explore the links between literature and healing, between reading and repair. Her project of *reparative reading*, says Love, would have critics approach literary works "with loving attention and care rather than with wariness or skepticism," keeping themselves alert to a text's evocations of "positive rather than negative affect." It would mean restoring critical value to the discredited experience of readerly joy.

That is a tall order for a discipline that attaches such high prestige to negative feelings. But Love suggests it may be possible for criticism to give pleasure its due even in full awareness of the hard facts of material suffering. She develops this line of argument by pursuing an unlikely connection between Sedgwick and the Marxist philosopher Theodore Adorno. On the face of it, nothing could be further from Sedgwick's project of repair than Adorno's project of "critical *askesis*" in *Minima Moralia* (1951), a work determined to face the worst horrors of modernity without consolation or hope of redress. But Love finds "surprising resonances" between the two, particularly in their insistence on maintaining the closest possible proximity and affective attunement to their objects. Even Adorno's "melancholy aphorisms on the end of the world," she says, may be read as poetic openings onto positive affect in extremis, a kind of joy that manifests only when "snatched quite literally from the jaws of death."

Love concludes her essay by acknowledging that, even with the examples of Sedgwick and Adorno before us, we in literary studies and critical theory lack the conceptual tools needed to grasp in their full complexity the relationship of pleasure to pain or the mutual dependency of positive and negative in the realm of human flourishing. It is fair to say that this volume as a whole contributes more points of ambiguity and hesitation to the study of well-being than it does decisive advancements. Literary scholars are drawn more readily to the problematic than to the decidable. Our hope is that by dwelling on the trouble spots in a field of inquiry still largely confined to the sciences, we are helping to assure it a more interdisciplinary future.

Works Cited

Achor, Shawn. *Before Happiness: The 5 Hidden Keys to Achieving Success, Spreading Happiness, and Sustaining Positive Change.* Random House, 2013.
Achor, Shawn. *The Happiness Advantage: The Seven Principles of Positive Psychology That Fuel Success and Performance at Work.* Crown, 2010.

Adorno, Theodor. *Minima Moralia: Reflections from Damaged Life*. Translated by E. F. N. Jephcott, Verso, 1974 [1951].

Ahmed, Sarah. *The Promise of Happiness*. Duke UP, 2010.

Annas, Julia. *The Morality of Happiness*. Oxford UP, 1993.

Aristotle. *Nicomachean Ethics*. Translated by W. D. Ross, Clarendon, 1926. Internet Classics Archive, n.d., http://classics.mit.edu/Aristotle/nicomachaen.html.

Bal, P. Matthijs, and Martijn Veltkamp. "How Does Fiction Reading Influence Empathy? An Experimental Investigation on the Role of Emotional Transportation." *Plos One*, 30 Jan. 2013, https://doi.org/10.1371/journal.pone.0055341.

Baldick, Chris. *The Social Mission of English Criticism*. Clarendon Press, 1987.

Cabanas, Edgar, and Eva Illouz. *Manufacturing Happy Citizens: How the Science and Industry of Happiness Control Our Lives*. Polity, 2019.

Caston, Ruth R., and Robert Kaster, editors. *Hope, Joy, and Affection in the Classical World*. Oxford UP, 2016.

Cohen, Joshua. "Social, Emotional, Ethical, and Academic Education: Creating a Climate for Learning, Participation in Democracy, and Well-Being." *Harvard Educational Review*, vol. 76, no. 2, 2006, pp. 201–37, https://doi.org/10.17763/haer.76.2.j44854x1524644vn.

Crum Alia J., et al. "Rethinking Stress: The Role of Mindsets in Determining the Stress Response." *Journal of Personality and Social Psychology*, vol. 104, no. 4, 2013, pp. 716–33, https://doi.org/10.1037/a0031201.

Fulkerson, Laurel. *No Regrets: Remorse in Classical Antiquity*. Oxford UP, 2013.

Harris, William V. *Restraining Rage: The Ideology of Anger Control in Classical Antiquity*. Harvard UP, 2001.

Hilliard, Christopher. *English as a Vocation: The* Scrutiny *Movement*. Oxford UP, 2012.

Hunter, Ian. *Culture and Government: The Emergence of Literary Education*. Palgrave Macmillan, 1988.

Hunter, Ian. "History Lessons for English." *Cultural Studies*, vol. 8, 1994, pp. 142–61.

Konsatan, David, and N. K. Rutter, editors. *Envy, Spite, and Jealousy: The Rivalrous Emotions in Ancient Greece*. Edinburgh UP, 2003.

Kurnick David. "A Few Lies: Theory and Our Method Melodramas." *ELH*, vol. 87, no. 2, 2020, pp. 349–74, https://doi.org/10.1353/elh.2020.0011.

Laam, Kevin. "Shakespeare and Happiness." *Literature Compass*, vol. 7, no. 6, 2010, pp. 439–51, https://doi.org/10.1111/j.1741-4113.2010.00711.x.

Latour, Bruno. *An Inquiry into Modes of Existence: An Anthropology of the Moderns*. Translated by Catherine Porter, Harvard UP, 2013.

Longcraine, Patricia. *Skybound*. Picador, 2018.

MacIntyre, Alasdair. *After Virtue: A Study in Moral Theory*. 1981. 3rd ed., U of Notre Dame P, 2007.

Miller, D. A. *Narrative and Its Discontents: Problems of Closure in the Traditional Novel*. Princeton UP, 1981.

Morrison, Toni. Acceptance Speech, Nobel Prize Banquet. Stockholm, Sweden, 10 Dec. 1993, https://www.nobelprize.org/prizes/literature/1993/morrison/speech/.

Noddings, Nel. *Happiness and Education*. Cambridge UP, 2003, online edition 2009, https://doi.org/10.1017/CBO9780511499920.

Norton, Brian Michael. *Fiction and the Philosophy of Happiness: Ethical Inquiries in the Age of Enlightenment*. Bucknell UP, 2012.

Nussbaum, Martha C. "Flawed Crystals: James's *The Golden Bowl* and Literature as Moral Philosophy." *New Literary History*, vol. 15, no. 1, 1983, pp. 25–50.

Oades, Lindsay G., et al. "Towards a Positive University." *Journal of Positive Psychology*, vol. 6, no. 6, 2011, pp. 432–39, https://doi.org/10.1080/17439760.2011.634828.

Peterson, Christopher, et al. "Group Well-Being: Morale from a Positive Psychology Perspective." *Applied Psychology*, vol. 57, no. 1, July 2008, pp. 19–36, https://10.1111/j.1464-0597.2008.00352.x.

Potkay, Adam. *The Passion for Happiness: Samuel Johnson and David Hume.* Cornell UP, 2000.

Potkay, Adam. "The Career of Joy in the Twentieth Century." *The Eudaimonic Turn: Well-Being in Literary Studies*, edited by James O. Pawelski and D. J. Moores. Dickinson UP, 2014, pp. 247–64.

Rosenfeld, Jessica. *Ethics and Enjoyment in Late Medieval Poetry: Love after Aristotle.* Cambridge UP, 2010.

Sanders, Ed. *Envy and Jealousy in Classical Athens: A Socio-Psychological Approach.* Oxford UP, 2014.

Seligman, Martin. E. P., and Alejandro Adler. "Positive Education." *Global Happiness and Wellbeing Policy Report: 2019*, edited by Layard Helliwell et al., Global Council for Wellbeing and Happiness, 2019, pp. 53–72, https://s3.amazonaws.com/ghwbpr-2019/UAE/GH19_Ch4.pdf.

Seligman, Martin E. P., and Mihaly Csikszentmihalyi. "Positive Psychology: An Introduction." *American Psychologist*, vol. 55 no. 1, 2000, pp. 5–14, https://doi.prg/10.1037/0003-066X.55.1.5.

Seligman, Martin E. P., et al. "Positive Education: Positive Psychology and Classroom Interventions." *Oxford Review of Education*, vol. 35, no. 3, 2009, pp. 293–311, https://doi.org/10.1080/03054980902934563.

Soni, Vivasvan. *Mourning Happiness: Narrative and the Politics of Happiness.* Cornell UP, 2010.

Taylor, Charles. *Sources of the Self: The Making of Modern Identity.* Cambridge UP, 1989.

Williams, Raymond. *Culture and Society, 1780–1950.* Hogarth , 1958.

Wilson, Eric G. *Against Happiness: In Praise of Melancholy.* Crichton Books, 2009.

Withington, Tim. "The Invention of Happiness." *Suffering and Happiness in England 1550–1850: Narratives and Representations: A Collection to Honour Paul Slack*, edited by Michael J. Braddick and Joanna Innes, Oxford UP, 2017, pp. 23–44, https://doi.org/10.1093/oso/9780198748267.003.0002

PART I
HAPPY READING
Literature without the Academy

1

Bibliotherapy and Human Flourishing

Leah Price

Around the turn of this millennium, as scientific journals migrated online, their index entries on "reading" ballooned. Cognitive scientists, neurobiologists, epidemiologists, and statisticians vied to compare print-reading with screen-reading, book-reading with magazine-reading, fiction-reading with non-fiction-reading, literature-reading with the reading of whatever genres they identified as antonyms to the literary.

Doctors had long blamed books for tired eyes, hunched backs, or fevered minds. Now, psychiatrists entrusted self-help books to mitigate anxiety and depression. More surprisingly, natural and social scientists began to credit the curative power of reading to its *medium* (print vs. online), its *scale* (immersive prose vs. snippeted listicle), or its life expectancy (*durable* book as opposed to *ephemeral* news).

Thus literary fiction garnered testimonials from an unlikely quarter: science ("Book Reading"). Or more precisely, *Science*. In 2013, that journal published a study concluding that reading about fictional characters correlates with more sophisticated theory of mind. More specifically, reading about characters in formally ambitious "literary" fiction did—for the authors discovered experimental subjects to be better at identifying the emotions expressed on faces or at understanding others' false beliefs when they had just read prizewinning short stories than when they had just read less esthetically ambitious popular fiction (Kidd and Castano 2013). This latest version of the centuries-old attempt to distinguish trashy escapism from intellectually challenging and therefore morally respectable fiction was widely reported by journalists with their own investment in reading.

Neuroscientists drilled down, wedging readers inside fMRI scanners to measure novels' effect on brain function and structure (Berns et al. 2013; Tamir et al. 2015). Social scientists scaled up, as when psychologist Steven Pinker's 2011 book *The Better Angels of Our Nature* correlated a centuries-long decline in violence with an increase in fiction reading. Some surveys

Leah Price, *Bibliotherapy and Human Flourishing* In: *Literary Studies and Human Flourishing*. Edited by: James F. English and Heather Love, Oxford University Press. © Oxford University Press 2023. DOI: 10.1093/oso/9780197637227.003.0002

measured effects on health; others on wealth; yet others on civic virtue. Back in 2004, data aggregated by the National Endowment for the Humanities suggested that Americans who read outside of work and school were likeliest to vote and volunteer. Four years later, a meta-analysis connected the frequency with which Canadians read books to the rate at which they donated and helped their neighbors (Capriotti and Hill 2008: 2). Also in 2008, a British study correlated pleasure reading inversely with divorce (Clark and Dugdale 2008: 7). Madame Bovary would have been surprised.

The questionnaires behind these studies asked about wanting to read and about acting on that desire. Their subject, therefore, was the choice of reading more than the act of reading itself. Where the *Science* study concerned identification *with* fictional characters, these social-scientific studies concerned identification *as* a reader. Conversely, even those lab interventions that pinpoint the neural mechanisms attending reading pleasure have little to say about pleasure reading. A letter announcing a lottery win wouldn't count as "pleasure reading" by the NEH's definition, which makes enjoyment mutually exclusive with grades or pay. The corollary seemed to be that a novel assigned in a course or the notetaking performed by the teacher who assigns it constituted reading for pain.

Beyond the classroom and the office, longform reading became the domain of very young and very old Americans, replacing the middle-class women whose time was once of equally little value. In the lab, though, college students paid by the hour to act as research subjects read for work *and* school at the same time. Even ergonomically, these 18- to 25-year-olds remain anomalies, cramped flat in an apparatus rather than curled up with the proverbial book or gooseknecked over a smartphone.

The emerging division of labor between scientists, policymakers, and bibliotherapists rules out lumping the kinds of reading against which we literary scholars define our own role under the single umbrella of a negatively defined "common reader." Where once literary criticism aspired to fashion its own methods into a science, it's now likelier to outsource rigor. Invoking cognitive scientists' or epidemiologists' findings about our objects of study risks reducing us to curators of their raw materials.

* * *

The 2013 theory of mind study focuses on literary form, but other research shows more interest in delivery device. A lab intervention measuring melatonin levels, for example, found offline e-ink reading (as on an earlier-generation Kindle) to have more in common with print than with the use of blue-lit phones (Rangtell et al.). Still other researchers consider the medium alongside the message. A study comparing three groups of teenaged girls—those assigned a book about healthful eating, those given a book on another topic, and those not asked to read at all—found not just that the first group ended up with a healthier body-mass index than the second but also that the second fared better than the third.

Whether you read has consequences for your body and the body politic, these studies suggest—but so does what you read about, in what linguistic register, on what device, at what length. In 2016 a team of epidemiologists correlated reading with longevity (Bavishi et al.). This held even after correcting for the fact that readers skew rich, white, and female—and more specifically that in the United States as in other high-income countries, digital media have done nothing to change the several-centuries-old fact that men read less overall but read a higher proportion of short-form news than do women. Plotted against life expectancy—after correcting for gender—news-reading turned out to fall somewhere between reading books and not reading at all.

As striking as what the researchers considered is what they didn't. These weren't books *about* characters living to a ripe old age, or even gory depictions of smokers' lungs. Nor did the blue-light study distinguish *Goodnight Moon* from *Gone Girl*. When a study of teenagers finds that "major depressive disorder is positively associated with popular music exposure and negatively associated with reading print media *such as books*" (Primack et al. 2011, my emphasis), or when readers' heart rates and muscle tension are measured to prove books "68% better at reducing stress levels than listening to music" ("Reading Well Evidence Base"),[1] the researchers don't ask about the words contained in either. A formalist interest in medium at the expense of message sets those research studies apart from the largest effort to translate research on reading into policy. That effort goes by the name of book prescription.

* * *

In 2005, a Cardiff psychiatrist named Neil Frude saw his patients waiting months to be prescribed antidepressants, and years to receive talk therapy.

---

[1] The Reading Agency explained in "Mood-Boosting Books 2012" that "our . . . promotion is aimed at adults, particularly those who might have experienced mild to moderate mental-health conditions linked to stress, anxiety and depression" (emphasis mine).

He noticed, as well, that they were filling those days and months of waiting with furtive forays to the self-help section of the bookstore, or, in the privacy of their local library, with what was then coming to be known as Googling. Of the more than 100,000 books on sale that offered psychiatric advice in layman's language, at least some seemed to help. If randomized trials could identify which books those were, Frude realized, doctors without specialized psychiatric training would be able to recommend them.

Soon, "recommend" ratcheted up to "prescribe." In NHS Wales's Book Prescription program, any primary-care physician who diagnoses "mild to moderate" depression can scribble a title on a prescription pad. The patient takes the torn-off sheet not to the pharmacy but to her local library, where it gets exchanged for a copy of *Overcoming Depression* or *The Feeling Good Handbook*. Now that depression is only one of over a dozen conditions treated, libraries across Wales stock *Mind over Mood, Overcoming Traumatic Stress, Getting Better Bit(e) by Bit(e)*, and *The Worry Cure*. Those made anxious by all that required reading can choose between *Stop Worrying about Your Health! An Introduction to Coping with Health Anxiety: A Books on Prescription Title* (Frude 2011).

By 2011, doctors in Wales were issuing 30,000 book prescriptions a year (Frude). Whether or not those books were ever opened, many of them at least got as far as the circulation desk. By 2013, a third of libraries' top ten most borrowed titles were self-help books (Brown 2013). A public library system suffering even more drastic budget cuts than the health service was in no position to turn away the foot traffic, funding, and legitimacy that Book Prescription supplied. No wonder that in 2013, Books on Prescription began to spread beyond Wales. England's Reading Well initiative was launched by a nonprofit rather than its own health service, but the doctors who participated were paid by the NHS. Within three months, English libraries had lent over 100,000 copies of the prescribed titles—20,000 more than *Fifty Shades of Grey* ("Most Borrowed Books").

From a medical vantage, many of books' selling-points are negative. The money they don't cost, the side effects they don't produce, the addictions that they don't engender—all these allow them to beat out drugs and talk therapy alike. Unlike the antidepressants taken by over 12.7% of Americans and 6 million Britons, reading doesn't increase weight or decrease libido. It can't even trigger nausea, unless you happen to be in the car.

Compared to one-on-one counseling, meanwhile, bibliotherapy looks almost absurdly cost-effective—for while randomized trials suggest that therapists outperform books by a narrow margin, books underbid therapists by a much wider one. A 2012 study that compared anxiety sufferers stuck on a therapist's waitlist to those prescribed self-help books found a significant effect size in favor of self-help but cautioned that "comparison of self-help with therapist-administered treatments revealed a significant difference in favor of the latter" (Lewis et al. 2012). Translation: a book does worse than a therapist, but better than nothing—which, in an NHS reeling under budget cuts, is what many patients would otherwise get.

The NHS-Wales version of bibliotherapy emphasizes the experience of reading less than the information that happens to be vehicled by print— and could just as well (though more expensively) emanate from a mouth or a smartphone app. Or more precisely, what matters is the mental operations prompted by the book's verbal content, whether that means a set of workbook exercises or a self-styled bibliotherapeutic picture book like *My Beautiful Mommy* (2008), which invites children of patients undergoing elective cosmetic surgery to identify with the narrator. Here, "therapy" is the central term, with "biblio" being a mere convenience.

In the NHS program as in the research studies whose authority it invokes and for which it creates demand, "biblio" sometimes denotes verbal content ("a book about depression"); sometimes material form (longform print as opposed to apps, mp4s, leaflets, and bullet-pointed PDFs). Somewhere in the middle of that spectrum lies the claim that the *verbal* form affects health— that the reading of narrative, or of esthetically ambitious texts, or of patterned poetic language, itself has curative powers (Martin 2012).

Consider a companion program to Books on Prescription, Mood-Boosting Books. Funded by England's beleaguered library system in collaboration with a patchwork of social-service agencies, but administered by NHS-employed doctors, this program also recommends "good reads for people who are anxious or depressed." The "reads" in question, though, are fiction, poetry, and memoirs. Only some represent anxiety or depression.

What does get consistently thematized in its titles is the power of reading. A novel enrolls its characters in a reading group (*The Guernsey Literary and Potato Peel Pie Society*); an autobiography chronicles a footballer's journey toward literacy (*Tackling Life* by Charlie Oatway). Protecting books—censored in the first title, marginalized in the second—becomes an image for loving and caring for an equally threatened self. In other selections, though, the underdog is more literal. Mood-Boosting titles like *The Bad Dog's Diary* and

My Boy Butch: The Heart-Warming True Story of a Little Dog Who Made Life Worth Living Again read like printouts from PetTube.com.

In the same year the Nobel Committee named Alice Munro Laureate in Literature, Mood-Boosting Books selected her short story collection *Too Much Happiness* as an Uplifting Title. The first honor seems easier to understand than the second, since Munro's mood-killing stories turn, more specifically, on the power dynamics brokered by books. One story's naked heroine is tricked into reading aloud to a fully clothed man. Another story depicts a postoperative radio announcer, eyes bandaged, listening to books read aloud by a sinisterly unidentified woman. A third protagonist "hated to hear the word 'escape' used about fiction. She might have argued, not just playfully, that it was real life that was the escape." Also in *Too Much Happiness*, a character writes a book of short stories with "some title like a how-to book," *How Are We to Live*. The character's "mission in life is to make people feel uncomfortable."

Bibliotherapists often quote Kafka's ambition to make his books an axe to break the frozen sea within readers. A more accurate metaphor for their uses of literature might be an icepack. Carried captive by comfort: instead of inciting readers to rage (as a critic might have done a generation ago) against the patriarchal logic of the sonnet, a bibliotherapy course at University of Warwick instead uses poems to "calm" and "reassure" readers ("Literature and Mental Health"). What's therapeutic here is the reading of literature—but not literary reading.

* * *

Bibliotherapy's reach can be measured by the ragtag range of institutional settings that it's coming to inhabit. Mood-Boosting Books's "uplift" (if I can borrow a term from David James's essay in this volume) finds its trickle-up equivalent in feepaying bibliotherapy. At London's archly named School of Life, two bibliotherapists named Susan Elderkin and Ella Berthoud scribble faux prescription pads with recommendations ranging from the allopathic (racing through a nail-biter like *The Postman Always Rings Twice* heals apathy) to the analogic (short stories treat diarrhea). More simply, patients can identify with similarly suffering characters. Your tooth aches; so does Count Vronsky's.

While self-help books provide a cheaper alternative to face-to-face treatment, "biblioconcierges" (the 2014 coinage of an American imitator) emerged on the contrary as an upmarket alternative to what librarians have long done for free. And then there are the hidden costs. "Buy *The Enchanted April*," Elderkin and Berthoux's 2014 bibliotherapy manual commands, "then book a villa in Italy and read it on the way out" (241). If making your own reservation proves too onerous, its authors will chaperone you and your airport novels to a 1,600-pound oceanfront "bibliotherapy retreat." This kind of bibliotherapist sounds more like a sommelier than like a doctor—"therapy" as in "aromatherapy," not as in "chemo."

Book boosters don't always cater to the worried well-off. Some activists defend marginalized readers by championing persecuted books. In Texas, Librotraficante distributes banned books in low-income communities where book ownership is a rarity. (How many books a household owns turns out to be a better predictor of children's success in school than parents' education level (Evans et al. 2010).) Others bypass the library and the bookstore for less bookish settings. That includes the waiting room: "Reach out and Read," founded in Boston in 1989, gives doctors and pediatric nurses picture books to hand to patients. And the tops of dryers: Libraries Without Borders places paperbacks in laundromats in the Bronx, the only borough in New York without an independent bookstore. In the UK, "Give a Book" places new books, Gideon-style, in police station holding cells.

Not content to distribute texts, some programs mandate how and when they're discussed. In the United States, an alternative-sentencing program called Changing Lives Through Literature conditions probation on offenders' attendance at a single-sex reading group. Like the probation officers and judges who told me that their lives, too, were changed by arguing over photocopied short stories (for even middle-class men have few other opportunities to read Hemingway), the court-ordered participants whom I interviewed for my book *What We Talk about When We Talk about Books* mixed a Christian language of "turning-points" with New Critical identification of "epiphanies." The difference is that the offenders can be sent to jail if they fail to show up or—in theory at least—if they fail to do the reading.

Censorship is force-reading's obverse. The same justice system that requires the men in this room to read or go to jail forbids prisoners from being sent certain books: hardbacks that can be used as weapons; texts that preach violence; books not available through the businesses that have negotiated a monopoly on supplying goods to prisons. Casting books as a weapon of the weak, the one place where otherwise powerless readers can escape all social constraints, obscures how often the choice to read comes from above as much as within.

No less than for-profit biblio-baristas, the biblioactivists whom I met claimed to defend individual choice against academic coercion. (This held true even, or especially, for those who had the weight of a criminal-justice system or medical bureaucracy behind them.) Many claimed, more specifically, to champion for common readers' common sense against literary-critical jargon. To thrust books into readers' hands, they first needed to wrest them out of the hands of the killjoys like me who make a living chaperoning booklovers' natural urges.

If literature cultivates empathy, I asked Jane Davis, the author of a dissertation on George Eliot who went on to found an NGO that gathers ill, incarcerated, or isolated people to take turns reading photocopied literature aloud in real time, why do I leave every faculty meeting wanting to strangle my English department colleagues? She parried neatly with a question in return: had I heard of molecular gastronomy? By trying to learn *about* texts rather than *from* texts, she told me, you and your colleagues are cooking up the intellectual equivalent of snail-flavored porridge.[2] Davis's metaphor departs from the traditional complaint that the academic study of literature doesn't make a difference. The celebrity chef analogy suggests instead that criticism commits active harm by draining legitimacy from uses of literature that do support well-being.

Even or especially when they emerge from activist communities, bibliotherapists' disavowal of academic critique upends the form of political engagement invented by Cold-War–era cultural studies. In the second half of the twentieth century, critics claimed a social function by declaring literature a training ground for critique. The skills honed on literary texts, they hoped, could ultimately be directed to nonliterary objects, such as advertising or political oratory or other forms of propaganda. Rescuing lit from crit, bibliotherapists' project of making literature more usable to lay readers risks making literary criticism less so.

Critics who value literature as something good to think with may, however, have one thing in common with therapists who treat it as good to feel with. In its refusal to be embarrassed by sentiment, identification or instrumentalization, bibliotherapy mirrors new currents within literary criticism itself. As Beth Blum points out in this volume, card-carrying English professors themselves are increasingly replacing critique by "reparative" or "surface" or "descriptive" reading (Marcus and Best 2009; Love 2010; Felski

---

[2] Interview with Jane Davis, London, 11 Sep. 2013.

2015). In comparing "weak theory" within the academy with extra-academic attacks on charisma (geek chic, #MeToo), Blum makes it possible to recognize that bibliotherapy shares with emerging styles of literary criticism its emotional tone, not just its object. As professional reading comes to exceed the boundaries of the literary professoriate, the boundary between amateurism and expertise no longer maps onto the boundary between thematic and formal approaches (Vadde 2017). What's less clear is how the academic study of literary form can contribute to bibliotherapeutic projects—except by getting out of their way.

Works Cited

Bavishi, Avni, et al. "A Chapter a Day: Association of Book Reading with Longevity." *Social Science and Medicine*, vol. 164, Sept. 2016, pp. 44–48.

Berns, Gregory S., et al. "Short- and Long-Term Effects of a Novel on Connectivity in the Brain." *Brain Connectivity*, vol. 3, no. 6, 2013, pp. 590–600.

Berthoud, Ella, and Susan Elderkin. *The Novel Cure: From Abandonment to Zestlessness: 751 Books to Cure What Ails You*. Penguin Books, 2014.

Best, Stephen, and Sharon Marcus. "Surface Reading: An Introduction." *Representations*, vol. 108, no. 1, 2009, pp. 1–21.

"Book Reading." Humanities Indicators, May 2015, https://humanitiesindicators.org/content/indicatordoc.aspx?i=92.

Brown, Mark. "GPs to Prescribe Self-Help Books for Mental Health Problems." *Guardian*, 31 Jan. 2013.

Capriotti, Kathleen, and Kelly Hill. *Social Effects of Culture: Detailed Statistical Models*. Report, Statistical Insights on the Arts series, vol. 7, no. 1, Hill Strategies Research Inc., 2008.

Clark, Christina, and George Dugdale. *Literacy Changes Lives: An Advocacy Resource*. National Literacy Trust, 2008.

Evans, Mariah, et al. "Family Scholarly Culture and Educational Success: Books and Schooling in 27 Nations." *Research in Social Stratification and Mobility*, vol. 28, no. 2, 2010, pp. 171–97.

Felski, Rita. *The Limits of Critique*. Chicago UP, 2015.

Frude, Neil. *Book Prescription Wales 2011—A Strategy for Enhancing Treatment Choice for Mental Health: Prescriber Information Booklet*. Wales National Health Service, 2011, http://www.wales.nhs.uk/sitesplus/documents/829/BPW%20Prescriber%20Information%20booklet%20.pdf.

Kidd, David Comer, and Emanuele Castano. "Reading Literary Fiction Improves Theory of Mind." *Science*, vol. 342, no. 6156, Oct. 2013, pp. 377–80, https://doi.org/10.1126/science.1239918.

Lewis, Catrin, et al. "Efficacy, Cost-Effectiveness, and Acceptability of Self-Help Interventions for Anxiety Disorders: Systematic Review." *British Journal of Psychiatry*, vol. 200, no. 1, 2012, pp. 15–21.

"Literature and Mental Health: Reading for Wellbeing. " Future Learn, https://www.futu relearn.com/courses/literature.

Love, Heather. "Close but Not Deep: Literary Ethics and the Descriptive Turn." *New Literary History*, vol. 41, no. 2, 2010, pp. 371–91.

Martin, Meredith. *The Rise and Fall of Meter: Poetry and English National Culture 1860–1930*. Princeton UP, 2012.

"Mood-Boosting Books 2012." Reading Groups for Everyone website, http://readinggro ups.org/news/mood-boosting-books-2012.html. Accessed 1 July 2018.

Munro, Alice. *Too Much Happiness*. Chatto & Windus, 2009.

Pinker, Steven. *The Better Angels of Our Nature: Why Violence Has Declined*. Penguin Random House, 2011.

Price, Leah. *What We Talk about When We Talk about Books: The History and Future of Reading*. Basic Books, 2019.

Primack, B. A., et al. "Using Ecological Momentary Assessment to Determine Media Use by Individuals with and without Major Depressive Disorder." *JAMA* vol. 165, no. 4, 2011, pp. 360–65.

Rångtell, F. H., E. Ekstrand, L. Rapp, et al. "Two Hours of Evening Reading on a Self-Luminous Tablet vs. Reading a Physical Book Does Not Alter Sleep after Daytime Bright Light Exposure." *Sleep Med*, vol. 23, 2016, pp. 111–18, https://doi.org/10.1016/j.sleep.2016.06.016.

"Reading Well Evidence Base." The Reading Agency, http://readingagency.org.uk/adults/impact/research/reading-well-books-on-prescription-scheme-evidence-base.html. Accessed 1 July 2018.

Tamir, Diana I., Andrew Bricker, David Dodell-Feder, and Jason P. Mitchell. "Reading Fiction and Reading Minds: The Role of Simulation in the Default Network." *Social Cognitive and Affective Neuroscience* vol. 11, no. 2, 2015, pp. 215–24.

To Read or Not to Read: A Question of National Consequence. Research Report 47. National Endowment for the Arts. 2007.

Vadde, Aarthi. "Amateur Creativity: Contemporary Literature and the Digital Publishing Scene." *New Literary History* vol. 48, no. 1, 2017, pp. 27–51.

"Which Were the Most Borrowed Library Books in 2012–2013?" DataBlog. *Guardian*, 14 Feb. 2014.

2

Bad Habits on Goodreads?

Eclecticism vs. Genre-Intolerance among Online Readers

James F. English, Scott Enderle, and Rahul Dhakecha[1]

This chapter presents some findings from work we have done on the social reading site and Amazon subsidiary, Goodreads. In discussing this work we hope to connect literary reader studies to the study of human flourishing by way of three questions. The first is methodological and concerns a basic challenge in the empirical social sciences that has made its way into literary studies via digital humanities: how to build datasets adequate to support generalizations about readers and reading (generalizations such as: reading contributes to well-being). The second is a sociological question, arising out of work that began in the 1990s: whether readers today are inclining toward broadly tolerant habits of reading, replacing the ideal of narrowly "good taste" with that of eclecticism, and establishing creative curation as the basis of a flourishing relationship to books. Our third question links the other two by asking whether digital platforms such as Goodreads, besides being rich sources of data about readers and reading, might themselves, through their ever more comprehensive algorithmic mediations, be affecting this entire scheme of values, preferences, and readerly well-being.

[1] Note on authorship: Most of the writing for the Mining Goodreads project has been done by James English, the corresponding author (email: jenglish@sas.upenn.edu). A majority of the technical work discussed in the present chapter was performed by Rahul Dhakecha and Scott Enderle. Dhakecha and Enderle also contributed significantly to the discussion and analysis of findings as presented here. Earlier technical work on data-mining of Goodreads was done by Tianli Han and Sharvin Shah with input from Lyle Ungar. Popular genre booklists were curated by Daniel Sample, Alex Anderson, Amy Stidham, and Samantha Lambert. James Pawelski served as Project Manager during the first phase of work, with input from Louis Tay.

James F. English, Scott Enderle, and Rahul Dhakecha, *Bad Habits on Goodreads?* In: *Literary Studies and Human Flourishing*. Edited by: James F. English and Heather Love, Oxford University Press. © Oxford University Press 2023. DOI: 10.1093/oso/9780197637227.003.0003

The Data of Literary Reception

Problems of scale and selection in data gathering are not germane to every branch of well-being studies, any more than they are to every branch of literary studies. But the rationale for expanding research and curriculum on human flourishing drives the field as a whole toward research questions that are inherently empirical. Well-being science justifies itself with the promise to discover new knowledge that can enhance individual and collective life. It seeks such knowledge through rigorously observed demonstrations of cause-and-effect, where certain sharable skills and practices may be shown to increase chances for social connectedness, self-actualization, and achievement of non-trivial, "higher" states of happiness. The Positive Psychology Center at the University of Pennsylvania, for example, promotes a set of "21 empirically validated skills" that enhance resilience.[2] The recurring hypothesis that reading literature counts as a positive human activity, that doing it is good for us (as the "bibliotherapists" discussed in Leah Price's chapter contend), ultimately depends, at least for some vectors of its validation, on data about actual readers and the kinds of reading they actually do.

Yet the datasets used to support claims for the positive effects of reading seem woefully deficient. Neuroscientific and other empirical cognitive studies of literary processing—such as the widely publicized "Your Brain on Jane Austen" experiment at Stanford (Phillips 2012)—involve sample sets so small and socially narrow as scarcely to improve on Norman Holland's pilot experiment of the mid-1970s, which sought to discover "the nature of literary response" (Holland 1975) by studying just five student readers in an academic setting.[3] Where the sample sets are large, as in national-scale social scientific studies, breadth of social reach is achieved at the cost of considerable imprecision. Interpreters of the Cultural Capital and Social Exclusion survey in Britain, for example, or of the Everyday Cultures survey in Australia—two of the best large-scale studies—must accept respondents' self-reported habits and preferences as a proxy for their actual reading practices, despite evidence

---

[2] These twenty-one skills constitute the "Resilience Skill Set" in the Penn Resilience Program. Positive Psychology website, ppc.sas.upenn.edu/resilience-programs/resilience-skill-set.

[3] Natalie Phillips's 2012 study of reading and forms of attention involved graduate student test subjects reading a chapter of *Mansfield Park* two different ways, casually for entertainment and closely as though in preparation for an academic assignment. Her finding that the two modes of reading involved radically different patterns of brain activity was widely popularized according to the "Your Brain on Jane Austen" formula, foregrounding the unsupported inference that canonical literature provides an especially beneficial cognitive workout.

that people often misconstrue or mischaracterize their relationships to literature. Scholars using the NEA surveys of Public Participation in the Arts to study American readers have had to settle for rudimentary classifications more appropriate to literacy studies (mapping of readers vs. nonreaders) than to research on literary reception per se (mapping of readers to different varieties of literary experience or habits of literary consumption). The NEA counts a person among "adults who read literature," for example, if she has read just one story, play, or poem "not for work or school" in the previous year (NEA 2004, ix). Reception studies cannot do much with a statistic like that.

Scholars working on reception from within literary studies proper have struggled with the paucity of good data, as well. Book historians have used publishing industry sales figures, library borrowing records, and other data to infer general patterns of consumption over time or across different nations and regions. But it is difficult to derive from aggregate statistics of this sort a good sense of how readers' judgments of taste are organized or how their different experiences of reading are socially distributed—key questions for reception studies. The ethnographic approach pioneered in literary studies by Janice Radway (1984) is limited to small-group analysis, focusing on geographically compact communities of like-minded readers. Radway's study of romance readers was based on surveys and interviews of just forty-two women who acquired their books from a single bookseller in a small Midwestern town. Elizabeth Long threw an only marginally wider net for her study of women's book clubs (Long 2003). Long conducted fieldwork across several dozen women's groups and interviewed more than 130 subjects, but her research remained strictly local in scope: the clubs were all in the Houston area. The findings of these small-group case studies could be interestingly sharpened and amplified through analysis of comparative samples: Midwestern male readers of science fiction, say, or women bookclub members who are neither Southern nor white nor rural. Indeed, the methodological gold standard might be a coordinated set of parallel field studies addressed to different populations, each combining analysis of survey responses with participant-observer descriptions and ethnographic interviews. But our discipline isn't equipped to undertake such work. Rather than building on existing datasets, we fall back on our standard procedures, viz., to extrapolate and generalize from our own reading or the reading reported anecdotally by other scholars, critics, literary journalists, or students. Literary studies has learned to do a lot with this unmethodical approach to "the reader." A book like Rita Felski's *Uses of Literature* draws on highly evolved disciplinary skills and provokes new ways to think and talk about the act of reading. But the book's force is rhetorical rather than evidentiary; Felski's explicit statements about "ordinary" and "typical" readers (Felski 2008, 39, 41, 70, 102) rest on the common sense, or common prejudice, of an atypical academic, and lack standing on the ground of statistical demonstrability. The same could be said for the way readers are invoked throughout this volume. None of us really knows what we mean when we speak of *ordinary* readers, or even whether we ourselves should be included in that category.

The branch of literary studies that has been most exercised about inadequately representative data of reception is a strain of digital humanities (DH) that Alan Liu and Ted Underwood have labeled DH's "sociological" zone: the zone where computational text analysis is used to "model social boundaries" (Underwood 2015). This is a methodological space that seems well-disposed for an encounter between literary research and the science of well-being, and our small team has been attempting initial experiments along these lines. Supported by Penn's Price Lab for Digital Humanities and the Humanities and Human Flourishing Project,[4] we have been extracting and analyzing data from the Goodreads social reading and curation site. With its 50 million unique users per month, rating and reviewing the books they read, arranging them on personalized "shelves," and forming into fan clubs, friend networks, and discussion groups, Goodreads is an enticing resource for empirical reader studies. The reviews for any given book are generally more relevant, more detailed, and many times more numerous on Goodreads than on Amazon, which became its parent company in 2013 but maintains a front-end separation between what consumers write about a book on the shopping site and what booklovers write about it on the "social cataloging" site.[5] In Amazon, for instance, Chimamanda Ngozi Adichie's *Americanah* has 3,900 ratings and reviews, including off-topic rants about same-day delivery or damaged packaging. In Goodreads, *Americanah* has 17,000 reader reviews and nearly 170,000 ratings, most of these linked to a user page where the user's full collection of books and all attendant links and commentary

[4] Research connected with the Humanities and Human Flourishing Project was supported in part by a grant from the Templeton Religion Trust. The opinions expressed in this chapter are those of the authors and do not necessarily reflect the views of the Templeton Religion Trust.

[5] Dmitrov et al. (2015) performed a comparative computational analysis of book reviews on Amazon and Goodreads restricted to the nonfiction genre of biography. Their study confirmed that reviewers on Amazon tend to use more language about the quality of their shopping experience (e.g., "buy," "bought," "purchased," "price") while reviewers on Goodreads use more language about the quality of their reading experience (e.g., "interesting," "pretty," "funny").

may be found. For social scientists who favor "naturalistic study of reading" (NSR) over the artifice of laboratory experiments, having all that data in one place represents a potentially massive shortcut to the expensive and time-consuming business of chasing down readers "in the wild."[6] Literary DHers have likewise found Goodreads hard to resist; scholars who have crawled the site include Andrew Piper and colleagues at McGill (Dmitrov 2015) and Katherine Bode's team at Australian National University.[7]

Alluring though it is, Goodreads is no easy gold strike for data miners. The site presents major legal restrictions and technical constraints, which became progressively more severe during the period of our research, forcing shut-downs of some of our most promising lines of inquiry. Crawling the site's profile pages yields only meagre demographic information about users, ruling out research into major areas of sociological interest. An attempt by the Humanities and Human Flourishing Project's Louis Tay to supplement profile data via survey questionnaire foundered on yet more legal and technical impediments. While Goodreads is eager to tout its "massive" user base of 50 million booklovers, only a small fraction of those are regular readers who habitually rate and review the books they read—and even those readers' reviews often contain just a few words of text: "thumbs up!" or "didn't like it." Working on Goodreads puts paid to any naïve hope that the mere existence of bigger datasets such as may be scraped from social media sites can solve the problem of sample bias or that of defining and operationalizing the "ordinary" reader. These are not problems that literary scholars and researchers of human flourishing can evade by means of big data. But the sheer scale of the repositories means that learning how to derive useful information from them could be an important undertaking for both fields: an ongoing shared challenge.

The Mining Goodreads project at Penn, which focuses on readers of contemporary fiction, has built a database comprising nearly 3 million reviews, together with corresponding ratings (on a 5-star scale), and metadata on the books, authors, and (to a much lesser degree) users themselves. We have gathered all the reviews in Goodreads of 500 bestsellers and 1,300 novels that made the shortlists of major awards since 1960, plus a substantial

---

[6] Mike Thelwall is pioneering this kind of web-based sociological work with his "statistical cybermetrics" group at the University of Wolverhampton, UK.

[7] Bode is studying Goodreads data as part of a larger project on Australian literature in the digital age called "Reading at the Interface" (https://katherinebode.wordpress.com/projects/reading-at-the-interface-project/).

cross-section of the reviews of curated top-200 lists of twenty-first-century mystery/crime/detective fiction, science fiction, and chick lit/modern romance novels. In addition, we have compiled all the reviews written by a random set of 1,672 highly active Goodreads users, who between them have read more than 200,000 unique works of fiction across the full range of popular and not-so-popular genres.[8] We have refined and structured this data, some of which, along with the attendant code, may be shared with other researchers pursuing their own questions about contemporary readers, tastes, and values.[9]

Divisions on the Field of Reading

What might be learned from all this Goodreads data? Our initial experiments focused on the traditionally assumed polarity of literary commerce vs. literary status: popularity vs. prestige. Is the literary field still describable in terms of a "great divide" between the space of bestsellers, with their masses of undiscriminating readers, and the space of legitimate literary art, esteemed by critics and consumed by a cultural elite? If so, that would suggest that when we talk about reading and its benefits we may be conflating two different and opposed modes of practice, envisioning a space of cultural divergence and even antagonism as a unified, harmonious field.

Such a division does seem to express itself in the data of online reception. Reviews and ratings of novels that succeed commercially look different in many respects from reviews and ratings of novels that garner critical praise. The NRC Word–Emotion Association Lexicon, EmoLex, an algorithm designed to measure the emotional orientations of language, finds that reviews of bestsellers tend to involve more frequent use of words in the categories of "surprise" (e.g., "amazing," "interesting," "entertaining," "wow") and "anticipation" ("what," "suspense," "mystery," "plot," "new"), while reviews of prize-listed books tend to use more words in the "trust" category (e.g.,

---

[8] The initial scrape was based on a random selection of 2,000 prolific reviewers (>150 reviews). Of these, 328 were eventually excluded due to personal privacy firewalls, giving us a sample of 1,672 prolific Goodreads reviewers. Review counts for some of these users are well below 150 because for most of our analyses we have set aside reviews of nonfiction and of fiction aimed at children or young adults.

[9] Given the Goodreads licensing statement, which seeks to place far-reaching restrictions on use, our project data is locked in a secure server and we have anonymized all users in our visualizations and other outputs.

Rank	Bestseller r	(p) N freq
0	Surprise 0.218	(0.0000) 1084 6533073
1	Anticipation 0.155	(0.0000) 1084 4730037
2	Disgust 0.028	(0.4102) 1084 9429944
3	Anger −0.020	(0.5002) 1084 5643934
4	Fear −0.039	(0.2604) 1084 5684769
5	Sadness −0.061	(0.0722) 1084 3308934
6	Joy −0.070	(0.0433) 1084 4346488
7	Trust −0.126	(0.0001) 1084 8854387
Rank	Bestseller r	(p) N freq

Figure 2.1 Analysis of a corpus containing all the 4- and 5-star Goodreads reviews of 500 top-10 annual bestsellers and 1,300 prize-listed novels published between 1960 and 2016. The NRC Word-Emotion Lexicon (EmoLex) finds words relating to "surprise" and "anticipation" are strongly overrepresented in reviews of bestsellers compared to the full corpus, while words relating to "trust" are strongly overrepresented in reviews of prize-listed novels (p-values below .05 indicate significant correlation).

"character" "love," "life," "relationship," "others")[10] (Figure 2.1). This seems to confirm a traditional notion of bestseller lovers as people who read for the plot, as distinguished from readers of literary fiction, who read for development of character and relationships. A more all-purpose tool of linguistic analysis, LIWC, yields the further finding that reviews of prize-listed novels are most distinguished by a high incidence of language in the categories of *perception* ("beautiful," "strange," "haunting"), *space* ("close," "distant," "among"), and *insight* ("sense," "believe," "interpret"), whereas reviews

[10] Known as EmoLex, the NRC Word-Emotion Association Lexicon counts words, according to a weighted scheme, into eight basic emotion categories (anger, fear, anticipation, trust, surprise, sadness, joy, and disgust) and two valences of sentiment (positive and negative). For access to tool and commentary, see Mohammad and Turney.

of bestsellers are most strongly distinguished by a high incidence of language connected with *work* and *reward*—a somewhat counterintuitive finding that turns out mainly to capture the tendency of bestseller reviewers to foreground the bare fact of having "read" the "book," as well as to appraise a novel in comparatively blunt terms such as "good," "great," "favorite" (Figure 2.2).[11]

Some of the most basic patterns of contrast are evident even in a simple comparison of word frequencies using the Differential Linguistic Analysis (DLA) toolkit, which lacks any fixed lexicon or weighted system of moods and topics. The cloud visualizations in Figure 2.3 show the individual words or punctuation marks that are most distinctive of each set of reviews, with font size indicating the strength of the correlation. (A color difference, blue indicating a word appearing with lower frequency in the database and red a higher frequency, is not discernible in these grayscale images.) In contrast to the bestseller-review emphasis on the activity of book-reading itself ("read," "book," "books") and the yield of plot-derived excitement or entertainment, the prize novel reviews are distinguished by attention to the writing, the prose, the sentences, the narrative voice and its affective particulars. This again tends to confirm a traditional and hierarchical division (appreciation of literary language being rarer and more elevated than enjoyment of a good story), as does the fact that the bestseller reviews are slangier, making more use of exclamation marks, smiley faces, the internet shorthand LOL, contrasting with the prize novel reviews' much heavier reliance on commas and prepositions (of, in, and, or). These latter are indicators of formality, more elaborately or pedantically constructed sentences with more subordinate clauses.[12]

One way to interpret these findings is as a difference of education, readers of bestsellers seemingly writing at a lower grade level, further from the norms of college English. One might also infer differences of age and gender, with the bestseller readers younger and more female. In sociolinguistics, the history of language is sometimes understood to be one of decreasing formality, where the young are ahead of the old, anticipating where usage is headed, and men, perhaps being more distant from the young, or more invested in the status quo, tend to lag behind women.[13] With respect to our dataset, the

---

[11] LIWC is the acronym for Linguistic Inquiry and Word Count, a tool developed by James Pennebaker et al. in the early 1990s which has been much refined and updated over the years and is very widely used in psychology and psycholinguistics. We used LIWC2015, described in Pennebaker et al. 2015.

[12] Formality is a vast and complex area of linguistics research. For an overview, see Dewaele and Heylighen 1999.

[13] This interpretation was suggested to us by Lyle Ungar, a senior consultant on the project. For discussion of relevant recent research, see Flekova et al. 2016. See also the paragraphs on gender in Heylighen and Dewaele 1999.

TOP LIWC CATEGORIES				DLA MOST DISTINCTIVE WORDS		

Rank	Bestseller r	(p) N freq		Rank	Word	Rel freq
				1	BOOKS	110
0	REWARD 0.466	(0.0000) 1435 1799376		2	READ	96
1	WORK 0.408	(0.0000) 1435 4674314		3	GOOD	93
				4	GERAT	71
2	POSEMO 0.378	(0.0000) 1435 5392039		5	STILL	62
3	LEISURE 0.340	(0.0000) 1435 3253552		6	:)	61
				7	EXCITING	61
4	TIME 0.334	(0.0000) 1435 5645409		8	ONE	60
5	INFORMAL 0.330	(0.0000) 1435 824566		9	FAVORITE	59
				10	I	58
6	ASSENT 0.328	(0.0000) 1435 195367		11	BOOK	56
7	NETSPEAK 0.304	(0.0000) 1435 222146				
8	I 0.295	(0.0000) 1435 5147989				
9	NUMBER 0.294	(0.0000) 1435 1422342				
10	AFFECT 0.262	(0.0000) 1435 8031372				

Figure 2.2 The Linguistic Inquiry and Word Count 2015 tool (LIWC, on the left) finds that words pertaining to *reward* and *work* are much more frequent in reviews of bestsellers than in reviews of prize-listed novels. Using differential linguistic analysis (DLA, on the right) to identify the specific words that most sharply distinguish bestseller reviews from prize novel reviews shows that the LIWC finding is driven by words about the *work* of book-reading itself, with the evaluative terms "good," "great," and "favorite" registering heavily in the LIWC category of *reward*.

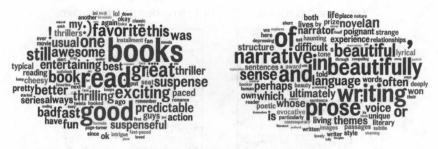

Figure 2.3 Most distinguishing words in reviews of bestsellers (left) and prize-listed novels (right). Font size indicates the strength of a word's correlation with that set of reviews.

assumption would be that we are dealing here with two different populations of reviewers, a younger and/or more female set and an older and/or less female set. Such assumptions can lead to dangerous forms of circular reasoning in which researchers appear to extract from social data confirmation of a stereotype that has in fact been built into the research.[14] But given that the three most reviewed novels in our collection are the bestsellers *The Hunger Games*, *Gone Girl*, and *Mockingjay*, novels aimed at young women readers, we might in this case be prepared to relax our critical vigilance.

That would be a mistake, though, for in fact the difference in linguistic register persists even if we correct for a population gap. We filtered the reviews down to users who read and review *both* kinds of book, and filtered those down to the ones who actually like both kinds of book (excluding all reviews attached to ratings of 3 or below), and then ensured that from each of these readers we took an equal number of reviews, equally divided between bestsellers and prize novels.[15] This produced a single population, of whatever median age and gender mix, each reviewer carrying the same statistical weight as the others, and that weight evenly balanced across the two sides of the corpus.

Outputting DLA analysis of these population-balanced samples as word clouds, we find the differences are muted, but still discernable (Figure 2.4).

---

[14] On the risks of circularity and overgeneralization in computational gender attribution, see Koolen and van Cranenburgh 2017.

[15] As we mention further on in the discussion, since more than two-thirds of all the ratings in our database are 4 stars or above (a ratio close to that of the Goodreads site as a whole), even a 3-star rating may be regarded as negative.

Figure 2.4 Most distinguishing words for reviews of bestsellers (left) and prize-listed novels (right), 4- or 5-star reviews only. For each bestseller review there is a corresponding prize novel review written by the same reader. Font size indicates the strength of a word's correlation with that set of reviews.

The exclamation mark and the smiley are still distinctive of the bestseller reviews, the marks of formality (the comma, colon, and semicolon, the prepositions) still distinctive on the prize novels side. When someone who happens to have written a positive review of a bestseller writes a positive review of a critically distinguished novel, they don't just adopt a different, more elevated set of aesthetic values (e.g., those of "beauty" and "lyricism" in the prose rather than "speed" and "suspense" in the plot); they also write in a different, less formal or mature-sounding linguistic register.

The fact that we have controlled here for demographics does not mean that social categories such as gender are irrelevant to the binary division of the field. A traditionally gendered status hierarchy ensures the alignment of systems for classifying linguistic registers with systems for classifying literary genres and styles. The same gender stereotypes that shape linguistic assumptions about formality and informality, maturity and immaturity in natural language shape the literary assumptions about seriousness and frivolity, art and entertainment in literature. Today's major US and UK fiction prizes are about 50 percent more likely to go to a male than a female author in any given year, and if a woman author does win, her protagonist is 50% more likely than not to be male (Griffith 2015).[16] In other countries represented in our dataset the male tilt is even sharper. The genre that is most dominated

---

[16] Recent work in *Cultural Analytics* (Kraicer and Piper 2019) shows how thoroughly woven into the texts of novels themselves is the pattern of male overrepresentation and female marginalization. The authors do not, however, find large differences in this respect between prizewinning novels and bestsellers.

by women authors, romance, is the least respected by critics and the least represented on prize shortlists. The economy of symbolic rewards in literature is gendered such that the reader who discusses a critically esteemed book, expressing herself in the space of artistic legitimacy, will feel encouraged to adopt a voice closer to the masculine stereotype than she would for discussing a work of mere commercial entertainment.[17]

With respect to the putative "great divide" in the space of literary reception, then, we have a double finding: the gap separating bestsellers from critically respected fiction on Goodreads is not so absolute that a reader can't roam across it; at the same time, the symbolic force of that gap is strong enough that readers who do cross over are compelled to don a kind of linguistic camouflage. It is noteworthy as well how very small a fraction of Goodreads reviewers do actually make that crossing, contributing positive reviews to both sides of the contrastive set. It is expected that a social media crawl of this kind will capture a large number of users who contribute very little and a small number who contribute a lot; that's the normal pattern. In our bestsellers-vs.-prize-listed database, 400,000 readers contributed just a single review; only 23,000 contributed 10 reviews or more. But we assumed that the major share of these 23,000 high-volume reviewers would be pretty eclectic in their reading habits. The average high-volume reviewer, with 21 reviews of our books, will have written 200 reviews of other books that aren't in our database, that is, books that are neither bestsellers nor prize contenders. This would seem to point away from a simple bifurcation of readerships toward more various, broad-minded patterns of consumption, what Richard Peterson famously described as a tendency toward "omnivorousness" (Peterson 1992).

The Omnivore Concept and Genre-Intolerance

Indeed, Peterson, a founding figure in the sociology of culture, introduced the concept of the cultural omnivore specifically to complicate the standard binary scheme of reception. A sociologist of music working in Nashville,

---

[17] As the corpus linguists Sally Johnson and Astrid Enselin have argued, wherever a distinction is made between "male language" and "female language" it is likely to be hierarchical, placing higher value on male language and valuing female language only to the extent that it departs from "stereotypically" female language., i.e., where it more closely resembles "male language" (Enselin and Johnson 2013).

he was observing that the most avid and sophisticated music listeners were not, as the old high/low model would have it, devoting themselves entirely to classical and avant-garde music. Rather, they were mixing and matching, building complex portfolios of preference and expertise in a number of different musical forms up and down the supposed high/middle/low scale: modern classical, perhaps, but also country, and maybe big, block-buster Broadway musicals as well. These listeners still constituted an elite, but their distance from the ordinary mass consumer was to be measured by the greater complexity of composition of their cultural appreciation profiles, not by their rejection of popular and middlebrow forms.

The concept has been widely assimilated and repurposed in cultural sociology, as has Peterson's finding of generally increasing omnivorousness, according to which all groups, and not just this retooled elite, are broadening the spectrum of their preferences.[18] This widening of consumer appetites is, in Peterson's view, a "society-wide," "long term secular trend," affecting all the fields of culture, from popular music to art and literature (1996, 904, 901).

If, as Michèle Ollivier has said, Peterson's coining of the terms "omnivore" and "univore" represented a "paradigm shift in cultural sociology" ("Revisiting Distinction" 263), it is because these new terms provided a way for sociologists to reimagine the way taste related to core questions of hierarchy and freedom. Through his innovative application of multiple correspondence analysis (MCA) to map the data of the 1960s French Kodak and Taste surveys as a "cloud of individuals" in the "space of lifestyles," Pierre Bourdieu had shown in *Distinction* (1979) that people's tastes in art, music, literature, film, furniture, food, and sport fall into certain patterns of correlation both with each other and with such particulars of their social position as the rank and industry of their employment, their income, their own and their fathers' highest level of education, and other factors. The symbolic hierarchy of good vs. bad aesthetic taste was homologous with a range of other hierarchies of value (healthy vs. unhealthy food; finesse sports vs. sports of suffering), including the material hierarchy of more vs. less capital. One's tastes were not an exercise of individual discernment and personal choice so much as a baked-in feature of one's position in this social space of lifestyles, more

---

[18] Peterson and Kern found that the young "highbrow" cohorts were diversifying their tastes most rapidly, but that young "non-highbrow" cohorts were following a similar pattern (Peterson and Kern 1996, 900–907). For more recent attempts to confirm the breadth of the trend toward omnivorousness, see Lahire 2008 and Ollivier 2008.

rigidly and predictably bound up with one's economic and cultural inherit-
ance than anyone wanted to admit.

Peterson made no use of MCA and did not directly address himself to
Bourdieu's model of social space. Nonetheless, in its many subsequent
versions and offshoots, the omnivore concept has seemed to open pathways
out of Bourdieu's depressing prison of correspondences. Even in Peterson's
own comparatively un-utopian analysis, which stressed the persistence of
distinctions between higher and lower social strata, there is said to be more
"mixing" of "people holding different tastes," and a decline in the use of "the
arts as markers of exclusion" (Peterson and Kern, 905). More recent research
has extended this upbeat view of the changing patterns of taste, observing
greater eclecticism and a more curatorial disposition toward culture as part
of a "wider democratizing shift" that can be said to "invalidate, or at least
threaten, Bourdieusian processes of cultural distinction" (Friedman et al.,
2). Some scholars link this development to the unfolding of late modernity
as described by Anthony Giddens (2013), whereby the increasingly global
circulation of modern ideas, images, and narratives of the self is weakening
traditional, nationally embedded status systems such as those investigated by
Bourdieu. The rise of digital technologies, with their transformative impact
on systems of cultural production, dissemination, and reception, has likewise
been seized on as a driver of omnivorousness.[19] The upshot, as David Wright
summarizes, is that the omnivore appears today as "increasingly unremarkable," indeed, a perfectly "mundane" figure who, on the "more fluid" cultural
fields of the twenty-first century, happily "ranges across traditional hierarchies" (356). In reading as in other domains, the exercise of taste has come
to be seen as a mode of active self-definition, occurring within a "general
ethos of cultural 'openness' and 'tolerance,'" rather than a quasi-automatic
reinscription in cultural space of existing social divisions and relations of
status and stigma (Friedman et al. 2).

We rehearse all this old news in order to highlight the place of the omnivore concept in an uplifting vision of contemporary cultural consumption, a vision that we think underpins some of the common ideas about how
reading relates to well-being or flourishing, why it is good for people and
should be promoted and subsidized. Through reading, people expose themselves to new ideas and experiences, they open themselves to others, they

---

[19] Peterson and Kern were already arguing in the pre-internet era that the "increasingly ubiqui-
tous mass media have introduced the aesthetic tastes of different segments of the population to each
other" (905).

stretch themselves: they grow, in ways that benefit the society as well as the individuals.

To test that vision in a thoroughgoing way would require far more abundant information about readers than we have managed to extract from Goodreads.[20] Our data lets us pursue only the most basic quantitative question about reading tastes, corresponding to Peterson's starting point with music: How eclectic *are* readers' tastes? How likely are today's active readers, the true book lovers, to extend their reading beyond a single favored portion of the literary field? We have approached that question in various ways, and from what we can see, our best answer to it is: somewhat, but not as much as we—or they—might think.

Our first look at the data focused on users who reviewed ten or more novels on our combined lists of bestsellers and prize-listed novels. Nearly half of these people did more than 80 percent of their reviewing on one side or the other of the collection. Ten percent of them reviewed books on one side exclusively, some reviewing as many as fifty or sixty prize-listed novels and not a single bestseller, or vice versa. Only about a quarter of the reviewers presented "balanced portfolios" of between 40 and 60 percent of each kind of book. And these were just the numbers at first glance. They began tilting even further away from the vision of readerly eclecticism when we made some tweaks to the way we were counting. In Goodreads, even 3 stars is quite a low rating; 68% of the ratings in our dataset are either 4 or 5 stars. We reasoned that a user who reviewed, say, twelve bestsellers and four prize novels, but whose bestseller ratings were nearly all 4 or 5 stars while the prize novel ratings were 3 stars and below, is not a reader whose taste actually accommodates both kinds of fiction. So we excluded negative reviews—with the result that some of our seemingly bilateral readers had to be reclassified as one-sided. We also excluded reviews of crossover novels that managed the rare feat of landing on both a prize list and an annual bestseller list, reasoning that the reviews of books like *The Corrections* and *Paradise*, catapulted onto the bestseller lists by Oprah, could misleadingly suggest eclecticism among readers who are in fact just sticking to their favored cultural terrain. After

---

[20] Friedman, et al. (2018) are right to stress the need for greater "methodological pluralism" in the study of cultural consumption, omnivorousness, and evolving forms of cultural distinction and social advantage. The task of gathering better quantitative data about "what people consume" needs to be joined to qualitative enquiry into "how people consume" (6). Goodreads does give us some access to this question of the "modality of consumption," but the emphasis on ratings and recommendations tends to constrain users' discussion of their desires and experiences as readers or the relationship of their reading to other dimensions of their social lives.

making these refinements, the predominant pattern conforms even better to the old division between high and low, elite and popular readerships. What appears "mundane" and "unremarkable" in our data is not the figure of the omnivore but the reader who displays a strong preference either for commercially successful or for critically esteemed works of fiction.

It might seem that by designing the experiment the way we did, adopting the binary logic of commercial value vs. aesthetic value, the axis of economic capital vs. the axis of symbolic capital, we were looking for eclecticism in all the wrong places. What about all the tens of thousands of books, and all the millions of acts of reading, that fall somewhere "in between" the handful of blockbusters and the handful of critically acclaimed masterworks? Isn't the reading done in that vast middling space likely to be less rigid, more flexible and adventurous? Actually, our guess is that the opposite is true. As the two most widely disseminated forms of literary "judgment device," prize lists and bestseller lists both function to guide readers through the thousands of new novels being published every month toward the tiny handful that become *part of the conversation* at any given moment, whether that conversation is in the literary journals and book reviews or at the office watercooler. Shouldn't we expect more rather than less than a typical amount of overlap between the readerships of these two most visible and widely discussed sets of novels?

Maybe—but we don't really know how readers distribute and comport themselves across the vast space of contemporary genre fiction. To develop a sketch of that terrain, we first drew up 200-book sample lists of crime fiction, science fiction, and chick lit, each sample containing a mix of novels that won genre-specific awards (such as the Edgar for crime fiction or the Hugo or Nebula for science fiction), novels that sold particularly well (without being actual top-ten bestsellers), and novels that appear on prominent genre-specific lists of bests and favorites in Goodreads. We compared highly active reviewers of these three sets with highly active reviewers of the most recent 200 bestsellers and most recent 200 prize-listed novels. Looking at the distribution of reviews and reviewers across these 1,000 novels, the impression again was one of prevailing narrowness rather than breadth in reading habits. Two-thirds of the prolific bestseller reviewers in this dataset eschew prize novels entirely. And these bestseller fans display even less flexibility of taste with respect to the books on our sci-fi, chick-lit, and detective fiction shelves. We also found two-thirds or more (in some cases, much more) of the enthusiasts for each of those popular genres eschewing each of the other genres.

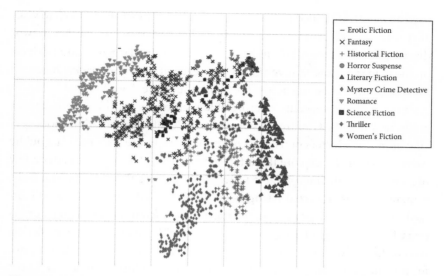

Legend:
- Erotic Fiction
× Fantasy
+ Historical Fiction
● Horror Suspense
▲ Literary Fiction
♦ Mystery Crime Detective
▼ Romance
■ Science Fiction
✦ Thriller
✳ Women's Fiction

Figure 2.5 Taste profiles by genre of 1,672 highly active Goodreads fiction readers (published at http://gr.pennds.org).

There is a serious problem with these findings, however. Whereas we were able to gather all the tens of thousands of reviews of our bestsellers and prize-listed novels, by the time we came to gather reviews of the novels on our popular genre lists, Goodreads had placed a constraint that limits users to seeing just 300 reviews per book, and those 300 chosen according to Goodreads' own unstated principles of selection. By skewing the data this way, Goodreads made it impossible for us to know what kind of a subset or cross-section of fiction readers we were looking at, and hence impossible to make any defensible generalizations about genre and reception.

To gain a sounder view of the distribution of readers across genres, we came at the problem from the opposite direction, defining a set of readers and then looking at their books rather than defining a set of books and looking at the readers. We then created an interactive visualization of the reviewing done by 1,672 Goodreads users randomly selected from among highly active reviewers who have published at least 150 reviews on the site (Figure 2.5). These readers' book reviews were distributed into ten genre categories based on the books' most common shelving assignments in Goodreads.[21] We then

---

[21] We first gathered the top six genre shelves for every book in our database, as listed on the books' Goodreads landing pages. We then consolidated the categories by folding less populated into more

used an algorithm called t-SNE and a presentation tool called Bokeh to visu-
alize readers' taste profiles as proximity or distance from one another in two-
dimensional space. Symbols indicate a reader's primary genre, and position
on the map indicates relative affinity with each of the other readers based on
the distribution of genres across the books they've reviewed.

This is not an especially interpretable picture; its real value to us is as a
guide back into the Goodreads site to obtain detailed information about specific users and clusters of users. (Our visualizations are archived on a public
website so you can explore them for yourself.)[22] But we may consider a few
of its more readily interpretable features. We can see that readers who favor
romance novels (inverted triangles, at the upper left) are the most balkan-
ized, the least omnivorous, and the most distant from readers who favor literary fiction (upright triangles, at lower right). The readers of literary fiction
would themselves be as sharply segregated as romance readers were it not
for the blurry borderland they share with readers of historical fiction (in orange). The extreme lack of affinity between the romance and literary groups
conforms with a classic high/low social division, romance being the least
critically respected of all popular genres and literary fiction being in a sense a
tautological category consisting of precisely those novels that attract critical
regard. The strong affinity that t-SNE discloses between literary fiction and
historical fiction conforms with what we know about the increasingly close
relationship between critical status and historical setting on the contemporary literary field.[23] And these patterns, much like those discerned in the language of reviews, conform with a conventional gender hierarchy. Women are
a clear majority of Goodreads fiction readers in general, but we find them
most heavily concentrated, approaching 100%, in romance.[24] By contrast,

---

populated shelves, e.g., by treating "dystopia," "dystopian," "apocalyptic," "post-apocalyptic," and "sci-
fi" as belonging to the larger category of "science fiction." This enabled us to distribute all the books
into fifteen genre categories, including "nonfiction," which we excluded from the analysis presented
here. We also excluded the tiny category of "Christian," as well as "young adult," "children's," and
"graphic fiction," since we are studying reading habits of adults and need to avoid conflating their
preferences with the preferences of children they read to or shop for.

[22] For interactive, color versions of these visualizations, point a browser at http://gr.pennds.
org. Note that public versions of our outputs are anonymized, with Goodreads-assigned user IDs
removed.

[23] This confirms earlier findings (in English 2016) about the increasingly close relationship between critical status and historical setting on the field of contemporary fiction.

[24] Male readers are heavily overrepresented in our data on nonfiction reviews, which we've
removed from the t-SNE analysis. Tony Bennett et al. analyze data on the gendering of nonfiction
readerships in the United Kingdom, showing men to favor biographies and autobiographies but not
self-help (Bennett 2009).

men are overrepresented in the literary fiction and historical fiction groups.[25] Mike Thelwall's team has shown that there is a further degree of segregation in that, whatever their favored genre, Goodreads users tend to prefer novels of that genre written by authors of their own gender (Thelwall 2017).

As for readers of the other genres, their taste neighborhoods appear less distinct, more integrated with one another. But our closer reading of individual users and small clusters of users suggests that this is an artifact of poorly defined, permeable genre categories rather than evidence of free-ranging tastes. Readers of fantasy (signified by x) occupy the center of our map because fantasy is the loosest and most ambiguous category, containing techno-futurist novels that appeal to a fraction of science fiction fans, paranormal romances that appeal to certain fans of romance and erotic fiction, and medieval-themed epics and steampunk Victoriana that appeal to some fans of historical fiction. Science fiction and romance readers have little direct affinity; studies have shown their readerships to be quite polarized.[26] But we can see in the bar charts of distribution by genre (Figure 2.6) that for both of them fantasy is the most common second-favorite genre.[27] This creates the appearance of affinity between readers who in reality would almost never read any of the same books. The point may be generalized: When we look closely at a user who appears on the map to be frequently roaming away from their generic home to explore a different genre-neighborhood, we tend to find someone whose tastes are actually focused on a particular kind of hybrid or crossover fiction: traditional detective fiction and historical mysteries, for example, or paranormal romance and "naughty sci-fi."

To see more clearly these false eclecticisms and hidden affinities, we created a second interactive Bokeh visualization based on a different use of t-SNE. Here we calculated the similarity or difference between two readers' tastes according to the specific books they have read rather than the genre-shelves of the books in Goodreads.[28] We then merged the two maps and

[25] Though even here, women readers are in the majority. For discussion of possible reasons for the persistent gender gap in literary reading, see Tepper 2000.

[26] Observing that in their study of UK readers, "women are almost 15 times more likely than men to choose romances as a preferred genre," Bennett et al. 2009 suggest that science fiction "might be interpreted as a popular form with similar potential uses as romances for men" (105).

[27] Note also that for romance readers "erotic fiction" is the third most common genre. This category probably should be regarded as a subgenre of romance.

[28] Our genre categories are left out of the calculations entirely. The code here generates a distance matrix by treating all the books and all the users as part of a bimodal "reader network"—that is, a network with two kinds of nodes that only connect to nodes of the other type. It then "imagines" a process: Suppose you talk to a random user and ask for a recommendation. The user randomly picks one of the books they've reviewed. Then you talk to other random users until you find one who has also reviewed that book, and ask them for a new recommendation . . . ad infinitum. The probability

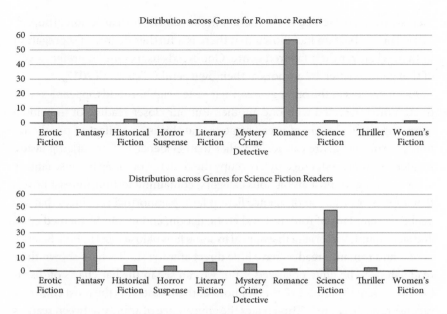

Figure 2.6 Distribution by genre of books reviewed by readers primarily of romance (above) and science fiction (below).

added a slider bar so one can observe the movement of all the reader-points as they are remapped from the location of their genre-profile to a position reflecting the actual books they have in common with other readers (Figure 2.7). Mousing over a point discloses a reader's "neighbor-self correlation" rank from 1 (remains closest to their initial neighbors) to 1,672 (moves farthest away from their initial neighbors).

At a glance, the reader network map, with its less sharply differentiated symbol-zones, could suggest that readers are not as genre-exclusive as our first projection indicated: that their reading tends toward exploration and eclecticism after all. Watching more closely what happens with operation of the slide bar, though, we see that romance and literary fiction readers remain quite stable in their polarity (each of these groups claiming half of the top

of connecting two users in this scenario is the "distance" between them (actually, it's 1–p instead of p). To make things work nicely, we posit that all the users have reviewed one amazingly popular book that we don't know the title of. This ensures all users are at least slightly connected in the network. You might say that this imaginary book is Goodreads.com. To make the map fit more readably onto the page we log-transformed the distances to yield the projection of Figure 2.7. The two visualizations are then merged, with a slider bar to display the movement of specific readers between the two mapping strategies.

Genre t-SNE (0) ↔ Reader Network t-SNE (1): **0.96**

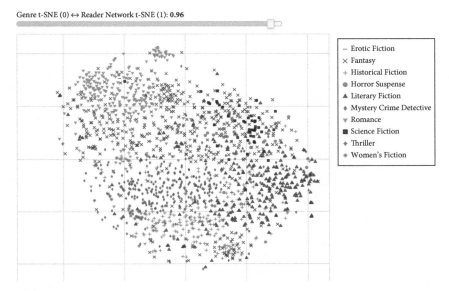

Figure 2.7 Taste profiles of 1,672 readers with slide bar from Genre map to Reader Network map at 96 percent (close to final reader-network positions). The interactive, full-color visualization is shared at http://gr.pennds.org/adult fictioncomparegraph.

ten most static user-points), while most of the movement across the center involves the division of large genre-groups into smaller but more narrowly partisan groups of subgenre-readers. The readers of historical fiction, for example, can be seen to separate into two main bands reflecting the two main "flavors" of fictions set in the past (Figure 2.8).

The more populous band consolidates toward the far right, intermingled with literary fiction, in the space occupied by readers of *Wolf Hall* or *The Underground Railroad*; the other band establishes separation from this literary zone, forming to the left, in the space occupied by readers of medieval-themed or mythopoeic fantasy such as *Game of Thrones*. The abandonment of original neighbors in such cases does not reveal an unsuspected eclecticism of taste but, on the contrary, an intolerance even of works that land on the same genre-shelf of Goodreads as one's favorites but that deviate subgenerically from one's overarching preferences.

These maps are just one way to present the complex information in our Goodreads data, and our interpretations of them are far from definitive. For sure there are some mixed taste portfolios on view here. Yet even those mixed

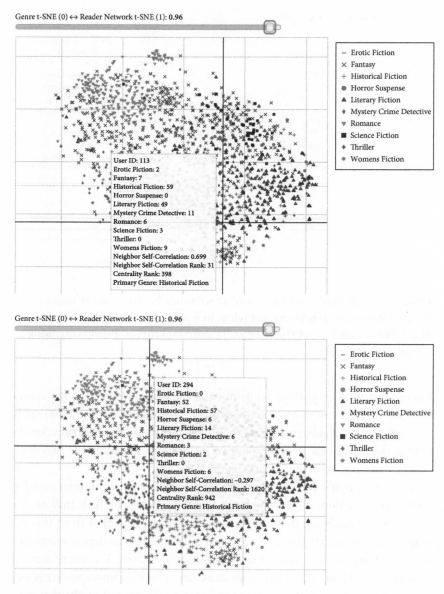

Figure 2.8 Two readers who favor historical fiction: User 113 (top) shares many books with readers of literary fiction; User 294 (bottom) shares many books with readers of fantasy fiction. The much higher neighbor-self correlation of User 113 (ranked 31st out of 1,672, vs. 1,620th) tells us that her position relative to other readers changes little whether we consider the specific books she reads or only their genres.

tastes seem to observe an underlying logic of strong and narrow preferences. We don't have a good way to describe this, rhetorically or statistically. There is no standard or point of comparison, no agreed upon "normal" or "expected" amount of eclecticism in reading habits. And the data of Goodreads does not lend itself to modeling historical change (to show that there is or is not more eclecticism among readers today than in the past). But if we are looking for evidence at this fairly large scale that omnivorousness has become a mundane feature of the field of literary reception, we have to be disappointed. And certainly it is hard to see how the overall patterns visible here could connect to the warm, positive terms that, in some accounts, have come to be bundled with the omnivore concept: openness, tolerance, democratization.

The Digital Fate of Eclecticism

Which brings us to the third question that literary studies might share with the sciences of human flourishing: whether digital platforms are at least encouraging greater eclecticism and openness of taste, heading us in the direction of an omnivorous future. Our study of Goodreads offers scant support for that view. To be an active user of Goodreads is to be shaped by its peculiar affordances, which put a premium on counting and compiling: Your profile page presents a bar chart of your progress toward an annual goal; your statistics page presents monthly and annual counts of the number of books you've read, the number of pages, books per author (Figure 2.9).

The site pressures readers to finish the book they're reading and move on to the next one, and the next after that: to keep an active queue and a shelf of to-reads. As Lisa Nakamura has observed, it organizes readers' collections by default around "a temporality of consumption" (241). It is not set up to be a "search" engine, where you actively look for titles or authors. Like Netflix, it is a "discovery" site, where what you discover ("your next favorite book"), right there on your landing page, is substantially determined by metrics of similarity: similar books, books read by similar readers. Coordinated as it is with its parent company, Amazon, and in particular with the Kindle Direct Publishing unit (essentially a factory for just-in-time production of micro-genre e-fiction), Goodreads seems designed to foster binge-reading, the kind of one-track, ultra-serial reading where even a book that is not part of a series is the next on a list—your list—of similars. And thanks to the sped-up production cycle and the vast output of fiction—several times as many new

Figure 2.9 Reading by the numbers: stats tracking on Goodreads.

novels per year as at the turn of the millennium—there will always be plenty of similars.

These developments point to a curious tension in contemporary culture, which has become evident in our attempts to interpret the data of Goodreads. The actual circumstances of cultural consumption, including the new forms of its technological mediation, appear to discourage eclecticism, at least where reading is concerned.[29] But those same circumstances seem to be installing eclecticism more firmly than ever as a contemporary ideal. Sociologists of culture are not the only ones who have come to associate eclecticism with the

---

[29] We are not the first to note that literary reading may be an outlier as regards patterns of consumption. Reading is known to follow a social pattern distinct from TV watching or popular music listening. Most people, even in economically advantaged nations, do not read books at all. The NEA finds that about half of adult Americans are not even "capable of reading and understanding most novels, short stories, poetry, or plays" (*Reading at Risk* 15). Of the minority that does read at least a few books a year, only a fraction reads novels, and only a small fraction, consisting mainly of college-educated, middle-class women, reads novels at all regularly. Literary reading of any sort is an asset, a rare and distinguishing form of capital, and its uneven distribution features prominently in larger systems of stratification. For this reason, as Tony Bennett and colleagues observe in the course of their large-scale study of cultural consumption in the United Kingdom, "tastes in reading have been less central than, for example, music in recent debates about social class and mobility," and "reading has been marginal to the development of the thesis of the omnivore" (96).

values of openness, tolerance, and democratization—in short, with human flourishing. Goodreads users themselves tend to emphasize eclecticism in the "About Me" and "Favorite Books" sections of their profiles, describing their preferences as "quirky," "all over the place," unconstrained by standard patterns of taste. A 30-something woman with nearly 500 reviews on the site describes herself as someone with "eclectic reading habits" who "devours books from humor to autobiographies to erotica." Her tastes, she says, are "personal": "I read for myself, regardless of what is popular or what others think of my choices and preferences." But 82 percent of the books she has reviewed are shelved in Goodreads as Romance or Contemporary Romance, with a further 11 percent belonging to Erotic Fiction—essentially a subgenre of Contemporary Romance. The few books (just 7 percent) that fall on other shelves consist mostly of Fantasy novels with paranormal romance plots, such as *Wicked Werewolf Night* in Lisa Renee Jones's Werewolf Society series, or mystery novels of the romance-hybrid kind publishers call "romantic suspense": *Armed and Fabulous* and *Who Glares Wins* in Camilla Chafer's Lexi Graves series, *Thug Guard* and *Lip Glock* in D. D. Scott's Cozy Cash series, and *Stillettos and Scoundrels* in Laina Turner's Presley Thurman series. Statistically speaking, this reader's tastes are not eclectic or idiosyncratic in the least. She is a dedicated reader of contemporary romance, whose choices in mystery and fantasy betray a predictable intolerance for nonromance narratives and track closely with fellow readers of her favored genre, placing her among the 22 percent most neighbor-correlated readers in our dataset. Yet for this reader as for many, it seems natural to disavow her orientation toward a keen and narrow enthusiasm so as to claim eclecticism as the true shaping logic of her taste profile. And it seems natural in turn for us, scholars surveying data that highlights the preponderance of these keen and narrow enthusiasms, to lament contemporary readers' genre-intolerance, this sad compulsion to repeat. We condemn the technology of digital curation for discouraging a presumed happier disposition toward bold explorations of the literary terrain, hampering the process of self-realization through readerly encounters with the new.

No doubt we should be prepared to resist the mechanisms of algorithmic tracking and prediction that channel us into small, separate neighborhoods of literary reception. But shouldn't we also direct some critical vigilance toward the orthodoxy of eclecticism itself? When exactly did the heterogeneity of one's reading become the measure of one's readerly health? When did an overweening preference for one genre of literature to the exclusion of others come to seem a bad habit, a kind of literary binging, a readerly sickness? And how has it been possible for eclecticism to spread so widely as a cultural creed when so few readers seem actually to enact it in practice? Historicizing the fate of eclecticism in our era, as has been done for the Victorian age,[30] could help us push back against its force as the unacted common sense of contemporary culture. And this could open space for some less reflexively dismissive appraisals of digital platforms like Goodreads, allowing for their positive as well as negative affordances. Some readers clearly are flourishing on Goodreads, and not despite but because of their bad, univore habits. For them, Goodreads represents a thousand micro-niches of amateur expertise, online positions where readers excluded from the more strictly gated forms of cultural distinction may be credited with a critical voice and power of judgment. From the vantage of those positions, the downbeat story of genre tribalism might be usefully complicated by a counternarrative of emerging literary communities, new spaces of attachment and respect. Both literary studies and well-being science will need that sort of double vision if they are to make an honest appraisal of literature's role in shaping systems of social belonging and exclusion.

Works Cited

Bennett, Tony, editor. *Culture, Class Distinction*. Routledge, 2009.

Bolus-Reichert, Christine. *The Age of Eclecticism: Literature and Culture in Britain, 1815–1885*. Ohio State UP, 2009.

Dewaele, Jean-Marc, and Francis Heylighen. *Formality of Language: Definition, Measurement, and Behavioral Determinants*. Internal Report, Free University of Brussels, 1999, http://pespmc1.vub.ac.be/Papers/Formality.pdf.

Dmitrov, Stefan, et al. "Goodreads versus Amazon: The Effect of Decoupling Book Reviewing and Book Selling." *Proceedings of the Ninth International AAAI Conference on Web and Social Media*, 2015.

English, James F. "Now, Not Now: Counting Time in Contemporary Fiction Studies." *Modern Language Quarterly*, vol. 77, no. 3, Sept. 2016, pp. 395–418, https://doi.org/10.1215/00267929-3570667.

Felski, Rita. *Uses of Literature*. Blackwell, 2008.

Flekova, Lucie, et al. "Analyzing Biases in Human Perception of User Age and Gender from Text." *Proceedings of the 54th Annual Meeting of the Association for Computational Linguistics (Volume 1: Long Papers)*, Association for Computational Linguistics, 2016, pp. 843–54, https://doi.org/10.18653/v1/P16-1080.

---

[30] Christine Bolus-Reichert describes a slow passage "toward acceptance and tentative celebration of eclecticism" in the nineteenth century, for most of which "the words eclectic or eclecticism . . . carried strongly negative connotations" (4).

Friedman, Sam, et al. "Cultural Sociology and New Forms of Distinction." *Poetics*, vol. 53, Dec. 2015, pp. 1–8, https://doi.org/10.1016/j.poetic.2015.10.002.

Giddens, Anthony. *Modernity and Self-Identity Self and Society in the Late Modern Age.* John Wiley & Sons, 2013, *Open WorldCat*, http://nbn-resolving.de/urn:nbn:de:101:1-201412104570.

Griffith, Nicola. "Books about Women Don't Win Big Awards: Some Data." *Nicola Griffith*, 26 May 2015, https://nicolagriffith.com/2015/05/26/books-about-women-tend-not-to-win-awards/.

Hill, Kelly, et al. *Reading at Risk: A Survey of Literary Reading in America.* Diane Publishing Co., 2004. *Open WorldCat*, http://www.arts.gov/sites/default/files/ReadingAtRisk.pdf.

Holland, Norman Norwood. *The Nature of Literary Response: Five Readers Reading.* Yale UP, 1975.

Johnson, Sally, and Astrid Ensslin. "'But Her Language Skills Shifted the Family Dynamics Dramatically': Language, Gender and the Construction of Publics in Two British Newspapers." *Gender and Language*, vol. 1, no. 1, Apr. 2013, pp. 229–54. https://doi.org/10.1558/genl.v1.i1.17192.

Koolen, Corina, and Andreas van Cranenburgh. "These Are Not the Stereotypes You Are Looking For: Bias and Fairness in Authorial Gender Attribution." *Proceedings of the First ACL Workshop on Ethics in Natural Language Processing*, Association for Computational Linguistics, 2017, pp. 12–22, https://doi.org/10.18653/v1/W17-1602.

Kraicer, Eve, and Andrew Piper. "Social Characters: The Hierarchy of Gender in Contemporary English-Language Fiction." *Journal of Cultural Analytics*, 2019, https://doi.org/10.22148/16.032.

Lahire, Bernard. "The Individual and the Mixing of Genres: Cultural Dissonance and Self-Distinction." *Poetics*, vol. 36, no. 2–3, Apr. 2008, pp. 166–88, https://doi.org/10.1016/j.poetic.2008.02.001.

Long, Elizabeth. *Book Clubs: Women and the Uses of Reading in Everyday Life.* U of Chicago P, 2003.

Mohammad, Saif, and Peter Turney. NRC Word-Emotion Association Lexicon. https://saifmohammad.com/WebPages/NRC-Emotion-Lexicon.htm.

Nakamura, Lisa. "'Words with Friends': Socially Networked Reading on *Goodreads*." *PMLA*, vol. 128, no. 1, Jan. 2013, pp. 238–43, https://doi.org/10.1632/pmla.2013.128.1.238.

National Endowment for the Arts. *Reading at Risk: A Survey of Literary Reading in America.* 46, National Endowment for the Arts, 2004.

Ollivier, Michèle. "Modes of Openness to Cultural Diversity: Humanist, Populist, Practical, and Indifferent." *Poetics*, vol. 36, no. 2–3, Apr. 2008, pp. 120–47, https://doi.org/10.1016/j.poetic.2008.02.005.

Ollivier, Michèle. "Revisiting Distinction." *Journal of Cultural Economy*, vol. 1, no. 3, 2008, pp. 263–79.

Pennebaker, James, et al. *Linguistic Inquiry and Word Count: LIWC 2015 Operator's Manual.* Pennebaker Conglomerates, 2015, https://s3-us-west-2.amazonaws.com/downloads.liwc.net/LIWC2015_OperatorManual.pdf.

Peterson, Richard A. "Understanding Audience Segmentation: From Elite and Mass to Omnivore and Univore." *Poetics*, vol. 21, no. 4, Aug. 1992, pp. 243–58, https://doi.org/10.1016/0304-422X(92)90008-Q.

Peterson, Richard A., and Roger M. Kern. "Changing Highbrow Taste: From Snob to Omnivore." *American Sociological Review*, vol. 61, no. 5, Oct. 1996, p. 900, https://doi.org/10.2307/2096460.

Phillips, Natalie. "Literary Neuroscience and History of Mind: An Interdisciplinary fMRI Study of Attention and Jane Austen," Zunshine, pp. 55–84.

Radway, Janice A. *Reading the Romance: Women, Patriarchy, and Popular Literature.* U of North Carolina P, 1984.

Tepper, Steven J. "Fiction Reading in America: Explaining the Gender Gap." *Poetics*, vol. 27, no. 4, 2000, pp. 255–75.

Thelwall, Mike. "Reader and Author Gender and Genre in Goodreads." *Journal of Librarianship and Information Science*, vol. 51 no. 2, May 2017, pp. 403–30, https://doi.org/10.1177/0961000617709061.

Underwood, Ted. "Seven Ways Humanists Are Using Computers to Understand Texts." *The Stone and the Shell*, 4 June 2015, https://tedunderwood.com/2015/06/04/seven-ways-humanists-are-using-computers-to-understand-text/.

Williams. "The Age of Eclecticism: Literature and Culture in Britain, 1815–1885, by Christine Bolus-Reichert." *Victorian Studies*, vol. 53, no. 3, 2011, p. 531, https://doi.org/10.2979/victorianstudies.53.3.531.

Wright, David. "Making Tastes for Everything: Omnivorousness and Cultural Abundance." *Journal for Cultural Research*, vol. 15, no. 4, Oct. 2011, pp. 355–71, https://doi.org/10.1080/14797585.2011.613222.

Zunshine, Lisa, editor. *The Oxford Handbook of Cognitive Literary Studies.* Oxford UP, 2015.

PART II
FLOURISHING BEYOND REASON
Literature's Augmented Realities

3

Flourishing Spirits

Christopher Castiglia

Flourishing is a possibility that haunts me. When I was a child, my mother, claiming to be clairvoyant, preoccupied herself with Tarot cards, palm reading, and, most powerfully, a Ouija board, on which she and her siblings—also supposedly clairvoyant—channeled communications from the Other Side. I remember one particular instance in which my mother, aunt, and uncle contacted a sailor who had drowned at sea. He gave his name, which appeared again many years later when another relative researching the family history found a nineteenth-century ancestor by the same name who had been a sailor drowned at sea.

There are many ways to read this incident. All three of the siblings were sexually abused as children, and all suffered psychologically as a result. That the history they resurrected involved the sensation of going under, gasping for breath, flailing in mad efforts to survive, is not surprising. They needed another world, a place that might await their unhurt spirits as they left behind bodies that represented, for them, pain, guilt, danger, uncertainty. A world from which secrets from the past emerge without danger. My mother grew up in two worlds, the one she lived in, filled with dark, vicious, insidious demons, and the spirit-world, which brought her pleasure, confidence, reliability, and control. The only time I saw my mother and her siblings together was when they became clairvoyant: able to put down for a time the shared history that filled them with shame, anger, and confusion that kept them otherwise separate. Their hands were touching when the spirits came.

It's possible, then, to read these experiences of the spirit-world as projections of trauma, bodies robbed of spirit imagining spirits robbed of bodies. That is a feasible interpretation, the siblings' accounts of their traumatic experiences as spirit presences enacting the therapeutic redescription Beth Blum describes elsewhere in this volume. The question I want to ask in this chapter is *why*, beyond its therapeutic value, the siblings chose *spiritualism* to reckon with their traumatic pasts, how that choice enabled not

Christopher Castiglia, *Flourishing Spirits* In: *Literary Studies and Human Flourishing.* Edited by: James F. English and Heather Love, Oxford University Press. © Oxford University Press 2023. DOI: 10.1093/oso/9780197637227.003.0004

just a bearable response to loss but an active and joyful *gain*, and what we might learn from their flourishing spirits about belief and the ways people like my mother and her siblings keep it alive, strengthen it even, in the face of what might otherwise be dispiriting circumstances. Each time my relatives sat down to contact spirits, they were not only escaping trauma or working it out through projection. They were regenerating their *will to believe*. Whether or not they *really* believed in spirits is beside the point. What they believed in is the power of belief in itself, and that belief required and reinforced tremendous willpower, given the circumstances they faced daily that threatened to kill belief once and for all. This chapter is a reckoning with disenchantment, will, and belief, and how they find their medium—pun intended—in the spirit-world. It is a chapter that argues that belief is central to—perhaps even the most essential feature of—a flourishing spirit.

The times when my family communicated with spirits are among my most vivid childhood memories, and so it is hardly surprising that, inspired by an overdetermined curiosity, I've recently begun reading about nineteenth-century Spiritualists and the spirits *they* contacted. Reading accounts of séances, I can easily understand why many saw and continue to see séances as hoaxes perpetrated on the gullible and needy. No doubt many attended as curious thrill-seekers who didn't care whether they were being hoodwinked or not so long as the experience was new and tantalizing. But séances were not always consoling or enjoyable. Sometimes they were downers. It's possible, however, that, knowing that what they heard from the spirits might be anything but uplifting or pleasurable, at least some who attended séances did so for the experience of belief itself, which they received not despite but *because* the disturbing things they heard from the spirit-world so often contradicted Spiritualist doctrine, and even defied belief.

On April 7, 1860, *The Banner of Light*, a Boston-based Spiritualist newspaper, published a poem by "R. Thayer."

> Wife, mother, sister, friend is gone
> Where none e'er weep—where none ever mourn,—
> But all are blest;
> Now, freed from earthly noise and strife,—
> From all the storms and ills of life,—
> She is at rest.
>
> Though from all earthly scenes removed,
> She's still with those whom here she loved,—

And day and night
Her spirit watches round their way,
To guard them lest they e'er should stray
From paths of right.

In the bright sphere where now she dwells,
Where light the darkness all dispels,
She now doth wait
To welcome us, as one by one—
When each the work of life has done—
We reach that state.

From her abode she looketh down,
Waiting for us to share the crown
Which she now wears;
Where kindred spirits sweetly blend,—
Where we eternity shall spend,
Released from cares.

When we death's narrow stream shall cross,
Then we shall know "death is no loss,
But endless gain:"
May we like her just passed away
No longer wish on earth to stay,
And heaven attain. (Thayer 6)

All the elements of Spiritualist doctrine are here: After death the body and its cares are left behind, as are all earthy concerns, as the spirit enters a realm of harmony and light from which it keeps benevolent watch over the living. When we think of Spiritualism today, this is the schmaltz we're likely to imagine.

Despite the promise of a reassuring realm where, "freed from earthly noise and strife,— / From all the storms and ills of life," spirits go "Where light the darkness all dispels" and "Where kindred spirits sweetly blend," in fact the spirits sometimes proved to be a whiny, pushy, petty, vengeful, distraught, and disrespectful lot. Spirits say things like, "I'm a poor, unhappy spirit. . . . That I'm unhappy, I can't deny; that I'm disappointed, I must own, too" or "I believe the rheumatism will stick to me through all eternity" (*Banner* 5 May, 28 April). The spirit of Daniel Ransom, who suffered in life from a bad stutter, complained, "I thought, when I got rid of the old body, I should get rid of this inconvenience, any way." But he finds this is not the case, and, eternally disabled, must adjust his means of communication. He promises, "the next time I make an engagement to talk, I'll write. By the Gods, there ain't no stammering in writing, that's a sure thing" (*Banner* 7 April). Spirits push and shove, try to keep each other from speaking, deliberately send false messages, and wait impatiently for their chance to speak. William Bancroft comes from the spirit-world to communicate with his children, but is so angered by what the previous spirit has said that he berates him instead (*Banner* 7 April).

Sometimes the spirits are affable in giving their information, as with one spirit who offers, "They [séance attendees] may be interested to hear something of my entrance here; it's a good story" (*Banner* 28 April). But more often they're resentful, even hostile. One spirit complains, "Don't hurry a body. I was hurried into the grave, and I won't be hurried now. To your business, and I'll attend to mine" (*Banner* 28 April). Another declares, "I will give you my full name when I get ready well," and yet another demands, "Well, what do you want of me? My name? Just as though you didn't know! . . . I may as well wait for the sun to move out of its place, as to wait to talk through this medium" (*Banner* 28 April). An Irish spirit named Bridget Conlan refuses to speak through a Protestant medium, asking for a "praste" instead (*Banner* 7 April). Ella Augusta McFarland urges her medium to publish her message in the *New York Ledger* rather than in the Spiritualist newspaper, since the former comes out more often and costs only twenty-five cents (*Banner* 7 April). One cranky spirit says, "I wish I hadn't come. Tell my story? Well, my story is, I am dead" (*Banner* 12 May).

More frequent than these amusing messages are the personal and detailed stories spirits tell involving suicide, childhood abuse, spousal violence, poverty, abandonment, betrayal, and ostracism. They are not shy about displaying hurt, resentment, and rage. The spirit of Catherine Young Bates begins her message, "I have seen the rough side of life." Forced by poverty as a young girl to work in a sailors' boarding house, she began drinking rum. "I couldn't help it," she says; "I might as well fight against the world," and, refusing shame, she states, "I believe it was well for me to do it." Claiming he can't live with her drinking, Catherine's husband throws her out and, leaving behind her two children, she heads to New York to find an institution for the care of the sick and poor. The matrons of a Christian institution ask her if she is married. She considers lying but admits the truth, and they tell her to go home and let her husband take care of her. She again appeals to him for aid, but he refuses and she dies a pauper.

Catherine Young Bates has come back with blood, not rum, in her mouth. "I am not going to curse him [her husband]," she claims, but "will do the next thing to it; and that is, to let him know I can come here, and that I ain't quite lost sight of him, and he is not going to be so terrible happy as he supposes he is when he dies." Although her husband knew she needed help and refused, she states, "he had the impudence to kneel down and pray God to have mercy upon me, when he would not have mercy upon me himself." If God heard his prayer, she continues, "He would have said: I called on you to have mercy upon that woman, and you refused; now don't expect me to open the gates to Heaven for you." Despite her ill treatment, however, Young Bates is unashamed, asserting, "I will here say I did the best I could, and I don't care whether I did well or not," adding, "I am smart enough to take care of myself now." As she leaves the séance, Young Bates gives the medium a message for her husband: if he seeks to speak with her through a séance, "I will not come near him" (*Banner* 12 May).

Nathaniel Hill's spirit tells another painful story. The death of his mother and his father's drunkenness leave him in the care of an uncle who regularly beats him. Hill says of his uncle, "no matter, but I don't want to see him, hear from him, or know about him—always makes me mad to think of him." Possibly disabled—he was barely five feet tall and "stooped"—Hill laments, "I wasn't started right—I didn't get the right kind of a shipping in this world—no, I didn't." Nor is the afterlife much better. Referring to fellow spirits, he reports, "they told me I must not speak too hard about one person. I wish I hadn't promised, for I haven't forgot." When more advanced spirits lecture Hill about his sins, he responds, "I told them it was my business, not theirs, and they left." "Teachers come round once in awhile," he reports, "but what's the use of wanting to know anything?—the more you know, the more unhappy you are. I don't want to know anything, I tell you. If I knew what was going on in some other place I should be more unhappy than I am." Hill's resentment of how, as a poor man, he was treated in life (and beyond) is apparent when he signs off: "Don't forget my letter, will you?" he requests, then adds, "Mine is of just as much consequence as anybody's else" (*Banner* 14 January).

As Hill's message shows, spirits struggle, too, with the same social prejudices they faced while alive. Poverty is a consistent theme in spirit messages. Spirits tell of losing jobs and homes, receiving poor or no education, and doing menial labor. More than the spirits of men those of women acknowledge hesitation to speak. Immigrants apologize for their accents, and the spirits of African Americans ask questions such as, "Do you treat n------ as well as white folks here? Send their letters same as white folks?" (*Banner* 14 January).

How do we account for these surprising messages and, more to the point, why people attended séances to hear them? When the spirits so often contradicted Spiritualist claims about the end of suffering, benevolent care of the living by the dead, and the joys of spirit life—claims promulgated by fiction such as Elizabeth Stuart Phelps's *The Gates Ajar* (1868)—why did Spiritualist newspapers like *The Banner of Light* publish them and, knowing they might hear such disheartening stories, why did readers of those extremely popular newspapers flock to séances? I want to offer a speculative answer to these questions: perhaps people went to séances not to confirm any belief in particular but rather to undergo the phenomenon of belief for its own sake. If this was the case, it helped that the messages were *not* reassuring, for reasons I'll discuss shortly, but challenging, even disturbing. This was particularly the case when attendees were also social reformers, as they often were, for whom the phenomenon of belief strengthened their commitments to ideals of social justice. It's possible, then, that experiencing belief allowed séance participants to flourish, even when the spirits they encountered had not. Based on their experiences, I would go so far as to argue that human flourishing is impossible *without* the phenomenon of belief. To explain what I mean by "the phenomenon of belief," I turn to William James, a séance attendee who offers an account of how and why the experience of belief becomes "a new zest which adds itself like a gift to life" (*Varieties* 485).[1]

From Spiritualism's inception it was plagued by demands for proof by those who sought to cast light on the shadowy stagecraft of ghostly melodrama. In lecture 10 of what was published in 1896 as *The Will to Believe*, however, William James provides a more nuanced account of the relationship between evidence and truth. James challenged the assumption that what

---

[1] Although James attended séances, he ultimately attributed the ability of mediums to supply accurate information to séance participants to telepathy. He also believed that what is perceived as paranormal experience might be the subconscious disrupting the order of the conscious mind. Yet, as James O. Pawelski observes, James "contends that religious experience, including conversion, cannot be sufficiently explained by psychology and that experience argues for the continuity of our consciousness with a larger spiritual world," which he saw manifested in, among other phenomena, "automatic writing and speech and of mediumship and possession" (91). Pawelski also notes that James also acknowledged that "conversion can occur through, among other sources, 'experiences which we shall later have to designate as 'mystical' " (79).

cannot be proven empirically is therefore not worthy of believing in or that what we currently know to be factual is the endpoint of what belief might show to be true. Fact and belief, in other words, are not necessarily mutually exclusive, and James wrote *The Will to Believe* to challenge William Clifford's claims to the contrary. In particular, James challenged Clifford's assertion that what cannot be proven through rational consideration of evidence must be rejected as error. In opposition to Clifford, James contends that religious faith is personal and "passional," the result of individual experience rather than cognition. Experiential truth, James argues, exists beyond empirical cognition. It is not that belief contradicts the validity of empirical investigation, but neither is it reducible to such empiricism. While it might be valid to empirically show some forms of occult activity to be trickery, James might have argued, it would be wrong therefore to condemn *all* belief as trickery because it cannot satisfy current practices of rational investigation. James responded to Clifford not only by claiming that experiential belief did not need proof, but also by claiming that Clifford's insistence that it did itself constitutes a belief system. A key element of that system is the insistence that *real* empiricism is always objective and therefore true in all places and times, which denies the diverse experiential truths to be found in "passional" belief. Posing a rhetorical question, "Objective evidence and certitude are doubtless very fine ideals to play with, but where on this moonlit and dream-visited planet are they found?" (14), James contends they can be found nowhere. The insistence that they can be found is made despite all evidence to the contrary, and is therefore, by Clifford's own definition, not a naming of empirical truth but an expression of belief.

If the choice is not between truth and error, then, but between two belief systems whose desires produce different "reals," why choose the Spiritual option over that of skeptics James called "faith-vetoers" (26)? The first answer comes in James's account of why skeptics both hold their belief and refuse to acknowledge it *as* belief. His answer is simple: fear. A person like Clifford who says, " 'better go without belief forever than believe a lie!' merely shows," James argues, "his own preponderant private horror of becoming a dupe" (18). A true believer, on the other hand, "may think that the risk of being in error is a very small matter when compared with the blessings of real knowledge, and be ready to be duped many times in your investigation rather than postpone indefinitely the chance of guessing true" (18). James confesses, "I have also a horror of being duped," but adds, "I can believe that worse things than being duped may happen to a man in this world" (18–19).

For James, skepticism has negative consequences both for the believers it dismisses and for the "faith-vetoers" themselves. The consequences of skepticism for the believers skeptics dismiss are relatively obvious. Skeptics force their own viewpoint on others, insisting that everyone accept as objective truth what are, in the end, one's particular beliefs. "To preach scepticism [sic] to us as a duty until 'sufficient evidence' for religion be found," James argues, "is tantamount therefore to telling us . . . that to yield to our fear of its being error is wiser and better than to yield to our hope that it may be true. It is not intellect against all passions, then; it is only intellect with one passion laying down its law" (26–27). Skepticism is for James a "command that we shall put a stopper on our heart, instincts, and courage" (28). But skepticism hurts not only those who believe differently but also, James warns, skeptics themselves. The nonbeliever, James writes, "would cut himself off by such churlishness from all the social rewards that a more trusting spirit would earn," (28). The result of "churlishness" and "snarling logicality" is a loss of trust and hopefulness, due to the willingness to relinquish one's belief in the "icy laws of outer fact" (7).

Given this analysis of skepticism, if those who went to séances were dupes, James might say, all the better for them, as their willingness to risk "error" despite the "icy laws" of facts allows them to move toward trust, hope, and courage, all of which are far preferable to fear. And they gain tolerance as well, since, understanding that beliefs are experientially various, they know that belief is not a universal law that must be imposed on everyone uniformly (hence Spiritualism's resistance to the institutional hierarchies and proscriptive rituals of established religions). When we reject the "command" of universal belief, James writes, "then only shall we have that spirit of inner tolerance without which all our outer tolerance is soulless, and which is empiricisms' glory; then only shall we live and let live, in speculative as well as in practical things" (30). In James's view, "No one ought to issue vetoes to the other, nor should we bandy words of abuse" (30).

James's theory of belief perhaps gives us answers to the puzzle of the motivation of séance participants who sought experiences that were not straightforwardly consoling. The first answer is, simply, that they wanted the experience of belief James describes. They sought, that is, belief for its own sake, belief in belief. Their presence at séances, more than anything that occurred *at* those meetings, testify to the desire for a literal suspension of disbelief in order to attain and have affirmed the trust, hope, and courage— the "zest"—that James claimed follow in the wake of belief. They were duped only if we assume it was the content of spiritual communication that they sought, not an opportunity to refresh their belief in belief.

But perhaps *after* the séance was when the real work of belief began. As James says of belief, "Not where it comes from but what it leads to is to decide" (17). That decision relies on the first term in James's title: *will*. For James, belief is a choice, and it is the capacity to choose belief, perhaps, that strengthened séance participants' will to act on behalf of belief. Many prominent Spiritualists, such as Isaac and Amy Post, advocated for the abolition of slavery, the enfranchisement of women, relief for the poor and ill, and other progressive social causes. To imagine that social ills of such staggering magnitude could be overcome, to imagine it strongly enough to continue to fight to overcome them despite discouragement, took the will born of belief (and vice versa). And when their experiences of belief joined with spirit messages detailing exactly the social problems reformers addressed, reform must have seemed the only appropriate enactment of trust, tolerance, and courage. If souls continue to suffer from the injustices among the living, all the more reason to fight to redeem "souls" (a word often used for those living persons requiring reform) from social ills among the living that might, if left unchallenged, persist through eternity.[2] That might have been an overwhelming motive, if it had not been conjoined with belief. "If this life be not a real fight," James wrote of belief, "in which something is eternally gained for the universe by success, it is no better than a game of private theatricals from which one may withdraw at will. But it feels like a real fight—as if there were something really wild in the universe which we, with all our idealities and faithfulness, are needed to redeem" ("Is Life Worth Living?" 61). Although its critics belittled séances as no more than "private theatricals," for some participants these practices, authentic or not, produced the belief that enabled the "real fight" to make the world otherwise that it was.

At the same time as he encouraged courageous belief, however, James was clear that courage is not the same as rigidity, or belief the same as doctrine. If a belief is held too unyieldingly, it becomes brittle and "dead." For a belief to

---

[2] Pawelski contends that for James, "Health-minded persons respond willfully, warring against the very presence of evil, while morbid-minded persons respond passively, allying themselves with a higher power that does not eradicate evil, but that promises victory over it" (72). We might therefore speculate that at least some of those who attended séances were "morbid-minded," since, in recognizing the ongoing need for reform, they also conceded the ineradicability of evil. If this is the case, it becomes easier to see why the séance experience, particularly in its encounters with ever-existing evil, produced a "threshold state" that required and enabled the development of will enough to produce a conversion.

remain alive, it must be adaptable, able to confront contradictory evidence, adjust, and resume. It cannot simply ignore whatever doesn't uphold the belief. For James, then, encounters with such contradictions were essential to confirming the aliveness of belief, its capacity to adapt and bend without breaking. For those gathered at the séance table expecting to hear consoling stories of eternal bliss—the existential reward for reform efforts among the living—the stories told by the spirits might have seemed like challenges to their beliefs and, if the participants heeded and adjusted to those stories, their beliefs, although not identical to what they were at the outset, would be stronger and better able to face difficulties among the living. It was important for James that belief not be a turning away from the world, but an engagement with it. If the "spirit-world" had been a fantasy unrelated to the conditions of the world, it would have been the former. Because it encountered the possibility of eternal suffering and persisted *because*, not despite, of that possibility, the beliefs of those at séance tables would have been, for James, alive.

To talk about the malleability of belief, however, is really to address the disposition of the believer. If beliefs are "passional," related to the desires of the believer, then that passion must change in order for a belief to do so. The adaptability of belief is also, in other words, a moment of self-transformation, an askesis, in which the outlook of the believer shifts and adapts. A belief that becomes stronger, more alive, is in the end a sign of a believer in the process of becoming more confident in the capacity to hold beliefs, a psychological as much as a metaphysical development. For James, one can choose whether to remain in a "pining, puling, mumping mood" (89) or be "converted into a bracing and tonic good by a simple change of the sufferer's inner attitude from one of fear to one of fight" (88). James acknowledged that such acts of conversion are rarely "simple," though, since they require that one pass through despair and suffering, a "radical pessimism" (144), in order to reach an earned and *critical* well being, or what James describes as an "abstract way of conceiving things as good" (88). The messages sent from the beyond might have represented a "radical pessimism," causing in séance participants uncertainty and unhappiness. But in doing so they also offered the choice between despair and *living* belief, one that refuses to ignore the "evil facts" that "are a genuine portion of reality" and therefore "may after all be the best key to life's significance, and possibly the only openers of our eyes to the deepest levels of truth" (163).

The idea that spirits can transform psychological dispositions may seem arcane, if not downright silly. Yet that belief is at the heart of some of the most influential theoretical work being written today, especially under the rubric—ironic given spirits' ephemerally—of "new materialism." Those theorists invoke the occult to signify the intangible *felt* experience of belief, or what William Connolly calls "a positive existential spirituality" (197). As James had done a century earlier, these writers champion the occult in its battle against "faith-vetoers" who debunk what "people have learned to cherish" (Latour 236). For Bruno Latour, interaction with the strange and mysterious "seems to *overflow* with elements which are already in the situation coming from some other time, some other place, and generated by some other agency" (166). The spirits that spoke at séances were precisely such "strange and mysterious" beings, free from time and space, exercising agencies that were barely describable. The similarity here is not arbitrary, for Latour is taking his model of social reassemblage from those whose beliefs, religious or otherwise, persist beyond sanctioned models of social propriety or empirical objectivity. For Latour, the work of reassemblage requires social detachment, an effort that can be best achieved by a counterattachment to a no-space, an occult realm in which believers "have an uncanny obstinacy to speak as if they were attached to spirits, divinities, voices, ghosts, and so on" (234), an "obstinacy" that defies skepticism's scare quotes. Social reassemblage is, in short, an occult act, reliant on something closely akin to what James called the will to believe.

We hear echoes of James once again in Jane Bennett's celebration of a "'weakly messianic' urge to exercise one's capacity to see things as otherwise than they are" (76). For Bennett, those who can "see things otherwise" are motivated by what might be a contemporary iteration of belief, the imagination. Bennett writes, "Imagination energizes us with alternatives, with the power of the new and startling and wonderful. The burden of this task falls to the imagination," Bennett continues, "now that, unfortunately, the outside, everyday world—disenchanted of spirit—is utterly unable to inspire and enliven us. Imagination," Bennett concludes, "is a counter to 'the pressure of reality'" (76). To take Bennett's figurative language back to the séance table, "the disenchantment of spirit" might be less a noun than a verb: to disenchant *spirits* is to accept fact over vision, over imagination, and over belief. But *enchantment*, for Bennett, is still alive, as it was for séance participants, in the persistence of belief, or, as Bennett would have it, imagination.

And here we arrive where human flourishing intersects with literature. Explaining how best to vivify belief in disenchanted times, Latour turns to fiction, which comprises subjects who, like all believers once they are identified *as* such, are excluded from "real" life as "fanciful, arbitrary, out-dated, archaic, ideological, and misleading" (80). According to Latour, literature incites "the irruption into the normal course of action of strange, exotic, archaic, or mysterious implements" (80) that flourish in "the vast outside to which every course of action has to appeal" (244). Reading literature, then, is a potentially liberatory act, through which we "let out of their cages entities which had been strictly forbidden to enter the scene until now and allow them to roam in the world again" (239–40). In turn, those entities, or what Latour calls "invisibles" (240), may free *us* by requiring that we fill in the gaps within the visible, empirical, and normative, freeing our imagination from *its* cage in order to roam.

We could substitute "séance" for "literature" here, and Latour's description would work just as well. At the séance table, mediums filled in the gaps within the visible with presences that were nothing if not "strange, exotic, archaic, or mysterious," allowing for "irruption" by "invisibles" into "the normal course of action." Those seated around the table appealed to "the vast outside"—in their case the ultimate outside, the afterlife—to release those who are "strictly forbidden to enter the scene" to "roam in the world again." That Spiritualism and the reading of literature can be described in such similar ways suggests how both generate and strengthen the will to believe, the choice to surrender to what is not *there* but *might be*, producing meaning *beyond* what is evident. "Meaning," in other words, is a sign of a willingness to believe in meaning. Literature requires us to see a world that doesn't exist but that *might* do so if we, in tandem with the text, let imagination free us from the "cage" of disbelief. I don't mean that the content of literature gives us scripts for believing or goals to believe in (most literature does the opposite). Rather, I am suggesting that before delivering its content, literature requires a prior willingness to suspend disbelief in worlds that, like the sprit-world, are only partially seen.

Depending on one's relationship to conventional accounts of what is "real," literature also potentially offers what Bennett calls "strategies to combat the everyday" (76). To those for whom "strange" and "imaginative" are synonymous with "bad" and "trivial," literature, like imagination generally, is dismissed in favor of what is "real." But as Latour argues, social action is enabled when the strange "seems to overflow" the real with agencies from other times and places. And the experience of belief, like that of imagination, releases the discredited and disparaged—the social as well as the spiritual "invisibles"—to roam the earth, released from "social death" through the medium of literature.

In her 1852 poem *Shadow Land; or, the Seer*, the Spiritualist poet Elizabeth Oakes Smith asserts that belief in spirits is common among those whose "past has been embittered by care and disappointment." Smith claims, "The unfortunate are always superstitious; just in proportion as the calamities of life impair the freedom of the human mind," leaving "no hopeful vista to relieve the gloom of the present" (60). I would gloss Smith in this way: What the hopeless share is a sense of inevitability, a belief that what is will always be, *must* always be. As James might put it, for the hopeless there is no possibility for truth beyond the empirical, and what can be seen is mortifying. Hopelessness is the inability to imagine life otherwise, an understandable incapacity when the resources for flourishing are nowhere in sight, when the forces holding the cage shut are so strong and so violent. I can well imagine this was what my mother and her siblings felt in their youth, that there was "no hopeful vista to relieve the gloom," that their future, like their past, would necessarily be "embittered by care and disappointment."

Yet that turned out not to be the case, at least not entirely so, as they, like many who experience embitterment and care, survived their past in order to live lives previously unimaginable. How the unimaginable becomes imaginable is what I've been exploring in this chapter, and I think it involves what Smith means by "freedom of mind," what Latour and Bennett call imagination, what séance participants meant by clairvoyance, and what James means by belief. To change any lived condition, one must have a sense of what changed conditions might look like. One must, in other words, layer the real with the unreal, create a corrected real, an imagined future worth trying to conjure into the present. It is not easy to imagine life differently. Doing so requires the simultaneous deployment of three capacities that do not arise naturally but require determined development. The first, as I've just said, is the capacity to imagine life as otherwise than it is, as a *not-yet* life. This is the capacity perhaps best developed through the reading of literature, which requires that we see a world described by a text, that we give it life in the mind's eye because, if it were present in the lived real, it would not be understood *as* literature. It is for that reason, I believe, that Latour and Bennett turn to literature to free the captive mind to roam.

The second is the capacity to live with the seeming irreconcilability of the *is* and the *might-be*. This is the capacity for belief, a conviction of the truth of the *not-yet* in the face of the discouragement and derision James called faith vetoing. If imagination makes the world of the possible, belief is what attaches the imaginer to the imagined, instilling a patient anticipation of what may become manifest only in pieces, yet maintaining the believed-in whole that keeps the soul striving in the face of discouragement. And that striving is the third capacity, what James called *will*, the active maintenance of belief and, as I've argued in the case of reformers who attended séances, the drive to make the imagined triumph over the disenchanting here-and-now. When these three capabilities come together, what Smith calls a "vista" opens and survival—even flourishing—is possible. Without any of the three, the cages Latour speaks of remain locked.

We can understand the operations of these capacities on scales ranging from the individual to the world historical. On the individual level, we might take the basic structure of psychiatric therapy. Clients engage therapists often motivated by a sense of being trapped in a state of incapacity or inevitability severe enough to cause distress. They come, in other words, feeling hopeless. Therapists become placeholders for that hope, reminders to clients that, in seeking help, they had already begun the process of imagining other states of mind, that with help they might bring those imagined selves into being. If the phenomenon of seeking help, of experiencing one's own belief *in* flourishing, is an essential component *of* that flourishing, then the client, like those who attended séances, repeatedly generates the phenomenon of belief for its own sake. Imagination at that point joins with belief, therapists serving as placeholders for both until clients can engender both for themselves. At that point the therapeutic process has joined imagination, belief, and will, and, if undertaken with skill and rigor, the result is movement toward the realization of the previously only imagined "freedom of mind."

On a broader scale, we might recall what the activist, political prisoner, and literary critic C. L. R. James wrote about the Haitian revolutionary leader Toussaint Louverture: "Firm as was his grasp of reality, old Toussaint looked beyond San Domingo with a boldness of imagination surpassed by no contemporary" (265). Or we might think of the iconic speech of the US civil rights movement, in which Martin Luther King Jr. spoke of a world of harmony between peoples divided by hate as a "dream," not because it was self-delusion or escapism, but because it was visionary. Both men were, in Smith's term, seers who overcame firsthand experience of the most disenchanting violence. Whether it was a liberated Haiti or a racially integrated United States, both could imagine a world other than what they saw, could believe in the truth of those imaginings despite vicious faith-vetoers, because they had the *will to believe*, were enabled to act in the here-and-now to make the *could-be* and the *not-yet* manifest.

It's important that, as C. L. R. James said of Toussaint, one keep a firm grasp on reality, even as one exercises the will to believe. Perhaps that is why those who attended séances needed to hear the sad stories spirits told, in order to direct their belief toward progressive reforms or why literature in its content so often depicts the dire consequences of existing or dystopic social conditions at the same time as it invites imaginings of other ways worlds can be made. Without such restraints and conductors, belief can become an instrument of privilege at the expense of the disadvantaged. But the response to these dangers should be greater vigilance, not the abandonment of belief, imagination, and will as social forces. For the perpetual making of and faith in *otherwise* realities may be the best hope for human flourishing.

Works Cited

Banner of Light, vol. 6, no. 16, 14 Jan. 1860. L. Colby & Company, Boston.

Banner of Light, vol. 7, no. 5, 28 Apr. 1860. L. Colby & Company, Boston.

Banner of Light, vol. 7, no. 6, 5 May 1860. L. Colby & Company, Boston.

Banner of Light, vol. 7, no. 7, 12 May 1860. L. Colby & Company, Boston.

Bennett, Jane. *The Enchantment of Modern Life: Attachments, Crossings, and Ethics.* Princeton UP, 2001.

Connolly, William. "Materialities of Experience." *New Materialisms: Ontology, Agency, and Politics*, edited by Diana Coole and Samantha Frost, Duke UP, 2010, pp. 178–200.

James, William. "Is Life Worth Living?" *The Will to Believe and Other Essays in Popular Philosophy.* Longmans, Green, and Co., 1905, pp. 32–62.

James, William. *The Varieties of Religious Experience: A Study in Human Nature.* Longmans, Green, and Co., 1902.

Latour, Bruno. "Why Has Critique Run Out of Steam? From Matters of Fact to Matters of Concern." *Critical Inquiry*, vol. 30, no. 2, 2004, pp. 225–48.

Latour, Bruno. *Reassembling the Social: An Introduction to Actor-Network-Theory.* Oxford UP, 2007.

Pawelski, James O. *The Dynamic Individualism of William James.* State UP of New York, 2007.

Smith, Elizabeth Oakes. *Shadow-Land; or, The Seer.* 1852. Rpt. Wentworth Press, 2016.

Thayer, R. Untitled. *Banner of Light*, vol. 7, no. 2, 7 Apr. 1860. L. Colby & Company, Boston.

4

Sage Writing

Facing Reality in Literature

David Russell

Reading appraisals of the recent histories of both disciplines, it would seem that academic psychology and literary criticism have something in common: both avoid thinking positively. For Martin Seligman and Mihaly Csikszentmihayli, academic psychology's historical focus on the negative, on psychic *ill* health, has severely limited the scale on which human mental development might be imagined. Certainly, in Freudian psychoanalysis (as familiar to literary study) a picture of mere sanity—let alone Seligman and Csikszentmihayli's "positive individuals" who exhibit "optimal experience" in "human functioning"—is only available by inference (5, 8). The field of "positive psychology" would counteract a similar negativity in the academic subject. It aims to overcome the discipline's symptomatic "disease model," in order to locate the material from which to construct a picture of psychic health.

For positive psychology, this is where the humanities come in. An interesting implied suggestion of work in positive psychology is that a large and vital area of human experience has been neglected by science, and that this area of experience may overlap with—or even be identical to—those experiences represented or performed by the humanities. Could the much-discussed decline and neglect of the humanities be linked to the negative focus Seligman and others have found in psychology—a general underappreciation of the positive? Could a blind spot in one discipline help to address the tribulations of another? Perhaps a similar preference for the negative and symptomatic has obscured our vision of both the psychological study of sanity, and the benefits of humanistic study. By these, positive, lights, a deficit of data about human flourishing represents a shared problem for psychology and the humanities; the resources have been there all along, but it is as if an important task of attention and accumulation has been shirked.

David Russell, *Sage Writing* In: *Literary Studies and Human Flourishing*. Edited by: James F. English and Heather Love, Oxford University Press. © Oxford University Press 2023. DOI: 10.1093/oso/9780197637227.003.0005

This task may be essential to the very survival of humanistic study: "To refuse to look for ways to measure the empirical effects of the humanities is to be careless with the enormous cultural treasure they represent," James Pawelski has warned (212).

Yet one might be doubtful about how much help literary criticism can offer, and whether it possess the capacities to turn literature to positive account. For literary criticism, too, seems afflicted by a constitutional aversion to positive claims. Admittedly, this may be true of any kind of criticism, which is a word marked by a curiously negative progress: "it is an exceedingly peculiar but undeniable fact" the philosopher Raymond Geuss has noted, "that a term that originally ... referred merely to the process of separating that which was distinct, eventually developed in the direction of acquiring a distinctly *negative* connotation" (72–73). (Nobody says: thank you for your criticism of my cooking). But while the neutral sense of the word and its variants do survive in some specialized rather than ordinary language contexts (as in the art school "critique," for instance), in specifically *literary* criticism, as Raymond Williams has pointed out, the negative use of the word emerged early on, and has persisted as primary: "This has even led to the distinction of *appreciation* as a softer word for the judgment of literature," Williams comments (85). Literary criticism has, for a long time, had rather a negative attitude.

Recently, an interesting parallel to positive psychology's demand for a less negative focus can be found in the general impression in academic literary studies that the discipline's investments in "suspicious" reading and ideology critique have limited the scope of literary criticism. As with psychology, a diagnostic vision—something like Seligman's "disease model"—has been in the ascendant. The 2009 call by Stephen Best and Sharon Marcus for a "surface reading" in literary criticism, for example, has been framed as, among other things, an attempt to restore to it the resources of a neglected neutrality. A professional practice of reading against the grain, in order to expose the symptoms of literature's complicity with power, has revealed much about literature—and much about power. But, as Best and Marcus ask, what might it have obscured? What about (as a positive psychologist might ask) the ways literature could be good for us, and not only revelatory of the trouble we're in?

For all that there is a suggestive echo between recent internal critiques in academic psychology and literary study, I think it can only take us so far. But in this very limitation, something usefully specific about literary criticism is revealed. For there does seem to be something else about the study of literature that would resist recruitment to any positive plans for human well-being. There is a longer tradition in literary criticism that has refused to literature a positive status on a different basis than the hermeneutics of suspicion. Literary works do not, claimed Thomas De Quincey in a famous 1848 essay, supply "information" that might be accumulated and superseded (166). "The *Iliad*, the *Prometheus* of Aeschylus, the *Othello* or *King Lear*, the *Hamlet* or *Macbeth*, and the *Paradise Lost*, are not militant, but triumphant," he argues, because

> to reproduce these in new forms, or variations, even if in some things they should be improved, would be to plagiarize. A good steam-engine is properly superseded by a better. But one lovely pastoral valley is not superseded by another, nor a statue of Praxiteles by a statue of Michelangelo. These things are separated not by imparity, but by disparity. They are not thought of as unequal under the same standard, but as different in kind, and, if otherwise equal, as equal under a different standard. Human works of immortal beauty and works of nature in one respect stand on the same footing ... they differ not as better and worse, or simply by more and less: they differ by undecipherable and incommunicable differences, that cannot be caught by mimicries, that cannot be reflected in the mirror of copies, that cannot become ponderable in the scales of vulgar comparison. (166)

Not imparity, but disparity: De Quincey insists that literature, like other humanistic works, is valuable to us because of its recalcitrance to collation under a scale of value. It cannot be "caught" in a manner that would mirror them—and so reduce them to bounded summary. This nonscalability and nonreducibility of the literary work makes it useless to further any predetermined instrumental aim (this is the role of what De Quincey calls "knowledge"); rather, it conditions the effects a literary work has on us as readers (what he calls "power"). In De Quincey's wittily repurposed theological terms, it is not "militant" but "triumphant": not an aid to an already established struggle, but productive of a renovating vision. The question literature raises is not how it might contribute to a future aim, but how it is to be lived with now, as a given, as something complete in itself.

We might use De Quincey's distinction between knowledge and power, which was not an uncommon way to understand the quality of literature in nineteenth-century Britain, to think about the status of the "positive" in psychology and literature. I don't think that the category of the positive can be abstractly defined in the field of literature; but I do wonder what kind of positive De Quincey's sense of "power" might be. (It is not, in any obvious way, a sense of the word we would encounter in a "suspicious" reading.) Pawelski's useful survey of the word "positive" defines it as containing two distinct senses: as (an older sense) of "presence, with having a quality vs. lacking it"—as providing something in addition to what was already there; and (a newer sense) as "having to do with preference, with what is desirable, what is good." De Quincey defines literature's power very vaguely, as a function to "move" readers and a capacity to provide "expansion" to their latent forces. The key to his definition of the literature of power is not a particular content but its performance of something—something that is both evasive and expansive. Following De Quincey, we might think of the positive sense of literature as providing something in excess, in addition. Not an addition in the sense of accumulation (of like data under a standard); nor in the sense of scientistic progress (by which new information supersedes the old). But more radically in addition, as adding something so distinct as to be inassimilable to established scales of measurement and development. Might there be virtue to this recalcitrance—and particularly for the function of literature at the present time?

For we live today, the anthropologist Anna Lowenhaupt Tsing has suggested, in an ever more scalable world. "Scalability," Tsing proposes, is a feature both of modern science and of much contemporary business: "progress itself has often been defined by its ability to make projects expand without changing their framing assumptions" (38). Major corporations like Amazon are scalable because their rapid expansion is predicated on their not changing their frame. Scalability allows for rapid communications and expansions across distance and unlike terrain, but it also "requires that project elements be oblivious to the indeterminacies of encounter; that's how they allow smooth expansion." Thus scalability "banishes meaningful diversity, that is, diversity that might change things" while "the nonscalable" is relegated to the status of "an impediment" (38). In De Quincey's time, such "progress" would have been imperial. Today it is associated with multinational corporations and their powerful logics. This process has become such a recognizable feature of contemporary life that it often structures the political and institutional demands of those who want to change their social environment. Demands for modernization are often made in terms favorable to scalability, as when standardization and corporate best practices are called for in university administration, research, and teaching, for instance; while opponents of the impact of capital on communities can cite scalability as the evidence of this impact. When activist residents of Queens in New York City resisted Amazon's location of a headquarters there, it was on the grounds of defending the borough from becoming exactly like every other urban area where Amazon has a major presence. Scalability brings efficiency to capital and information flow, just as it diminishes the vitality and diversity of any specific ecology—whether we understand ecology in its primary sense, in describing a particular natural environment, or in its metaphorical applications to workplace or institutional culture, or to the health and diversity of a New York City borough.

Scalability as Tsing describes it is not an unmixed phenomenon; it is as welcomed by some as it is resisted by others. But it is a very significant phenomenon of our times—joining powerfully the logics of bureaucracy, capital, and science (or rather, scientism). Indeed, the power of its logic renders it difficult to think around or beyond. Progress in scalability narrows our world picture. It is perhaps the principle way that the increased efficiency of information and capital flow is mistaken for moral and social progress.

Given conditions of ever-increasing scalability, could we understand literature not—as many do—as an antiquated, if still useful, form of information technology, but as an alternative to scalable thinking? Could the particular mode of literature's nonprogressiveness, as De Quincey describes it, provide a salutary and expansive challenge? And is there a particular moment or area of literary history that could provide a useful example of such challenge? In what follows, I want to make use of De Quincey and Tsing's distinctions in order to draw attention to the role or aspect of literary and cultural criticism that makes claims for literature as somehow expansive in a "meaningful" sense, to use Tsing's adjective, and as "adding to the stock of available reality," to borrow a line from the critic R. P. Blackmur; but as doing this not in addition, along a single scale, but by insisting on other forms of relation or modes of apprehension than those a reader might have anticipated.

This aspect of criticism repudiates attempts to insist on the value of the literary humanities by putting them to predetermined, measurable, all-too-scalable, use. Judged by the test of economic or scientistic uses, literature will usually fail. Or even worse: it could succeed. In a recent issue of the *New Yorker*, John Lanchester lists a series of recent popular books in economics and social science, all of which co-opt the humanities as data into their preexisting economic or biologistic formulae for progress. One of them makes the case for the uses of poetry as a remnant of mating rituals, by which the pleasure and attention of the powerful are attracted: the book proposes the example of Maya Angelou, who was so successful she snagged Bill Clinton and was invited to his inauguration. Lanchester, a novelist learned in economics, is obviously struck by the sheer absurdity of this proposition, but its logic is recognizable in many more subtle applications of literary "evidence" to scalable goals.

The tradition of criticism I am thinking of, on the other hand, proposes a role for literature that is somehow more vague and significant at once. Literature may not provide evidence or assistance for preexisting problems in science or morals—this is often to convert literature into another language, and so lose what makes it distinctive—but it might change our sense of what a problem is, and who we are to have such problems. This is one of the reasons Matthew Arnold called literature "criticism of life" and claimed that critics were voices in the wilderness: calling for new, as yet virtual modes of human relation. Indeed, I am thinking of a literary criticism whose proponents were treated as if they were setting themselves up as some kind of prophet: as a source of creative disparity as it was popularized by various "sage" figures (as they were dubbed in the 1950s) of the Victorian era, and also by dissenters from dominant cultures in the twentieth-century United States. It is possible to trace a line of criticism in the United Kingdom and United States—from John Ruskin and Matthew Arnold and George Eliot, to Lionel Trilling and James Baldwin and Susan Sontag—that insists on the necessity of a literary apprehension, and links it to the question of what passes for "reality" in a given culture, and how a fuller sense of reality may be faced, or seen with a wider vision.

Sage writing, as John Holloway dubbed it in 1953, places a remarkable faith in a literary prose; it is defined by a shared insistence on writing as performed wisdom, and a shared belief, in Holloway's words, that "acquiring wisdom is somehow an opening of the eyes, making us see in our experience what we failed to see before" (9). Literature, by this kind of critical writing, is joined to the task, if not of revelation, then of breaking through established modes of relation to the world. "There is a crust about the impressible part of men's minds," Ruskin wrote in "The Lamp of Power" in his 1849 *Seven Lamps of Architecture*, "which must be pierced through before they can be touched to the quick; and though we may prick at it in a thousand separate places, we might as well have let it alone if we do not come through somewhere with a deep thrust" (VIII.105). Sage writing gave itself this task.

Now, invoking the sages and prophets of literary history may sound a little grand, and it may arouse some unease. To do so may seem a return to outdated ideologies of culture: the same pious humanism, for instance, that it was one of the goals of a hermeneutics of suspicion to unmask. After all, as much criticism has shown us, insisting on wisdom in literature usually means endorsing the worldview of some people over others; talking about the human has always meant giving it a mold—usually bourgeois, white, straight, cisgender, able-bodied, and male—and denying full humanity to those who don't fit it. Many of the figures mentioned above have since been cut down to size by criticism. They are often read more as reflecting their times, places (the British or American empires) and privilege than as acting or performing anything through their language. It would be difficult to defend many specific opinions of Arnold or Ruskin, Trilling or Sontag. Moreover, this focus on a few individual writers might seem to be elitist: insisting on a kind of language that is privileged and particularly literary, all too invested in the prestige of the so-called canon; and on a kind of authority that is charismatic, rather than consensual, a concession to the great man or great woman model of cultural production. These prophet-critics were often difficult: often singular, egoistic, uncollaborative. One couldn't imagine peer-reviewing them.

There are good reasons for turning away from this kind of charismatic authority (rather like those cited by early analytic philosophers for turning to the collaborative and problem-focused methods and away from elitist grand theories). "[T]oday nobody wants to be seduced," Beth Blum remarks in her chapter on "Therapeutic Redescription" in this volume. She points to a "depreciation of the ideology of charisma taking place within the discipline and our culture-at-large." Blum's sophisticated reflections on charisma and criticism might lead us to wonder if an anticharismatic mode of "deflationary description" that seeks to give just the facts might actually be the most charismatically coercive mode of all. Data has its own seductions to offer. And, after all, as Ruskin pointed out in a famous essay in understanding literature as offering us ways of interpreting the world, we are bound to get it wrong. Literature seems to show how in the modern world we confuse emotion with thought, the subjective with the objective, and often read either too closely or too distantly. For Ruskin, the least useful response is the certainty sought through diminution, and an insistence on bare facts, which Ruskin attributes to "the man who perceives rightly, because he does not feel, and to whom the primrose is very accurately the primrose, because he does not love it." (Blum's essay concludes with the suggestion that even in the most restrained, stoical modes of reading, a keeping in mind of the finitude of what we are looking at may function to evoke love for the world.)

Even if we avoid such "careless habits of accuracy" (to borrow Wilde's phrase), one more imagined objection—a more general one—is to note how a case for literature's special effects risks a lapse into platitudinous truisms about how literature is good for people—or remedial to what's bad for people—in a way that damns with faint pieties. An observant critic herself may have noticed by this point that the terms are all rather vague: I have slipped several times between talking about literature to talking about a mode of criticism that is itself literary, and so somehow sits on the border between literature and criticism. To make the case for literature or the literary as having a special status may seem rather anachronistic. Why make the case about a particular kind of criticism (when nobody reads criticism anyway) and its possible social effects and not, say, about novels (which some people at least still read)? And isn't all this a way of introducing the utility of literature again, this time through the back door?[1]

Addressing these objections takes us to the stakes of this nonscalable literature, and to some points of contact with philosophical and social questions. I will turn from them to a specific example in the writing of John Ruskin. To take the last point first: I am not so interested in establishing a special high or literary mode of language as distinct from its low or ordinary uses. Nor am I that interested in the distinction between a primary literature and a secondary criticism. Rather, I am interested in a critical tradition that sought to use language in a particular way, and valued certain literature for its amenability to these particular uses. The writers in this tradition were not so much interested in a particular identity, genre, or set of information, but in particular modes of relation they thought literature could perform, and which they sought to perform in their own writing. These critics placed emphasis on a particular role for reading and writing, and it is this emphasis, more than any shared doctrine, voice, or opinion, that produces a family resemblance in them, and which directs their attention to particular works of literature, as more amenable to this emphasis than others.

This leads us to the question of the utility of literature. One of the roles of literature, this tradition claims, is in provoking or inspiring us to think about modes of use that we bring to a particular object (as we are about to see Ruskin do with the image of a sharp clean knife). It is not that literature is to be entirely divorced from the field of utility, to be placed in a separate, pure, realm of the aesthetic; rather, literature is described as intervening in

---

[1] I thank James English for this question.

this field. Literature is useful in what it does, potentially—in the way it offers particular tones, modes of attention and forms of relation—for the way we think about uses. It begins by unsettling assumptions about scalable and progressive definitions of use. It is these modes of relation, expressed through the individual voice and particular attention, that are missed by a scientistic, data-driven, and collaborative model of research (a dominant model, for instance, in British university funding now) that aims to pose and then solve specific problems though the supply of information. The historian of science Bruno Latour has identified this blind spot in his critique of what he calls "double-click communication," which he contrasts in his case not to literary, but to religious language, which "carries no messages, but transports and transforms the messengers themselves, or it fails to do so" (106). Literature shares a function with religious language here. Like religious language, literature has lost a lot of status in the modern world. (And perhaps for similar reasons: Simon During has recently proposed that after the decline of religion, the "second secularization" was of the belief in the power of culture, in which literature played a major role). We might have to update Latour's technological index now, but his contrast is useful. "Double-click communication," Latour explains,

> wants us to believe that it is feasible to transport, without any deformation whatever, some accurate information about states of affairs that are not present to us. In most ordinary cases, what people have in mind when they ask "is this true," or "does this correspond to a state of affairs," is just such a double-click gesture, allowing immediate access to information: tough luck, because this is what undermines ways of talking that are dearest to our heart. On the contrary, to disappoint the drive towards double-click— to divert it, to break it, to subvert it, to render it impossible—is just what religious talk is after. (106)

Preferring evocation to information, the sage writers I am interested in present another alternative to the knowledge-transfer, data-driven model of "double-click communication." This language that Latour calls dear to the heart— is a function of literature. It is this kind of communication that, as Tsing and others have argued, becomes ever rarer in the modern age of information and scalability (a modern age that began in the nineteenth century: nothing was supposed to be more scalable, from the outset, as were the "structures of understanding," as James Mill called them, that underpinned the expansion of the British empire).[2] Particular critics who take up this communicative role may be individually very dissimilar; but the issue this criticism seeks to keep in mind is not a set of facts—it always acknowledges we enjoy an abundance of facts, that we are drowning in information—but the question of how facts are faced. On this line of thinking, encountering a work of literature would be more like encountering a person than a set of data. Literary works, like people, are in excess of our plans for them. They can't be fully "caught by mimicries," as De Quincey put it, "or reflected in the mirror of copies." It is in this way that they are like what De Quincey calls "works of nature" ("scalability is not an ordinary feature of nature," Tsing reminds us; 38). We are in trouble when we understand the natural world according to our own uses for it. John Ruskin, on the basis of this principle founding his own criticism in the 1840s, made claims for the moral effects of the paintings of J. M. W. Turner, which themselves refused to bound their (often natural) subjects through predetermined uses—this virtue Ruskin thought people always had to relearn because they were always willfully forgetting it.

Exceeding the scalable, attending to forms of relation before facts, a function of literature may be to put into words a sense of reality beyond what is capturable by methods for problem-solving. Not as pieties about something ineffable, but as beginning from the contention—which is shared by a certain line in psychoanalysis, and in a certain branch of philosophy interested in "Ordinary Language"—that a sense of reality is something that for everyone has been achieved and is still being achieved. For Lionel Trilling, because literature is that "in which the things we cannot possibly not know live side by side with thought and desire," it must be "passionately" concerned with "reality" (276). Trilling, who was deeply interested in the "reality" line of psychoanalysis, proposed that the value in literature was its resources and capacities for taking readers to a site of confrontation with reality. What he means by what "we cannot possibly not know" is not a question of data but of relation; his essays are interested in what counts for us as what we cannot avoid, and how this relates to the way we live with the unavoidable, in our thought and desire, including the desire to go on engaging with reality. Literature does not reveal something to us we didn't know; it exceeds our current relationships to what we do know. It is about exposure to something that could be a stimulus for change.

---

[2] On Mill's "structures of understanding" in the nineteenth century, see Russell, *Tact*, 33.

Not new information, but new relations: The philosopher Cora Diamond has proposed that the place where we can see this exposure at work is in situations where one person can be moved, delighted or wounded, by a fact that leaves other people unaffected: they know it too, but as "the mere accepted background of life" (one of her examples is the way we treat animals in the food industry; Diamond 47). The difference between the affected and the unaffected response is not a matter of access to data; nor is it a matter of reasoned disagreement over facts. It is a variation between visions of the world. The philosopher Stanley Cavell calls this the experience of "inordinate knowledge" (Cavell et al. 95). One of his frequent examples is the experience of the separateness of other people, and so the experience of one's own dependence on the existence of others. Such experience is always being forgotten and relearned (see Cavell 2003). Both Trilling and Cavell relate this kind of experience to Freud's distinction from his essay on the unconscious, in which he remarks that "to have heard something and to have experienced something are in their psychological nature two different things even though the content of both is the same" (153). For Freud, the evocation of this experience is one of the aims of clinical practice, and a basis for psychic change; for Cavell, it is a reason why philosophy should attend to the ordinary—the material that we apparently all know, and the language which we apparently all share—much more than it does. Diamond calls the experience of being affected in this way "the difficulty of reality" (Diamond 47). Crucially for my interests, she thinks that literature is better than academic philosophy at taking us to the grounds of this problem: a particular use of literature reveals a blindspot in philosophy.

For Diamond, the virtual function of literature offers not the grounds of one particular subjective response, but a space of exploration. A work of literature is not a set of logical propositions, or an argument, or a set of facts. Indeed, Diamond calls "deflection" what happens "when we are moved from the appreciation . . . of a difficulty of reality to a philosophical or moral problem apparently in the vicinity" (57). Diamond understands one purpose of philosophical concepts to be the avoidance of reality (other forms of scientism could stand in just as well), while she awards literature the distinction of facing it. Diamond is arguing against the limitations of her own discipline's relational modes. The tradition of criticism I am interested in shares precisely this insistence on such exposures, and claims for it implications for their culture at large. But how does the critical approach to literature I have been describing seek to evoke and endorse such experience? There is a challenge to literary form here, because to deal with the boundary where something that seems overwhelmingly significant to some and seems ordinary or even banal to others, is to risk cliché. It cannot be a matter, either, of the right balance of positive or negative experience; it does not really make sense to say one is a little bit exposed. Are there rhetorical devices to be relied upon, or which recur, in this tradition?

Let us turn now to a particular example in the work of John Ruskin, who of the Victorian period was the "most sagacious of its sages," as his biographer Tim Hilton has claimed (10). Ruskin, said Tolstoy, "was one of those rare men who think with their hearts" (21.188). His writing is about the distinction between knowing something superficially, and knowing it in a way that it becomes part of one's feeling vision (so it becomes, in Latour's idiom, dear to our hearts). Again and again, his prose seeks to take his reader to the point where mere information is transformed into a new relationship to reality, as it is felt in the heart: not "head-work" or "hand-work" will suffice, he argues in conclusion to the *Stones of Venice* (1851–53), but "heart-work . . . is the one work we want" (XI.201). This aim accounts for the strangeness of Ruskin's prose, its repetitiveness, its evasion of logical proposition, as well as its sheer volume. Ruskin's writing seeks to reorient its reader rather than to prosecute an argument. Since his writing seeks to situate those who find it, it must flout convention, resist summary and continually strain to evade established modes of reading comprehension. It must keep itself—and us—on the move. As R. G. Collingwood observed in 1919, Ruskin was one of the least systematic or logical—the least philosophical—writers of his times; and yet despite (or rather because of) this eccentricity, he produced one of the most important philosophies of his age. His writing is not usually difficult, but it is demanding.

One of Ruskin's critical techniques is to overcome a facile knowingness by testing it against the difficulty of coming to certainty in questions of aesthetics. One of his preferred points of transition between these realms is the activity of composition—which Ruskin uses freely, metaphorically to mean both the making up of a picture and the making up of a society and even a psychology. It is such a useful metaphor, for Ruskin, because it is a site of what Diamond calls the difficulty of reality. "True composition," Ruskin explains in his *Modern Painters 5* (1860),

> is inexplicable. No one can explain how the notes of a Mozart melody, or the folds of a piece of Titian's drapery, produce their essential effects on each

other. If you do not feel it, no one can by reasoning make you feel it. And the highest composition is so subtle, that it is apt to become unpopular, and sometimes seem insipid. (VII.210)

Here again, is the salutary role of the possible change of aspect—as composing or recomposing the elements of a situation—which depends on relation more than information, and which always runs the risk, as we have seen Diamond suggest, of seeming too obvious, or clichéd to mention—what Ruskin calls "insipid."[3]

Much of the brilliance of Ruskin's criticism is found in the way he is able to bring this aesthetic predicament to a social situation. A good example is a lecture, "The Work of Iron," that he delivered in 1858 to an audience in the prosperous Kent town of Tunbridge Wells. This audience had asked Ruskin to address them on aesthetics and decoration—as an advisor, as it were, on "how to spend it."[4] Ruskin understands this role, and refuses to play along. He begins in ironic modesty, explaining that "it was a matter of some doubt with me whether I could find any subject that would . . . justify my bringing you out of your comfortable houses on a winter's night" (105). Instead of beginning a "mere talk about art," he cites the origin of the town's name in "the welling forth of the spring over the orange rim of its marble basin," because "it struck me that you might not be unwilling, to-night, to think a little over the full significance of that saffron stain." Instead of teaching connoisseurship as a means of making the comfortable more comfortable, he draws attention to something the people of the town have seen every day, but to which they have never really paid attention. This stain, Ruskin explains, which "is often thought to spoil the basin of your spring, is iron in a state of rust." The subject is the way Ruskin warms to his wider theme, which is his audience's mistaken relation to facts they already know. Ruskin goes on:

> Because we cannot use a rusty knife or razor so well as a polished one, we suppose it to be a great defect in iron that it is subject to rust. But not at all. On the contrary, the most perfect and useful state of it is that ochreous stain; and therefore it is endowed with so ready a disposition to get itself

---

[3] James Pawelski has pointed out to me how this formulation echoes William James's distinction between "knowledge of acquaintance" and "knowledge about" in Chapter 8 of his 1890 *Principles of Psychology*. Literature, as Diamond and others champion it, can offer ways of defending the former from subsumption by the latter.

[4] The consumer supplement to the British *Financial Times* newspaper is called "How to Spend it."

into that state. It is not a fault in the iron, but a virtue, to be so fond of getting rusted, for in that condition it performs its most important functions in the universe, and most kindly duties to mankind. Nay, in a certain sense and almost a literal one, we may say that iron rusted is Living; but when pure, or polished, Dead. (106)

Rather eccentrically, Ruskin attributes to iron a disposition. His rhetoric insists on a shift in attention from iron in one state to another: from the utility of a bounded object, a piece of technology, to the usefulness of rust, not as object but as condition: a relationship of lively diffusiveness. This assertion—a revaluation of assumed values—sets new terms of praise and blame. He suggests that within his audience's knowledge about iron and rust lies a known (but not really known) series of investments: in purity, in defenses against admixture, in keeping things separate. What at first seems a strange line of argument gains support when Ruskin turns to the role of iron in producing color:

You think, perhaps, that your iron is wonderfully useful in a pure form, but how would you like the world, if . . . all your arable ground, instead of being made of sand and clay, were suddenly turned into flat surfaces of steel—if the whole earth, instead of its green and glowing sphere, rich with forest and flower, showed nothing but . . . lifeless, excoriated metal. . . . It would be that . . . were it not that all the substance of which it is made sucks and breathes the brilliancy of the atmosphere; and, as it breathes, softening from its merciless hardness, it falls into fruitful and beneficent dust. (108)

Ruskin's didacticism has an odd tone and purpose; he doesn't reveal something hidden, but tries to make his audience see the value of what they have been treating as the mere background to their lives: "iron is the sunshine and light of landscape" (108). Most of Ruskin's work is about this seeing, a kind of revelation that makes you see nothing new, but which offers this nothing new in a way that proposes new relations. The significance of a stain, Ruskin claims, is an underappreciated source of joy and vitality. He continues:

I believe it is not ascertained on what the crimson of blood actually depends; but the colour is connected, of course, with its vitality, and that vitality with the existence of iron as one of its substantial elements. Is it not strange to find this stern and strong metal mingled so delicately in our human life that we cannot even blush without its help? (112)

Blood cells are red, as is rust, because of the interaction of iron and oxygen. Ruskin links the colour of the world, it's sheer liveliness, to the question of admixture, as opposed to purity—and then to what people do when they are embarrassed—to blushing.

Ruskin makes his audience stumble over the obvious, over accustomed uses, only so that they might relish being wrongfooted. The clean sharp knife is less valuable than the spreading rust that had seemed to diminish it. He then threads a new observation of value across a wider range of associations, to reveal it is integral to our lives—it couldn't, in fact, be more personal. It is in the blood. A certain pleased embarrassment is the place he wants to end up, and it is also the sign under which he speaks. But then his tone darkens. He wants his audience to go on feeling embarrassed; not only because they haven't noticed, in their mistaken scheme of values, the richness of the world around them, but because of the kind of behavior—humiliating behavior, that they have, in their obtuseness, perpetuated. For after listing the virtues of iron admixed with air, he returns to a functional use of iron, one that would have been very familiar to the people of Tunbridge Wells, and that is the iron railing which marks the bounds of their houses. The iron railing is

a thing which you can't walk inside of without making yourself look like a wild beast, nor look at out of your window in the morning without expecting to see somebody impaled upon it in the night . . . [it is] a useless fence—it can shelter nothing, and support nothing; you can't nail your peaches to it, nor protect flowers with it . . . it is also an insolent fence;—it says plainly to everyone who passes—"You may be an honest person, but, also, you may be a thief: honest or not, you shall not get in here, for I am a respectable person and much above you; you shall see only what a grand place I have got to keep you out of—look here, and depart in humiliation." (117)

Ruskin goes on to connect a town of iron railings to a world of exploitation, from domestic architecture to the imagined boundaries between people it implies, and the refusal to acknowledge wider forms of relation. Ruskin accuses his audience of living off the blood of others. People work at such disadvantageous terms; their labor is bought for such a cheap price by the rich that—and they must know—the "thing could not be offered you at that price, unless distress of some kind had forced the producer to part with it" (128). In particular Ruskin attacks "modern speculation" (a source of much of the town residents' wealth) that "involves much risk to others, with chance of profit only to ourselves," and he cites the effect of banking collapses, which harm the vulnerable most (129). Ruskin implies that these financial ties rely on a denial of that connection of the iron in the blood, and an affirmation of the purity of iron railings. It is the more reprehensible, Ruskin claims, that "we do our murdering, not with any pauses of pity or scorching of conscience, but in facile and forgetful calm of mind" (130). What Ruskin calls a "trade in unregarded blood" refers not just to the blood of disavowed yet murderous responsibility, but a disregard of the shared iron that joins people to one another, and to the earth. It is not a matter of what people know, but whether they admit of a shared reality: "be assured that the question is one of responsibilities only, not of facts" (131).

Against a disavowal of connection with others that would at the same time exploit it in labor relations, Ruskin proposes an ethics of dissolution. The "Work of Iron" is a good example of Ruskin's critical mode more generally, a mode that a critical focus on the accuracy or absurdity of his economic theories has tended to obscure. An aesthetic insistence on what is noticed and observed in ordinary life, the way ordinary things are related to, will lead to moral claims. And he tends to begin from what at first appears obvious and everyday—the stain on a well, the railings of a house—which have meanings that have gone unrecognized, in order to make an appeal to his audience. Ruskin's lecture seeks to dissolve its iron subject, to turn objects (like railings) into activities (new kinds of circulation), so that his listeners or readers may feel in a new relation to their everyday life. Ruskin's aim is that his audience might find themselves moved toward a radical sense of their interpenetration with others, and to a way of facing reality that could apprehend both the joy and outrage this interpenetration reveals.

Works Cited

Best, Stephen, and Sharon Marcus. "Surface Reading, An Introduction." *Representations*, vol. 108, no.1, Fall 2009, pp. 1–21.

Cavell, Stanley. *Disowning Knowledge in Seven Plays of Shakespeare*. Cambridge UP, 2003.

Cavell, Stanley, et al. *Philosophy and Animal Life*. Columbia UP, 2009.

Collingwood, R. G. *Ruskin's Philosophy*. Quentin Nelson, 1971.

De Quincey, Thomas. "The Works of Alexander Pope." *North British Review*, August 1848, pp. 163–82.

Diamond, Cora. "The Difficulty of Reality and the Difficulty of Philosophy." Cavell et al., pp. 43–90.

During, Simon. "The Second Secularization, or: the Humanities and Society Today." Utrecht University Humanities Graduate Conference, 11 Apr. 2019, Utrecht University, Netherlands. Keynote Address.

Freud, Sigmund. "The Unconscious." *General Psychological Theory: Papers on Metapsychology*. Simon & Schuster, 2008.

Geuss, Raymond. *A World without Why*. Princeton UP, 2016.

Hilton, Tim. *The Pre-Raphaelites*. Thames and Hudson, 1970.

Holloway, John. *The Victorian Sage: Philosophy and Rhetoric in the Work of Carlyle, Disraeli, George Eliot, Newman, Arnold and Hardy*. Norton, 1965.

Lanchester, John. "Can Economists and Humanists Ever Be Friends?" *New Yorker*, 23 July 2018, https://www.newyorker.com/magazine/2018/07/23/can-economists-and-humanists-ever-be-friends.

Latour, Bruno. *On the Modern Cult of the Factish Gods*. Duke UP, 2010.

Pawelski, J. O. "Bringing Together the Humanities and the Science of Well-Being to Advance Human Flourishing." *Well Being and Higher Education*, edited by D. W. Harward, Association of American Universities and Colleges, 2016, pp. 207–16.

Ruskin, John. *The Seven Lamps of Architecture*. *Library Edition of the Complete Works of John Ruskin*, edited by E. T. Cook and Alexander Wedderburn, 39 vols., Library Edition, 1903–1912, vol. 8.

Ruskin, John. "Of the Pathetic Fallacy." *Modern Painters III*, Library Edition, vol. 5.

Ruskin, John. *Modern Painters V*. Library Edition, vol. 7.

Ruskin, John. *The Stones of Venice*. Library Edition, vols. 9–11.

Ruskin, John. "The Work of Iron." *Selected Writings*, edited by Dinah Birch, Oxford UP, 2004, pp. 105–35.

Russell, David, *Tact: Aesthetic Liberalism and the Essay Form in Nineteenth-Century Britain*. Princeton UP, 2018.

Seligman, Martin and Mihaly Csikszentmihaly. "Positive Psychology, An Introduction." *American Psychologist*, vol. 55, no. 1, Jan. 2000, pp. 5–14.

Tolstoy, L. N. *Tolstoy Centenary Edition*. Edited by Maude, 21 vols., Tolstoy Society, 1928–37.

Trilling, Lionel. *The Liberal Imagination*. NYRB Press, 2008.

Lowenhaupt Tsing, Anna. *The Mushroom at the End of the World: On the Possibility of Life in Capitalist Ruins*. Princeton UP, 2017.

Williams, Raymond. *Keywords: A Vocabulary of Culture and Society*. Oxford UP, 1976.

PART III
FLOURISHING IN CRISIS
The Poetics of Disaster

5

Literature of Uplift

David James

"Everything else had faded away" for the elderly skater as he moved "with grace and poise around the ice" at 3:30 am (Barsby 75). At this hour, "the city was silent. The city was asleep" (75), and the outdoor rink is his alone. To venture onto the ice at all had from day one required a leap of faith. Learning to skate left him exposed at first, not only to his own "whispering doubts in his head" but also to incredulous onlookers: the teenagers, young mothers, and other rink-side regulars who, "staring at him" struggling through his first lesson, had wondered *"What is he doing here?"* (76). He once imagined them scoffing, "you're past it, old man" (76). But he had persisted, learned the ropes, and eventually this same audience "accepted him" (76). Now, before dawn, he goes a step further, fulfilling for himself that "vision of freedom and peace" he'd once sourced from a "glimpse of people gliding across the frozen water," a fortuitous snapshot of leisure and liberty snatched on a "diverted bus route home" (76). Night-skating like this, we learn, is his release from the drudgery of "the factory floor," along with "tinnitus and traffic"—those soundtracks to everyday routine from which "as he grew older he wanted to escape" (76). What once "remained a secret, a nugget he could retreat to when the noise all got too much," now became a reality as he "zoomed around the rink, faster and faster, unaware of anything apart from the sound of his skates cutting through the silence," uplifted in the absence of working life's "constant roar" (76, 76–77).

At less than three pages, its tautness reciprocated by a style that emits only flickers of ornamentation, Susan E. Barsby's "The Free Skater" revels in its own militant modesty. Yet its miniaturist scale belies its ambitious attempt to connect a rather idiosyncratic, personalized experience to collective structures of recovery. As feelings go, uplift couldn't be more apt for the 2018 volume in which Barsby's vignette appears: *24 Stories of Hope for Survivors of the Grenfell Tower Fire*, edited by the actress, playwright, and theater director Kathy Burke. The collection is described as "an anthology in aid of the

David James, *Literature of Uplift* In: *Literary Studies and Human Flourishing*. Edited by: James F. English and Heather Love, Oxford University Press. © Oxford University Press 2023. DOI: 10.1093/oso/9780197637227.003.0006

PTSD-related needs" of the Grenfell community, needs that are outlined in a foreword on the nature of trauma by Dean Burnett, a Cardiff-based neuroscientist, blogger, and author most recently of *The Happy Brain* (2018). The catastrophic fire on 14 June 2017 in the 24-storey North Kensington tower claimed seventy-two lives, leaving a further seventy-four hospitalized. Attention quickly turned in the aftermath not only to the local borough council's failings in maintaining the block's fire-safety standards but also to the inadequacies of the government's response, provoking Theresa May to concede a week after the disaster that there "was a failure of the state, local and national, to help people when they needed it most" (qtd. Kentish). If the ensuing scandal of systemic neglect unfolded in the context of residents' immediate rehousing needs, then *24 Stories* (published on the anniversary of the Grenfell tragedy) aligns itself with the longer-term psychological impact on those who lost friends and loved ones, and whose dispossessions are mental as much as material. By these lights, the volume undertakes an ameliorative act of collaborative redress: counterpointing with narratives of fugitive hope "a system that clearly didn't care" (Burnett 9).

To be sure, reading purposefully for moments of the kind that Barsby cultivates—where everything fades away, where vulnerable subjects are temporarily elevated above the travails of the day-to-day—might sound irresponsible. To some it might even seem unconscionable, as it surely would to disciples of a certain tradition of unshakably vigilant criticism that shares Herbert Marcuse's belief that in "the glow of great and beautiful words" readers are able to "overcome" life's "factual loneliness." Beguiled by writers who present "the counterimage of what occurs in social reality," such readers are uplifted by "the consolation of a beautiful moment in an interminable chain of misfortune." And because uplifting literature thereby "pacifies rebellious desire," its audience invariably "tolerates the unfreedom of social existence" (102, 121, 118, 121). It's surely not unreasonable to wonder who exactly this credulous reader is: so easily ensnared by books as to greet the world with complaisance, this figure apparently ignores the way literature "redeems the catastrophes of experience," as Leo Bersani once declared, "by the violence of its symbolic reconstructions of experience" (97). Unwittingly or indulgently, readers of this sort seek in their literary encounters a refuge from agitation and the consequences of their inaction, incapable of seeing how ethically bankrupt the uplift of aesthetic engagement remains.

24 Stories is a refreshing rejection of this rather condescending avatar of acquiescence, a rejection also shared by an emerging fictional mode that condones the minor redemptions of everyday life as perfectly acceptable subject-matter for contemporary writing: "Up Lit." A niche coined by publishers, this is less a new genre or wholesale shift in aesthetic temperament than it is a "new book trend," one that reveals as much about fluctuating reader preferences as it might do about changing ambitions among novelists themselves. Even if it would be overstated to call this a "turn," according to *Guardian* commentator Danuta Kean there's nonetheless something both aesthetically urgent and politically timely about the propensities shared by writing "with kindness at its core" (n.p.). As categories go, Up Lit is as loose as any: referring to novels that offer tales of solicitude, it embraces works as nationally and stylistically diverse as Rachel Joyce's *The Unlikely Pilgrimage of Harold Fry* (2012), Matt Haig's *How to Stop Time* (2017), George Saunders's *Lincoln in the Bardo* (2017), Gail Honeyman's *Eleanor Oliphant Is Completely Fine* (2017), and Joanna Cannon's *Three Things about Elsie* (2018). Cannon herself sums up Up Lit's efficacy as a counterweight to cultural dejection and social division, asserting that "if we all chose the words we speak with as much care as we choose the words we write, the world might be a much more bearable place in which to live" ("The Wrong" n.p.). That Cannon previously worked as a NHS psychiatrist has become a linchpin for appraisals, as critics like Hannah Beckerman celebrate the sense in which Cannon's former career "infuses her writing," throughout which "there is an intrinsic understanding of the quiet pain that accompanies loneliness." Accordingly, Beckerman praises *Three Things about Elsie* for the way Cannon "treats her characters with immense care and compassion, inviting the reader not merely to be interested in them but to show them concern and empathy" (n.p.). Modeling respect and attentiveness toward elderly individuals, Cannon's fiction sets high standards for real-world behaviors. And however moderately plotted or formally unostentatious, her writing carries Up Lit's sizable objective, namely, the simulation of micro-acts of concern for vulnerable selves—isolated in chronic ways by increasing infirmity or simply by their routine dislocation from the more socially and domestically fulfilled lives of their peers—acts that affirm, against the prevailing odds, that attentiveness to the everyday needs of others can still flourish in dark times.

But isn't this all very sentimental? Put more generously, wouldn't it be valid to view Up Lit's earnest concern with ameliorating structures of feeling as rebooting that central mission of literary sentimentalism from the eighteenth and nineteenth centuries, undertaking "a form of cultural work," in Jennifer A. Williamson's account, "by relying on emotional appeals to generate sympathy in readers"? This process of solicitation "serves a key rhe-torical function that allows a text to generate compassion for its subjects and subject matter to promote emotional and moral education for the reader." To borrow Williamson's terms, Up Lit "transposes" for readers reassuring "lessons" in compassionate care that parry an era of resurgent nationalism, stark regional-political divides, and state-sanctioned austerity (3). In Britain, systemic inequities continue to ramify materially and psychically for the eld-erly, the disabled, the racially marginalized, and the precariously employed. At the same time, following a fundamentally xenophobic Brexit campaign, one would be forgiven for thinking that cosmopolitan visions of sustain-able multiethnic communities have been split open on the anvil of pervasive and now-emboldened intolerance. In this climate, Up Lit seeks to provide a modicum of ethical-affective tuition: extending the sentimental tradition, it "creat[es] a metaphor" for alternative behaviors through its preoccupation with the affirming redress—however momentary—of ordinary lives, an in-structive metaphor "through which [the reader] views her role in society and her potential for transforming that society" (Williamson 3).

To the extent that such fictions—and, as I will go on to show, memoirs too—diegetically rehearse the tentative "promise of happiness" they emo-tively impart, we should not be surprised that it's "at times of crisis," as Sara Ahmed has shown, that such a "language of happiness acquires an even more powerful hold" (7). In an era marked by Teresa May's curation of deliberately hostile immigration laws, culminating in the 2018 "Windrush scandal"—an instance of systemic racism that in years since has only been made to ap-pear more gratuitous by contemporary Conservatism's increasingly hardline stance on immigration—the literature of uplift ventures to distribute kind-ness at a time when it may appear conspicuously scarce in political discourse and public life.[1] This hope is refracted by seemingly incidental, offhand asides in Cannon's *Three Things about Elsie*. Happenstance self-reflections, as in the following episode, make use of the second-person mode of address to invite mutual recognition from the reader. Florence, one of Cannon's retirement-home residents, has been hoarding cakes, without any memory of having accumulated a cupboard-full, which has now spilled out on to a careworker to whom she offered tea. Embarrassed and disoriented, she finds herself being consoled by the home's "handyman," Simon, who "always

---

[1] Prompted by the resignation of seven key members of the party over its own stance on Brexit and in the wake of its inadequate handling of internal antisemitism in 2019, the then deputy leader of Labour, Tom Watson, called on the party to become "kinder" (see Mason and Elgot).

appears slightly confused" to Florence but who now helps her clear up (177). This gesture of simple aid devastates her: "It's strange, because you can put up with all manner of nonsense in your life, all sorts of sadness, and you manage to keep everything on board and march through it, then someone is kind to you and it's the kindness that makes you cry" (180). Florence's conclusion to this emotional self-analysis could well double as a mission statement for a number of Up Lit novels, concerned as they often are with showing how it is "the tiny act of goodness that opens a door somewhere and lets all the misery escape" (180).

Turning these tiny, often-overlooked acts of goodness into something like a shared vision of compassionate responsibility defines Up Lit's more strenuous objective. To do so, such works rely on the extent to which the transmission of sympathetic involvement, as David Hume originally detected, can seem all but irresistible. Affection's communicability, observes Hume, makes it infectious in the context of our sympathetic engagement with another person's misfortune and uncertain recovery. "The passions are so contagious," he writes, "that they pass with the greatest facility from one person to another, and produce correspondent movement in all human breasts" (605). Up Lit capitalizes on this ease of emotional transfer; choreographing scenes of participatory reading is its core motivation. *Three Things about Elsie* does this in the aforementioned scene, with its sudden transition from first-person narration into a more intimate use of a "you" that bridges age and circumstance. Sketching a recognizable "act" of ordinary "goodness" that could affect us all, Cannon implicitly implicates her reader by suggesting that such everyday episodes of sustaining care rely not on the charismatic bestowal of sympathy in one-off gestures of self-elevating virtue, but upon the rather more selfless, unending labour of assiduously weighing and "choos[ing] the words we speak."

Ameliorative Sentimentalism

With this aspiration, Up Lit is nothing new. In one sense, its reminders of the reader's accountability to vulnerable or disenfranchised subjects would seem to confirm that twenty-first-century writing is actively harnessing the "driving force in sentimental texts" which, as Williamson writes, emanates from "the fear of loss, emotional connection, and the formation of utopian relationships that are grounded in affection and sympathy" (4). What *is* fresh is the conviction shared by these loosely affiliated writers that such a motive for writing needs urgently recuperating today with renewed purpose in response to the contemporaneous social and political backdrop I outlined above. But there are other contexts for this conviction too. For one, is there not also a compositional reaction here to the interminable self-referentiality and metafictional involution of postmodernism's formal gymnastics, which in their more ludic guise made the cultivation of compassion from linear plots and credible characters seem distinctly unfashionable? Speaking affirmatively about sentimentalism at the apex of postmodern theory would no doubt have seemed unfashionable too, and the legacies of its nonacceptance in critical discourse have endured. Among them, is the "superiority complex" that allows critics "to dismiss sentimentality," as Leslie Jamison has pointed out, with a certain degree of "self-righteousness." This dismissal insinuates that the professional reader's "emotional responses are more sophisticated than other people's," while passing over the uncomfortable recognition that "the anti-sentimental stance is still a mode of identity ratification"—one that yields its own healthy supply of intellectual capital (123, 127). If Up Lit represents an ethical corrective and a departure in form, then it also has the potential to parley with the critical advocacy of disaffection or estrangement, in part by exposing the pieties and generalizations that underly repudiations of sentimentalism as a purveyor of "feeling without the price of complication" (Jamison 119).

Up Lit thus represents a part-recovery, part-defense, and part-recalibration of some of sentimentalism's fundamental principles. In a more metacritical sense, it also offers an occasion for us to reassess customary misgivings about literature that holds out the promise of amelioration. If such writing both escalates and vindicates the indispensability of what James Chandler calls "the capacity of sentiment to represent *distributive* feeling" (334), then it's worth taking stock of whether literary studies can examine this phenomenon anew in more accommodating terms. This might certainly entail "asking what we can learn . . . *from* texts," in Leah Price's phrase, precisely in order to unlearn some of our suspicions toward writing that furnishes sentimental edification, thereby restoring "legitimacy" to specific "uses of literature that do support well-being." We might then get a little closer to understanding why contemporary writers are embracing a "sentimental aesthetic" which, in Emma Barker's phrase, "is communicative, its fundamental aim being to dissolve the barriers between the work of art and the observing subject, between fiction and reality" (11).

This sense of critical accommodation isn't easy to defend, of course, given that familiar charges against sentimentalism die hard. The view that "sentimentality" ought typically to be regarded "as a serious defect," in Robert C. Solomon's words, seems pretty pervasive. When dispatched with this indictment, sentimentality's fate is sealed: it becomes allied with emotional "kitsch," the superficial payoff of saccharine writing that "substitutes cheap manipulation of feeling for careful calculation of form or judicious development of character" (5). I could imagine writers like Cannon offering the riposte that sentimental narratives do not inevitably ask the reader to indulge an intrinsically sentimental*izing* view of the world. Converting poignancy into buoyancy, their work by no means dissolves the tough pathos and agonizing injustices that punctuate plots of recuperation; nor does it absolve readers of the ethical demands that come with their vicarious engrossment in the disadvantaged lives of others.

However, Up Lit's renavigation of the legacies of sentimentalism provides only one side of literary up*lift*'s recent story.[2] To discover amelioration in a work that is itself dark, a book ostensibly concerned with irremediable catastrophe rather than exemplary care, can usefully shift our critical parameters. Is uplift even legitimate in writing that encompasses devastating traumas of the kind that would appear only to underscore negativity as criticism's proper focus—thereby confirming D. J. Moores's suspicion that "the concern for well-being manifests" in literary scholarship invariably "as a preoccupation with its absence" (27)? How might an upliftingly upsetting work elicit responses that unsettle the correlation between affecting events and readerly edification, disarticulating the ravages of content from the meliorations of response? By behaving as such, would this text then prove James Pawelski's hunch that "if the subject of inquiry is negative, it does not necessarily follow that the inquiry itself is negative" ("Bringing Together" 210)? Turning to something of an extreme case for these questions, I consider for

---

[2] A word about my own invocation of the term "uplift" is in order. Reading the 2020 *Small Axe* film series, written and directed by Steve McQueen, as a pointed historicization of the structural racism that made the *Windrush* scandal graphic proof of "Black Britain's sense of erasure," Gary Younge praises the way the "films offer hope without descending into schmaltz or uplift propaganda" (10, 9). And for the purposes of this essay, I want to be clear about distinguishing uplift as it may be discerned in the works I place in conversation both from its affective-aesthetic association with cloying rehabilitation or saccharine optimism, as well as from its historical-material association with self-elevation in early twentieth-century African American culture, where uplift's "connotations," as critical race studies scholars such as Kevin Gaines have observed, pointed to "collective social aspiration, advancement and struggle" after emancipation, as "black elites made uplift the basis for a racialized elite identity" based on "improvement through class stratification" (xv).

the remainder of this discussion Rebecca Loncraine's *Skybound*, a posthumous 2018 memoir about her attempt to navigate the emotional aftermath of breast cancer through an impulsive desire to learn how to fly gliders. *Skybound* happens to complement the impetus of Barsby's vignette with which we began, albeit on a far more agonizing scale. Both texts are about taking corporeal gambles as avenues to release, voluntary leaps in the dark that are analogous to the physical execution and repercussions of writing itself: skating inscribes lines of sensory flight while leaving glinting marks on the ice that most early-morning commuters will overlook; gliding motivates Loncraine to rescript in order to comprehend a lacerated self, one that had remained unfathomable as her body recuperated from treatment.

By making this kind of move from fiction to memoir, of course, I'm raising unavoidable questions about stakes of generic difference. The creative context for uplift clearly matters in memoir's autobiographical scene of production in ways that may not obtain for the loosely grouped and remarkably different novels which coalesce under the banner of Up Lit. Moreover, to shift from fiction to memoir is also to shift from works that represent uplift as a shareable antidote for a prevailing cultural mood to the sort of writing that repossesses the experience of uplift as personalized antidote to individual mood. I've had more to say elsewhere about the larger political implications of memoir's affective individualism in this sense.[3] But for present purposes, certain generic promiscuities are worth entertaining, because transitions between fiction and life-writing expand rather than hinder the case for literary uplift's emergence as a twofold reason to unpick normative opinions about sentimentalism and to recontextualize the work it performs in contemporary culture.

Matt Haig is a case in point: an often-cited figure in accounts of the Up Lit trend, Haig has moved fluidly between writing books for children and young adults, alongside literary fiction and works that occupy the fringe between memoir, self-help, and existential counsel. An account of Haig's own acute depression aged 24, *Reasons to Stay Alive* (2015) set out to "lessen that stigma" which clings to depression and "to try and actually convince people that the bottom of the valley never provides the clearest view" (3). Reviewers celebrated the book not only as upliftingly "redemptive" in its confrontations with mental illness, but also as a wellspring of hope that "should be on

---

[3] See James, *Discrepant Solace*, 214–19.

prescription" (Haig, Personal Web).[4] This belief in the written word as a nostrum in its own right constitutes Haig's premise from the outset, where he asserts that "through reading and writing . . . I found a kind of salvation from the dark," while discovering too that "the oldest clichés remain the truest. Time heals" (*Reasons* 3).

And "healing" is the watchword for an online column that now archives ameliorative literature, compiling a directory of palliative poetry and prose that collates numerous genres. "A story needn't lift your heart in order to lift your mood," declares Hephzibah Anderson when outlining the case for medicinal reading ("Bibliotherapy"). Launching her BBC column, "Textual Healing," Anderson enthuses that the books she will recommend for various ills "are sure to speak to your predicament, offering insights and encouragement as well as a little escapism" ("Bibliotherapy"). "Think of it less as self-help than 'shelf help,' " she advises, inviting us to celebrate the fact, allegedly corroborated by psychologists, that "stories can console and trigger self-reflection" while also offering more intersubjective benefits by "enhance[ing] people's ability to register and read others' emotions" ("Bibliotherapy"). The "predicaments" for which Anderson assigns reading lists include anorexia, homesickness, lovesickness, wanderlust, loneliness, and grief. Recommendations for each "condition" typically narrate the symptoms head-on: suggestions for grieving readers, for example, include such iconic— because memorably unflinching—bereavement memoirs as C. S. Lewis's *A Grief Observed* (1961) and Joan Didion's *The Year of Magical Thinking* (2005). Without doubt, these are determinedly *un*sentimental works, their chiseled style dispassionately unpicking the imposed customs and (in Lewis's case) the theological compensations that may accompany as well as impede the business of fathoming grief. But however forthright they are, in joining the therapeutic archive of "Textual Healing" these books service a recognizably sentimental precept: that "sometimes a book's balm works by reminding us how much worse things could be" ("Unhappy Families?").

Elsewhere, Anderson's selected solace-providers are distinctly eclectic, as Anne Tyler and Rebecca Solnit rub shoulders with Ruth Ozeki. In many ways, their ostensible contrasts are used to accentuate the epistemic status they share for "Textual Healing" as an initiative. Irrespective of when or where they have been written, Anderson encourages us to treat novels, poems, and

---

[4] http://www.matthaig.com/books/reasons-to-stay-alive-2/: Haig is excerpting a review by BBC broadcaster Rev. Richard Coles.

memoirs as repositories of emotional wisdom, replete with apposite quotes that both encapsulate the malady in question and thereby soothe the reader who finds their distress mirrored thematically in what they read. This basic sentimental connection-through-recognition may seem thoroughly dubious to the professional critic, but it clearly remains central to the curative promise borne by any "biblio-therapeutic prescription" ("Unhappy Families?")

By appealing to this cross-section of genres, uplift remains a seemingly un-exceptional yet peculiar affect that overlaps quite idiosyncratic works of fic-tional and nonfictional prose. Generative of diverse strategies, uplift invites a comparative sampling of contrasting scenarios of psychological vulnerability and physical precarity where affiliated structures of feeling become legible—a sampling this essay has already initiated. Furthermore, uplift rarely exists, in my reading, merely to be admired, affirmed, condoned; instead, it's often captured in prose that sizes up its own ameliorative capacities, probing the promise of language to overcome ineffability in episodes of emotionally strenuous self-articulation. In this respect, the coming pages will supplement that corpus of therapeutically redescriptive texts that penetrate what Beth Blum calls "a nagging problem or theme," unraveling as they do equally pene-trating modes of self-inquiry. If the "candor with which they lay bare the effort and struggle of working on the self" is central to the way writers deploy ther-apeutic redescription, then this candor, perhaps unsurprisingly, is nowhere more poignantly felt than in memoirs of illness. For writers in this genre, however, the venture of "using redescription," in Blum's phrase, "to eman-cipate themselves from the power of imposed language and impressions" becomes also a means of challenging the perceived perimeters of affective description itself. Which is why I now turn, as promised, to *Skybound* as a work that presses back against the sacralization of putatively inexpressible experiences. This is a book about description as therapy and sentimental self-examination, yes; but it is also an exhibition of description's dissidence, its refusal to enshrine what at first appears inexpressible. Dissident texts aren't usually seen as salubrious, in part because we might assume that their aes-thetic militancy is also a measure of their refutation of sentimentalism as a beneficial aspect of literary experience. But why should that be so? Suppose we imagine instead a different fate for sentimentally charged amelioration as it is both enacted *within* the work and solicited *by* that work when the reader encounters its emotive contours. Suppose that this twinned creative and critical impact of ameliorative expression reconstitutes the possibilities of sentimentalism over the course of challenging time-honored assumptions about it. And in that case, suppose the uplift came with witnessing those preconceptions being vandalized by the very experience literary criticism has conventionally taught itself to distrust.

Language in Flight

Subtitled *A Journey in Flight*, Loncraine's *Skybound* it is also a voyage through self-grieving, a voyage from illness to fraught recovery that sets the coordinates for the book's twinned experiential and expressional exhibitions of uplift. Even as it becomes dramatically central to the events Loncraine recounts, uplift remains ontologically ephemeral. Yet for all its transience, uplift is arrestingly materialized in the book's language: when viewed in this sense as an affordance of style, uplift acquires a kind of legibility for her reader, becoming cumulatively palpable across the memoir even as she testifies to its evanescence. In its stylistic guise, uplift reminds us, as Hannah Freed-Thall has persuasively done, that "affect" needn't refer to "a single, structure-defying force or intensity" that evades representation, but may be analytically isolated in the sinews of literary form and therefore "must be *read* in all its specificities" (427n.12). With this mandate, I try to gauge the stakes of homing in on the formal particularities of uplift's emotional positivity in a memoir born from agonizing recovery. To do so, I feel, is to take one step toward refusing not only the sanctimony of maintaining that amelioration has no place in a work of trauma, but also the self-gratification of dismissing as merely sentimental writers who seek to document and impart affective counterpoints to pain. For if anything, *Skybound* suggests that more accommodating accounts of sentimentalism's contemporary conditions of critical and creative possibility are overdue.

Loncraine was no stranger to the promise of writing as a vehicle for rehabilitation. As an educator, she ran sessions for the charity Arts Alive Wales on "Creative Writing and Well-being." As her mother, Trisha, observes in a moving postscript, where Rebecca "was working with schoolgirls who struggled with dyslexia, funding has been found to continue the creative writing workshops" (300). A teacher-practitioner attuned to literature's role in human flourishing, Loncraine had to become instead the student of her own emotions, when debilitating treatment threatened the practice she loved. "I thought it had died during my illness"; but glider training revived the compulsion: "language cracks open again" and, "when I land, I'm itching to write while I can still feel the lift—flying and writing have become entwined" (91). Gliding becomes "a kind of writing into the sky, a surfacing of heart and head, a learning again" (92). It's "as though the sky has moved through [her] on to the page," where it motivates an "exhilarating" record of "sensations, physical and psychological," across notebooks that subsequently became "the origins of this book" (91)—a book that simultaneously memorializes the unconventional path to reinvigoration it plots. For the cancer from which Loncraine was seeking aerial consolation would return all too soon (she died, aged forty-two, in September 2016), an outcome whose pathos, as we'll see, returns acutely to the reader on the closing page.

Skybound thus compels us to read with a searing double vision. However immersive Loncraine's chronicle of "both learning to fly and beginning to write again" becomes, we concurrently sense that this is a proleptic elegy, one that mourns a writer for whom the very construction of the sentences we read facilitated self-*re*construction, supplying her with a compositional analogue of "finding some way to navigate the chaos" (92). As a result, the book's engagement with uplift as leitmotif and as precarious experience is offset, inevitably, against our encounter with it as a posthumous work; partially finished when Loncraine died, the typescript was brought to fruition by Trisha in collaboration with Rebecca's Picador editor, Sophie Jonathan. But as Trisha herself insists, that knowledge "doesn't change what *Skybound* is: a story about coming close to death, and learning to live and be joyful again" (301).[5] And in what follows, I construe this as an invitation to do justice to the arguments this memoir achieves as separable from the devastating loss to which we know it inexorably leads, arguments about the expression of otherwise incommunicable effects of illness.

By bringing into stunning legibility feelings that seem beyond words, *Skybound* confronts the critical sanctification of trauma's ineffability. Loncraine's language, as we'll see, disobeys the consecration of damage as that which literature's "symbolic reconstructions of experience" (to recall Bersani) cannot adequately evoke, let alone compensate or overcome. As such, her memoir offers a striking challenge to assertions about the alleged limits of affective representation, which became virtually axiomatic as

---

[5] Reviewing *Skybound* in the *Guardian*—notably, under the topic of "Health"—Arifa Akbar drew attention to the pathos of these twinned effects. Akbar suggested that "Loncraine seems simultaneously to be hoping for healing and to confront mortality," sustaining a "blend of light and shadow" across a "euphoric and courageous book about how to live joyously, and how to meet death" (15).

trauma studies reached its theoretical zenith through the 1980s and 1990s.[6] Pushing back against this paradigm—which posits trauma as inherently inexpressible and thus forever vulnerable to betrayal by literary efforts to evoke its psychological complexities—*Skybound* reveals "how narratives of illness," in Ann Jurecic's account, "invite reflection about the purpose and future of literature, the arts, and literary criticism." As Jurecic points out, the "academy has long rewarded readings that dismantle literature's illusions but, with regard to literary and amateur illness memoirs, it is also evident that critics need other options, interpretive approaches that enable them to assemble meaning in the face of life's fragility" (4). By observing ourselves as we observe the wrenching, brutally consoling journey on which Loncraine leads her readers as she flies into the turbulence of her own vulnerability, we have an opportunity to see what those other approaches might look like. For what critical adjustments might we need to make in order to apprehend without mistrust a book that is unequivocally devastating yet so adamantly life-affirming?

Loncraine's first experience of unpowered soaring left her "burning with a sense of uplift," a feeling that features in spectacular (and often unnerving) episodes of flight throughout the book but that also finds its stylistic correlative in *Skybound*'s lyrical promotion of the possibility of describing personal devastation that otherwise seems inexpressible (10). If the memoir movingly evokes her intimation that "flying might become part of my recovery, a way for me to escape the grief of my illness and treatment" (21–22), it also prompts us to theorize the way life-writing formally debates—precisely *through* its strenuous efforts to satisfy—the need "to find a language, a context, through which . . . suffering can speak" (22). By pursuing this bifocal grammar of suffering and recovery, Loncraine enters into conversation with

---

[6] Countering the premise that trauma is intrinsically resistant to depiction, Roger Luckhurst has suggested that contemporary literary and filmic "narratives have developed a repertoire of plots that explore both traumatic disruption and the possibility of release into narrative," even though for many critics this seems "at odds with some of the most influential cultural theories of trauma," which posit the term "*in opposition* to narrative." Consequently, there's now "a flat contradiction," notes Luckhurst, "between cultural theory that regards narrative as betraying traumatic singularity and various therapeutic discourses that see narrative as a means of productive transformation or even final resolution of trauma" (80, 82). Stef Craps follows Luckhurst's cue about the possibilities that trauma may open up in narrative, but warns against privileging modernist experimentalism as the only form of writing adequately equipped to evoke trauma's complexities. Just as Craps contends, then, that "trauma theory needs to become more inclusive and culturally sensitive by acknowledging the sufferings of non-Western and minority groups more fully," so he recommends that "trauma theory should take account of the specific social and historical contexts in which trauma narratives are produced and received, and be open and attentive to diverse strategies of representation and resistance which these contexts invite or necessitate" (38, 43).

a longer genealogy of illness narrative (pathography), one crucial episode of which points to Virginia Woolf's remarkable meditation from 1930, *On Being Ill*. Woolf begins by alerting us to scarcity of the very subgenre she's trying to occupy: "literature does its best to maintain that its concern is with the mind" and, as a result, "of all this daily drama of the body there is no record" (4, 5). More to the point, she observes, not only has the subject of ill-being historically taken second place to "the doings of the mind," but what tends "to hinder the description of illness in literature" further "is the poverty of the language" (5, 6). And the impoverishment extends across literary history. Maladies and ecstasies of the heart have landmark plays and poems at their disposal, so that the "merest schoolgirl, when she falls in love, has Shakespeare or Keats to speak her mind for her"; by contrast, with bodily incapacities we face a paucity of such resources: "let a sufferer try to describe a pain in his head to a doctor," writes Woolf, "and language at once runs dry" (6–7).

Loncraine comes close to this drought early in *Skybound* but finds in such linguistic depletion a reason to push the envelope of self-expression. In one sense, her venture would seem to confirm Woolf's conclusion that, rhetorically, "illness is the great confessional" (11); true enough, Loncraine confesses that if gliding provides "a place to feel uplifted" then it is also a bald form of escape. This confession, however, also applies to the way traumatic recovery serves as a creative incentive, when Loncraine begins to hone an uplifting "language in flying" that lends articulacy to the aftermath of what seem like unutterably painful experiences of rehabilitation (22). Utilizing that language, *Skybound* is no soother; it conducts instead a pathographically exacting inquest, delving into the reasons why Loncraine "continued to look upward to the sky and birds for solace" while making use of "free flying to build my resilience, to cope with what I face back on earth" (25, 249). With this prospect, she seems to concur with Woolf's injunction that "it is not only a new language that we need, more primitive, more sensual, more obscene, but a new hierarchy of the passions" (7).

One consequence of *Skybound*'s contribution to this adjusted hierarchy is that we're compelled to reassess usual misgivings about escapism as fantasy-fueled, too effortlessly voluntaristic, and above all self-deludingly sentimental. Loncraine is the first to admit that friends and family see her sudden obsession for flying as a mere "distraction from the pain of my illness and separation" (82). Yet the "truth," she insists, "is otherwise": the whole effort of "learning to fly" is a means of "getting more intimate with this pain" (82).

Although "soaring at altitude might look from the ground like a form of escape," for her it has become a "way of piercing the surface of my pain and going underneath it, into it" (82). Uplift begets self-excavation as much as escapism, because "feelings of flying" lead her "inward" with a force she has been "resisting" (82, 83); unyoked from mere assuagement, it aligns with the unusually consoling sublimity of being "overpowered, overwhelmed" by the "rapture of flying", as Loncraine is "carried aloft in its claws" (286). Addressing uplift as a close cousin of "ripping" awe, her sentimental journey skyward is compared to the feeling of being "carried away" whenever she spots raptors aloft—the experience of "upwelling is a splitting open, a tearing" rather than an ecstatic salve (286). Loncraine might have agreed with Woolf that if the "gigantic cinema" of the sky is "divinely beautiful," then "it is also divinely heartless"; its perpetually altering spectacles have "nothing to do with human pleasure or human profit." Rather, "it is in their indifference"—just like the inscrutable, ferocious birds of prey Loncraine so admired—"that they are comforting," insists Woolf (14, 15).

Uplift itself resists human profiteering, too: it cannot be planned, as Loncraine discovers; and it defies convenient instrumentalism. After leaving Wales for the Southern Alps in New Zealand to carry on her training through the winter months, she realizes that uplift isn't easily transportable either. Aboard her first flight in "one of the world's most extreme gliding landscapes," she finds herself "looking inward and finding a strange blankness" (157). Taken "aback" by "tears of frustration," she is "unmoved" and this "lack of fear seems to have closed off other feelings as well. There's no euphoria" (157). The clipped, denotative syntax reproduces this state of unemotionality in its dictional and rhythmic economy. A victim not of uplift's depletion so much as its outright deletion, Loncraine's "numb self, the self that has been shocked into silence by the horror of the last few years," is held in abeyance, "shocked into silence" (157). Only when she has full command of the glider's controls does the uplift return, leaving her "desperately grateful to feel again that buzz of ascending on the wind" (158).

After this disarming arrival, Loncraine's time in New Zealand turns out to be transformative, not just for her aeronautical apprenticeship but also for her meticulous descriptions, which specialize in convergences of ferocious topography and subjective turmoil, aerial astonishment and uncompromising introspection. To Loncraine, the experience alone of "flying on the energetic lift of the mountains" "re-enchants them," and her receptiveness to an enigmatic landscape that seems to exceed factual illustration leads her to embrace a position of negative capability. Consequently, "the dead materialism" of Loncraine's "secular imagination is lifted momentarily" in the presence of unprocessed awe (208–9). The lift, of course, also comes from the writing, with its synthesis of first-person topographical depiction and incisive self-analysis—that dead materialist turns out to be a lyrical impressionist "moving in and out of an almost trance-like state, quietly absorbing the extraordinary land and sky" (209). Climbing into this cloudscape enables striking analogies: "Learning to fly is like asking the universe a question: asking it to let me go into the world to live and soar with joy and the possibility of death. It is to ask to be graced with grace, filled with emptiness, to arrive and never arrive." In the end, she realizes that "greater intimacy with nature" is what she's "been searching for" (209), a sentimental quest that alights on the uplifting hypothesis that the "natural world can hold any hurt inside it, recognize it, gently turn it over in the palm of its hand like a precious stone" (209).

Loncraine's "experience of intimacy with the big mountains" of these Southern Alps modulates topographic depiction into anthropomorphizing dramas of commotion. No longer a matter of meteorology and aerial physics, "sky and mountains" are recast "in great conversation, embroiled in a dynamic, explosive interaction." This language of turbulent interaction creates its own variety of discursive replenishment, even though the terrain she delineates is inhospitable, barren—an unlikely habitat for rejuvenation. Metaphoric fertility takes over the book's existing facility for naturalistic perception, as though Loncraine's style conspires with animated "rocks, crags, and glaciers" whose "volatile, passionately unstable relationship with the air around them . . . creates the lift" (206, 207). Figured as "some giant unknowable body" (207), the Alps offer a treacherous site for continuing Loncraine's airborne physical re-education, a realm of maximal risk for "learning to really feel the new sensations of lift and sink," for "undoing some of the work of illness" by "re-possessing" her body "and learning to trust its signals" (79).

Such is the ambition of arresting works of life-writing from recent years, in which the relation between subjectivity and physiology becomes distressingly opaque, blunting the tools of self-description. As Christina Crosby attests in her queer memoir of experiencing sudden disability after a horrific cycling accident just after her fiftieth birthday, "figurative language helps us approach what's otherwise unapproachable or incommunicable" (12). "Writing offers," she insists, "not a way out, but a way into the impossible dilemmas of not-knowing" (200). Crosby's 2016 A Body, Undone conveys a private and professional life redefined in an instant by chronic neurological pain and irreparable physical damage. In describing this combination of impairments, she never denies that the "intricacies of bodymind interactions defy certainties and confound representation"; but as an artifact of affective expressivity fashioned from self-scrutiny the book also affirms that writing is "the most likely medium for addressing the imponderable" (21, 8). Attesting to what narrative *can* achieve in the face of seemingly ineffable pain, Crosby's memoir, like Loncraine's, gifts literary culture a testimony to aesthetic potential driven by the solace of being understood. "I see no other way to go on," insists Crosby, than by writing about affective extremities we assume are indescribable—"how else will I understand? How will you?" (21).

Loncraine too, it seems, saw no other way to go on. After being "blown open and off balance" by flying, for her the "only thing to do is to pursue this unravelling" (78), an inquiry that peaks in her movingly evanescent piece, "The Hurt Hare's Form." Sent to Bo Nilsson, her beloved gliding instructor, the fragment of text partially quoted here was found by her mother in a file called "Misc Writings." We will never know whether she intended to conclude the memoir with this inventory of personal flourishing amid the cross-currents of illness. But the fragment remains all the more affecting for being, precisely, just that: a fragment of self-knowledge, no less piercing for remaining unfinished, no less incisive for being so ephemeral. At once self-scrutinizing yet lyrically self-affirming, it stills the narrative—swelling like the shattering poise of one of Woolf's moments of being—to adjourn the tumult of personal excavation. Within this cocooning interval, Loncraine merges the fierce rapture that has often punctuated *Skybound* with a more serene kind of uplift that has been rare up to this point:

> We are lying, quiet, in a hare's form of flattened long grass and tall buttercups, which bend and bow around us in the breeze, waving to themselves. He sleeps, this man whose disappointment in himself stops him from realizing that he is one beautiful piece of this big new sky. . . . Perfect cumulus clouds bump and weave above us, towing along the wind, the ground, this very day with them. . . . I long to be up in the sky, but miss it less when he is with me, this man with the Scandinavian eyes, because he is of that element, from the north, where the sky is visible so much of the light side of the year, and where, when it's taken away during the dark months, people go mad with cold grief. No matter how broken and scarred I am, when I look up into a blue sky, which I now know I can navigate and

keep inside me, I feel repaired, revealed, consoled at least, enlivened, as
I jump off the cliff of my own pain again and again, to soar on its gale-force
currents and wave back at myself in my broken-hearted healing. We are all
broken; we are alright. (303)

In this beautiful sculpture of self-apprehension, Loncraine has no truck
with heroic resilience. Granted, her account of the trauma she's now able to
"navigate" would serve for some readers, perhaps, as an unambiguously sentimental testament to endurance; but the picture it leaves us of qualified survival is hardly triumphalist. Instead, Loncraine sketches a condition of fragile
continuity that allows her to access the uplift of ecstatic sky-reading, an uplift
that's reciprocated, as so often in this book, by syntax itself. In the penulti-
mate sentence, an assertive, paratactic catalog of self-revelation as gradual
reinvigoration enacts the momentum flying afforded when she faced "pain
again and again." This phrasal insistence is answered and elevated further
by an assonantal sequence of feelings (*repaired, revealed, consoled*), assem-
bling a kind of acoustic alliance against all that has hitherto seemed incommunicable about her suffering. Which is not say that "figurative language"
(to recall Crosby's terms) offers simply a tonic, a verbal equivalent to self-
redemption, whereby eloquence aestheticizes so as to anesthetize the des-
olation Loncraine recalls. *Skybound* resists that kind of deduction because
its style participates in rather than palliates the emotional and physical brokenness she probes throughout the book. Likewise, here, with its miniature
anatomy of "broken-hearted healing," this closing fragment instantiates a
type of "rupture," in Adorno's phrase, "which the work does not bridge but
rather, lovingly and hopefully, makes the agent of its form" (108). No less
"enlivened" throughout what is an inescapably plaintive postscript, style
supplies its own "gale-force" uplift to match the psychological soaring that
Loncraine arduously attained. A scene of expressive elevation and hard-won
consolation, it's all the more appallingly poignant because it could not have
anticipated the exquisite eulogy it now performs.

Critical Uplift

Arguably what a work like Loncraine's solicits in the end is nothing
staggering: simply a more accommodating disposition, one that permits
rather than proscribes the hope that literature might afford radiant if

necessarily wounded articulation—in a language, echoing Woolf, that's both "sensuous" and possibly "obscene"—to devastations that would otherwise appear to defy expression. It's a hope that Loncraine herself appears to foster in that final, crystalline fragment of reflexive sentimentalism I considered above, where the intensification of the reader's sympathy no longer feels like a supreme goal. The fragment isn't for us. It doesn't need us. Indeed, as Anna Metcalfe has intriguingly suggested, "'hope' is the opposite of 'sympathy.' Where sympathy seeks to take an abstract emotion and render it into a comprehensible category so as to allow us access to another person's experience, hope sustains the distance but keeps listening anyway" (18). Like hope, the kind of uplift that illness memoirs may crave, conjure, and contest with equal measure arises in this way from "an ongoing tussle between the recognisable category and the authentic abstraction" (18). Such is uplift's critical work in allowing us to disentangle the operations and provocations of contemporary sentimentalism: even as *Skybound* is able to "map some common ground for us"—offering readers unquestionably involving descriptions of physical and mental precarity that attest to our shared vulnerability—at the same time, the book checks our desire for easy identification. It thereby enables "us to maintain a certain distance" from the very idea of hope "so as to be able to place our creativity, individuality and subjectivity against it" (18).

Such talk of distance wouldn't sit well, of course, with accounts of literature's salubriousness that posit empathy as a source of emotional literacy and intercultural edification. But perhaps that same distance—whereby the objectifiable import of uplift appears most perceptible precisely when the text no longer presupposes our subjectively rewarding sense of identification—has something in common with the practice of eudaimonia itself. "Neither a fleeting feeling nor an ephemeral emotion," as Darrin McMahon reminds us, "*eudaimonia* was the product of discipline, dedication, and craft" (5). Disciplined training, a dedication to navigating formidable risk, and an unswaying devotion to aeronautical craft—such are the catalysts for Loncraine's confrontation with the despair of disease, out of which a vocabulary of reckoning flourishes that is as salutary as it is self-investigative. Clearly, uplift isn't always acceptable for the harrowed or unconsoled, for whom remedial stories of emotional bravery might be all the more questionable for being so courageous. What I've tried to show, nonetheless, is that the case of contemporary pathography compels us to reassess customary misgivings about books that are uplifting because they articulate the unspeakable; to unpick habitually pejorative responses to the ameliorative efficacy of sentimental strategies; to take a second look, as we do so, at affirmative structures of feeling that critique has traditionally earmarked as unsound; and ultimately to road-test other critical registers for engaging with narratives that excel at the intersection of well-being and ill-being, elevation and desperation, whose emotive forms enact that simultaneous need for and hesitation over expressing what seems inarticulable.

Where uplift is concerned, of course, its representation only really becomes credible when it imparts a foretaste of uplift's own intrinsic perishability. All buoyancy presages its eventual subsidence. Yet the writers who bookend this essay seem to be entertaining qualified relief, conjectural hope, and fugitive solace without solely mourning the provisionality of the ameliorative moments they illuminate. Consider Barsby's skater again. He acquaints us with a binocular vision of uplift shadowed by its own imminent recession, a vision that survives the despondency that (we might assume) trails it: "whirling, floating across the ice," he prolongs this episode to "an hour," knowing the exhilaration of "cutting through the silence" will pass (77). Before he leaves, he "repair[s] the hole he'd made" in the perimeter fence (77). Not simply covering his tracks, this improvised suture is a gesture of respect for the rink as a congregational zone for disparate inner-city constituencies, a communally diverse and unpredictable space that had "accepted him," had allowed him to flourish (76). A parable, perhaps, of reparative criticism? That's one inviting upshot of Barsby's story, certainly: if we assume that literary studies requires—like that fence—some mending if it is to develop sufficiently permissive methods for reading scenarios of thriving in addition to its usually afflictive fare. And if we assume that "part of the purchase of reparative reading," in Rebekah Sheldon's summary, may be "the license it gives readers to ignore or intentionally transform representations that might otherwise feel inimical to one's wellbeing" (174).

However, the metacritical lessons of Barsby's micro-sketch of felicity are less conclusive than that, as its closing sentences imply. "The skating marks on the ice glistened in the morning sun. The city woke and its people carried on with their daily routine" (77): two deceptively simple, declarative observations present two different modes of attention; the definite articles with which they both begin establish a register of impartiality that declines to offer any steer on what the takeaway of this perceptual contrast might be. The point of their juxtaposition, though, becomes sharper if we offset the rink's lingering spell, etched into those luminous marks, against an oblivious metropolis whose workers fulfill a habitual drill. If we're being presented here with an allegory of criticism's own forking paths, then portents of their fu-ture compatibilities remain. Responsible analysis, one might suppose, ought to be detached from the everyday, unseduced by writing that makes gritty places glisten, so as to decode the forces that coerce people to carry on in regimes that produce only an illusion of autonomy and thus inhibit their flourishing. From this perspective, appreciating the glinting remnants of one person's nocturnal excursion couldn't be less urgent. And yet, the very form of these equally weighted sentences (virtually the same length, refusing to endorse one vision over the other) potentially gives us pause before setting wonder again in opposition to demystification, before casting the beauty of a moment as the antithesis of critical engagement, before assuming we should always be looking at the city rather than the remains of a skating-spree, for fear that it would be irresponsibly sentimental for a critic to be doing any-thing else.

Despite their very different generic, emotive, and compositional purposes, Barsby and Loncraine share a concern with what we might call an aesthetic ecology of melioration, describing episodes of recess that refuse to slot into the parameters of what criticism is obliged to find useful when operating within the ideological remits of eagle-eyed inquisition. However, if they re-mind us of the "purchase" of reparative forms of reading works that in turn do much to repair the reputation of sentimentalism—both as a quality of af-fective engagement and as an affordance of affecting expression—then they never allow us to "ignore" what's "inimical" to flourishing; rather, they bring it into close-up, compelling us to reflect on our own sentimental proximity to what's emotionally and physically pernicious. Likewise, if these writers combat divertissement as they limn the lift reparative moments afford, they don't simply prescribe more virtuous ways of responding to scenarios that might conventionally be dismissed as too plangent, heart-rending, coer-cively poignant—in a word, sentimentalist. Instead, they waylay and incon-venience us. Tendering alternative, sometimes patently irreconcilable forms of vigilance and sorrow, hesitation and immersion, they model these states diegetically for a reader whose appetite for sure-fire methodological direct-ives is left unstated. Like the structurally twinned sentences that close "The Free Skater," the asseverations with which *Skybound* ends ("We are all broken; we are alright") replicate through collocation a version of those antinomies that in literary studies we're well-trained to identify, antinomies more often associated with literature's conflicts and symptomatic compromises than with its tangible aid. These texts hardly seek to remedy such culminating bifurcations of damage and well-being. Just as the uplifting instants they seize are invariably fringed with an inkling of impending cessation, these stories of (self-)elevation obstruct closure with the branching consequences of their final, syntactically adjacent declarations, stated so succinctly without gloss.

By retooling rather than abjuring sentimentalism such works seek to claim our affection with an intensity that for some might undoubtedly provoke distrust, and a wariness toward overinvolvement can quickly renew one's appetite for the solemn pleasures of prosecutorial reading. But in staking that claim, Barsby and Loncraine employ a sentimental aesthetic for which familiar gratifications of sympathy are no longer the principal quarry, as we've seen, while at the same time reminding us that it's equally gratifying to eschew uplift and find intellectual comfort in preserving literary studies as a heartland of the unconsoled. In this memo lies one last, rather paradoxical significance. Criticism, at its sternest, seems nowhere more sentimental than in its passion for avidly interrogating the (allegedly) sentimentalizing notion that literature might transmit alternative vocabularies of feeling for us to think and live by—that our "various negotiations with form" can also "represent our various capacities for hope, for inclusion, for participation, for possibility" (Metcalfe 18–19). For this reason, because we are so used to reading for broken worlds, it can be instructively uncomfortable to read for those that could be alright. Literatures of uplift lead us to the epicenter of such unease, and it's productively disconcerting to keep that critical prospect in sight.

Works Cited

Adorno, Theodor W. "Presuppositions." *Notes to Literature*, vol. 2, translated by Shierry Weber Nicholson, edited by Rolf Tiedemann, Columbia UP, 1992, pp. 95–108.

Ahmed, Sara. *The Promise of Happiness*. Duke UP, 2010.

Akbar, Arifa. Review of *Skybound*, by Rebecca Loncraine. *Guardian, Review*. 26 May 2018, p. 15.

Anderson, Hephzibah. "Bibliotherapy: Can You Read Yourself Happy?" BBC Culture: "Textual Healing," 6 Jan. 2015, http://www.bbc.com/culture/story/20150106-can-you-read-yourself-happy.

Anderson, Hephzibah. "Unhappy Families? A Novel Cure." BBC Culture: "Textual Healing," 11 May 2015, http://www.bbc.com/culture/story/20150511-unhappy-famil ies-a-novel-cure.

Barker, Emma. *Greuze and the Painting of Sentiment*. Cambridge UP, 2005.

Barsby, Susan E. "The Free Skater." *24 Stories of Hope for Survivors of the Grenfell Tower Fire*, edited by Kathy Burke, Unbound, 2018, pp. 75–77.

Beckerman, Hannah. Review of *Three Things about Elsie*, by Joanna Cannon. *Observer*, 14 Jan. 2018, https://www.theguardian.com/books/2018/jan/14/three-things-about-elsie-review-joanna-cannon.

Bersani, Leo. *The Culture of Redemption*. Harvard UP, 1990.

Burnett, Dean. "Foreword," *24 Stories of Hope for Survivors of the Grenfell Tower Fire*.

Cannon, Joanna. *Three Things about Elsie*. Borough, 2018.

Cannon, Joanna. "The Wrong Kind of Kindness." Blog, 3 Aug. 2017, https://joannacannon.com/2017/08/03/the-wrong-kind-of-kindness/. (accessed Jan. 2020; site inactive July 2022).

Chandler, James. *An Archaeology of Sympathy: The Sentimental Mode in Literature and Cinema*. U of Chicago P, 2013.

Craps, Stef. *Postcolonial Witnessing: Trauma Out of Bounds*. Palgrave Macmillan, 2013.

Crosby, Christina. *A Body, Undone: Living On after Great Pain*. New York UP, 2016.

Flood, Alison. "'Up-Lit' Gives Hope to Publishers at Frankfurt Book Fair." *Guardian*, 12 Oct. 2018, https://www.theguardian.com/books/2018/oct/12/up-lit-gives-hope-to-publishers-at-frankfurt-book-fair.

Freed-Thall, Hannah. "Heartsick: The Language of French Disgust." *Modern Language Quarterly*, vol. 79, no. 4, 2018, pp. 421–44.

Gaines, Kevin, *Uplifting the Race: Black Leadership, Politics, and Culture in the Twentieth Century*. U of North Carolina P, 1996.

Haig, Matt. Personal Website, http://www.matthaig.com/books/reasons-to-stay-alive-2/.

Haig, Matt. *Reasons to Stay Alive*. Canongate, 2015.

Hume, David. *A Treatise of Human Nature*. 1739–40. Oxford UP, 1976.

James, David. *Discrepant Solace: Contemporary Literature and the Work of Consolation*. Oxford UP, 2019.

Jamison, Leslie. "In Defense of Saccharin(e)." *The Empathy Exams*, Granta, 2015, pp. 111–31.

Jurecic, Ann. *Illness as Narrative*. U of Pittsburgh P, 2014.

Kean, Danuta. "Up Lit: The New Book Trend with Kindness at Its Core." *Guardian*, 2 Aug. 2017, https://www.theguardian.com/books/booksblog/2017/aug/02/up-lit-the-new-book-trend-with-kindness-at-its-core.

Kentish, Benjamin. "The Grenfell Tower Fire." *Independent*, 21 June 2017, https://www.independent.co.uk/news/uk/home-news/grenfell-tower-fire-theresa-may-apology-response-government-failure-state-latest-news-a7801246.html.

Loncraine, Rebecca. *Skybound: A Journey in Flight*. Picador, 2018.

Luckhurst, Roger. *The Trauma Question*. Routledge, 2008.

Marcuse, Herbert. *Negations: Essays in Critical Theory*. Translated by Jeremy Shapiro. Allen Lane, 1968.

Mason, Rowena and Jessica Elgot. "Labour: Watson Tells Corbyn He Must Change Direction to Stop Party Splitting." *Guardian*, 19 Feb. 2019, https://www.theguardian.com/politics/2019/feb/18/chuka-umunna-and-other-mps-set-to-quit-labour-party.

McMahon, D. M. "From the Paleolithic to the Present: Three Revolutions in the Global History of Happiness." *Handbook of Subjective WellBeing*, edited by E. Diener, S. Oishi, and L. Tay. DEF Publishers, 2018, pp. 1–10.

Metcalfe, Anna. *A Hope on the Wall*. Seam Editions, 2017.

Pawelski, James O. "Bringing Together the Humanities and the Science of Well-Being to Advance Human Flourishing." *Well-Being and Higher Education: A Strategy for Change and the Realization of Education's Greater Purposes*, edited by D. W. Harward, Bringing Theory to Practice, 2016, pp. 207–16.

Pawelski, James O., and D. J. Moores. "Introduction: What Is the Eudaimonic Turn? *and* The Eudaimonic Turn in Literary Studies." *The Eudaimonic Turn: Well-Being in Literary Studies*, edited by Pawelski and Moores, Fairleigh Dickinson UP, 2013, pp. 1–64.

Sheldon, Rebekah. "Reading for Transgression: Queering Genres." *After Queer Studies: Literature, Theory and Sexuality in the 21st Century*, edited by Tyler Bradway and E. L. McCallum, Cambridge UP, 2019, pp. 171–187.

Solomon, Robert C. *In Defense of Sentimentality*. Oxford UP, 2004.

Williamson, Jennifer A. *Twentieth-Century Sentimentalism: Narrative Appropriation in American Literature*. Rutgers UP, 2014.

Woolf, Virginia. *On Being Ill*. 1930. Paris Press, 2002.

Younge, Gary. "'What the Hell Can I Call Myself Except British.'" *New York Review of Books*, vol. 68, no. 7, 29 Apr. 2021, pp. 8–10.

6

Black Ecological Optimism and the Problem of Human Flourishing

Sonya Posmentier

In 1987, surviving cancer and many treatments for it, the self-described Black lesbian feminist poet Audre Lorde moved to St. Croix. She wanted a different kind of life and a warmer climate, and, as the daughter of immigrants from Barbados and Grenada, decided to return to the Caribbean. In 1989 Hurricane Hugo devastated the island territory. In interviews, letters, and poetry, Lorde documented this devastation and its effects on her own life and community, reflecting a prescient understanding of the ways environmental injustice, colonialism, racism, and misogyny intersect.

Lorde's accounts of survival raise a question also emergent at the intersection of Black literary history and the field of positive psychology: how is it possible for individuals or groups to "flourish" without collective freedom? One recent arena for responding to this question has been a debate over the persistence of what sociologist Orlando Patterson in 1982 termed "social death"—the distinguishing condition, he argued, of slavery—after legal emancipation. As I have argued in *Cultivation and Catastrophe* (2017), black ecological writing is a vital resource in this discussion, defining common ground between "what Jared Sexton and others have called Afro-pessimism, the theory that black diasporic subjects are conscripted within a modernity that enslaves, and what Fred Moten describes as black optimism, the idea of blackness as a persistent, resistant overturning of Western civilization, whose aim is also the recognition and reconstruction of its own possibilities" (Posmentier 14). While these thinkers have radically different responses to antiblackness, they share a fundamental critique of Enlightenment notions of freedom and (therefore) the potential for what we are calling human flourishing in the aftermath of transatlantic enslavement.[1]

---

[1] For a partial account of this debate, see Moten 2008, Moten 2013, Sexton 2011, and Sexton 2010.

Sonya Posmentier, *Black Ecological Optimism and the Problem of Human Flourishing* In: *Literary Studies and Human Flourishing*. Edited by: James F. English and Heather Love, Oxford University Press. © Oxford University Press 2023.
DOI: 10.1093/oso/9780197637227.003.0007

Drawing on Lorde's written responses to Hurricane Hugo, and working alongside such scholars as Katherine McKittrick and Christina Sharpe,[2] this chapter posits ecological tropes (the wind, a hurricane) as models for speculating about what it might mean to flourish while also acknowledging the structural, economic, environmental, and political conditions of un-freedom that have long shaped Black diasporic life. Rather than turning to the resiliency of the individual or to "the institutions that move individuals toward better citizenship"—said citizenship defined, according to Seligman et al., as "responsibility, nurturance, altruism, civility, moderation, toler-ance, and work ethic" (Seligman and Csikszentmihalyi 5)—Black writers from Zora Neale Hurston to Alice Walker, Lorde, and Sylvia Wynter often depict institutions as obstacles to flourishing (keeping in mind especially the "Peculiar Institution" and its afterlives). They theorize cultivation on the edges and outsides of institutions; flourishing that must resist the con-tainment of "civility, moderation, tolerance, and work ethic," and even citi-zenship. It might be argued that by imagining a place for human flourishing outside of institutions, such writers risk collapsing back into the ideology of individualism; but the model for survival Lorde imagines and creates is nei-ther institutional nor individual—rather, it is ecological.

Flourishing is itself an ecological trope. The verb to "flourish" means "to blossom or grow," from the Latin, *florere* (to flower, to blossom), derived from the word for flower (n.), *flos*. Commonly, the word is a metaphor used to describe not plant life but human success and well-being. Dwelling in the natural-world context of the metaphor's vehicle, we can understand "flour-ishing" as relational insofar as it is ecological. Put simply: to bloom, flowers require water, sun, soil, and otherwise supportive conditions. With an em-phasis on this literary valence, to attend to human flourishing is to take up the more relational calls for "positivity" articulated by positive psychology, and to challenge those definitions of "positive" focused on individual well-being. Positive psychologist James Pawelski usefully identifies a tension be-tween "prudential" and "moral" values at stake in these potentially divergent definitions of "positive":

When focusing on well-being, positive individuals, and positive subjective states, positive psychologists seem to be emphasizing prudential values.

---

[2] See especially McKittrick's analysis of "plantation futures" and Sharpe's formulation of the wake, the ship, the hold, and the weather as key tropes of modernity, all of which offer, in my view, parallel structures for thinking about the problem of flourishing in the context of the ongoing effects of trans-atlantic enslavement.

When focusing on flourishing communities, a just society, the good person and the good society, on the other hand, they seem to be emphasizing moral values (Pawelski 352–53).

Lorde's ecological optimism would teach us that there is no purely "prudential" positivity, and that there is, further, no nonethical or nonrelational flourishing. In response to Atlantic hurricane damage and human violence that disproportionately affects the well-being of Black diasporic communities, Lorde's writings foreground the need for communal care rooted in shared ecological experiences.

In an interview with Charles Rowell, a mainland-US-based Black scholar and the editor of the influential journal *Callaloo*, about a year after the hurricane, Lorde highlighted the interconnection between Caribbean and US-mainland economic and environmental circumstances, as well as the limits of state-based care.

> The point is, what happens on these islands is directly involved with what is going on with Black people on the mainland and all over the world. I am speaking politically and economically as well as socially. For example, how many people are aware that on this tiny Caribbean island is the largest oil refinery in the Western hemisphere, Hess Oil of the Virgin Islands? Larger than their refinery in Jersey, larger than the one in Texas. What does that mean? What does it mean that two days after Hugo leveled St. Croix, when there was no electricity, no telephone, no water, no food, no diapers, when 98 percent of the dwellings on this island were totally destroyed, the United States government came onto this island with MPs and U.S. Marshals and the F.B.I., and immediately guarded Hess Oil? What they first brought down were not emergency disaster relief supplies, but M-16s and military personnel. The U.S. military takeover of St. Croix reminded me of nothing so much as the U.S. military invasion of Grenada. (Rowell and Lorde 84–85)

The refinery in St. Croix to which Lorde refers would eventually have to pay millions in environmental damages for polluting the air and ground water. Lorde's account of the intersection of militarization, industrialization, global imperialism, and the slow violence of the oil industry echoes in our own century: in the federal neglect (we might say "islandization") that occurred after Hurricane Katrina in New Orleans, the impending deportation of Haitian-Americans with Temporary Protective Status (TPS) to Haiti, still reeling from the earthquake and cholera epidemic, and the tag-teaming of debt with Hurricane Maria in Puerto Rico. Lorde suggests we need a non-state model of survival, and that we already have the capacity to imagine our-selves living differently in time if only we can see how we are "involved" with one another.

Here, Lorde's writings open a window on a problem Scott Herring raises in another chapter in this volume, what he sees as positive psychology's over-emphasis on "character strengths" (particularly in the context of defining op-timal aging). Herring argues compellingly that by idealizing and normalizing such "good" values as "wisdom," this perspective pathologizes less standard ways of growing older. Like Herring I wish to orient our understanding of well-being away from the idea of "good character," and further, from the idea of "character" at all (insofar as character belongs to the individual actor). I want to suggest instead a positivity that must be held in common, even and especially when the commons is catastrophic.

While this essay focuses primarily on Lorde's explicitly ecological framings of collective survival in the context of natural disaster, I will begin by turning briefly to her reflections on the apparently more intimate and individual struggles of the body provoked by living with breast cancer. In both *The Cancer Journals* and her Hugo writings, the poet characterizes the relation-ship between the personal and political, between the sensory and affective experience of being in a physical body and the social, intellectual and envi-ronmental experience of being in community; and in turn she demonstrates the capacity for poetry to navigate that relationship.

Disaster and Survival: Cancer

In *The Cancer Journals*, a collection of essays recounting her diagnosis and survival, Lorde articulated in advance what was to be the necessary criti-cism of positive psychology's elision of real environmental, social, and eco-nomic factors in group and individual well-being. In the final of three essays (a screed against synthetic breast implants), she describes reading a doctor's letter in a magazine, "which said that no truly happy person ever gets cancer" (76). Lorde goes on to describe the dangers (for a cancer patient) of internal-izing such a facile idea of the mind–body connection: "Despite my knowing better, and despite my having dealt with this blame-the-victim thinking for years, for a moment this letter hit my guilt button. Had I really been guilty of the crime of not being happy in this best of all possible infernos?" Of course, this doctor's magical thinking is a far cry from the scientific logic of "positive psychology." Scholars of the latter have worked assiduously to distinguish their studies of well-being from the self-help branding of "happiness." But Lorde's response to the magazine article is nonetheless instructive for our thinking of the limits of positive psychology in the face of systemic oppression. For, she objects not merely to the idea of "happiness alone" but to an emphasis on the individual at the expense of engagement with the political. Along with the psychic damage of such guilt for patients, Lorde identifies the public consequences of theories of survival based on individual happiness or wellness. Such a theory, she writes,

> does nothing to encourage the mobilization of our psychic defenses against the very real forms of death which surround us. It is easier to demand happiness than to clean up the environment. The acceptance of illusion and appearance as reality is another symptom of this same refusal to examine the reality of our lives. Let us seek "joy" rather than real food and clean air and a saner future on a liveable earth! As if happiness alone can protect us from the results of profit-madness. (Lorde, *Cancer Journals*, 76)

"The acceptance of illusion and appearance as reality" displaces what will actually make us well: "real food and clean air and a saner future on a liveable earth." In recounting the internal monologue produced by the magazine article, Lorde produces a detailed and specific list of the structural and material impediments to well-being. "Was I wrong," she asks "to be working so hard against the oppression afflicting women and Black people?"

> Was I in error to be speaking out against our silent passivity and the cynicism of mechanized and inhuman civilization that is destroying our earth and those who live upon it? Was I really fighting the spread of radiation, racism, woman-slaughter, chemical invasion of our food, pollution of our environment, the abuse and psychic destruction of our young, merely to avoid dealing with my first and greatest responsibility—to be happy? (Lorde 76–77)

Only a "depraved monster," she concludes, could be happy "in this disastrous time, when little girls are still being stitched shut between their legs, when victims of cancer are urged to court more cancer in order to be attractive to men, when 12-year-old Black boys are shot down in the street at random by uniformed men who are cleared of any wrong-doing . . . ." Lorde rejects the idea that there are two distinct ways to think of happiness—as individual on the one hand, or as "ethical" and "relational" on the other—and suggests further that an individualistic emphasis on happiness can in fact damage collective well-being.

I would maintain, however, that Lorde is optimistic, even positive, if in a different key. For in Lorde's (sardonic) list of "wrongdoings" she finds a way to render care for the earth, care for other women, and care for the self as interdependent. To speak out, to fight against violence and environmental toxicity: these are the transformative powers of poetry and political action she believes we must engage in order to be well.

Lorde's understanding of cancer as environmentally produced refuses an understanding of the body as purely private or individual; so, too, her account of surviving cancer and mastectomy is insistently *environmental*. Upon waking from the invasive biopsy procedure through which doctors diagnosed her cancer, Lorde felt (and later wrote about insistently and repetitively) "the cold, the terrible cold of that first hour" (27). Because the hospital did not supply extra blankets, "our friends came and were there, loving and helpful and there, brought coats to pile upon my bed and then a comforter and blankets." In the longer run, Lorde also saw her survival as a matter of interdependence. One particularly provocative example of this is her lengthy criticism of prosthetic breast augmentation, not as a personal decision, but rather as the encouragement of "false and dangerous nostalgia" emphasizing normative ideals of female beauty at the expense of adequate research, knowledge, and power.[3] Survival depended neither on "false happiness" nor on "false breasts" but, instead, on "time and the loving support of other women" (78). Rather, as Angela Hume has elaborated, in the case of both cancer and hurricane, "survival constituted a repudiation of capitalist state-sponsored environmental injustice" (213). This, I want to suggest, is the ground upon which Lorde allows us to imagine "flourishing."

---

[3] Lorde develops this idea over the course of the chapter of *The Cancer Journals* titled "Breast Cancer: Power V. Prosthesis," in which she draws not only on her personal experience considering (and refusing) prosthesis but also on analysis of the written and treatment-based discourse of the American Cancer Society and other organizations and individuals that advocate prosthesis and reconstructive surgery as essential parts of women's healing (56–79).

In the wake of (and in constant anticipation of) disaster both personal and environmental, Lorde would have us develop a relational sense of well-being. This relational or even communal well-being took on an expanded environmental sense after Hugo, when the afflictions of environmental disaster affected an entire community simultaneously. Shortly after surviving Hurricane Hugo, Lorde wrote a letter to friends on the mainland, published in *Aché: The Bay Area's Journal for Black Lesbians*. Here, Lorde draws an explicit connection between the world-making required by environmental change, and the project of Black feminist community.

> The earth is telling us something about our conduct of living as well as about our abuse of this covenant we live upon. Not one of us can believe herself untouched by these messages, no matter where she lives, no matter under what illusion of safety or uninvolvement she pretends to hide. Each one of us has some power she can use, somewhere, somehow. (Lorde, "A Letter from St. Croix," 5)

For readers of Lorde's well-known essays, the passage evokes her oft-quoted assertion of intersectional feminist solidarity from her 1981 lecture "The Uses of Anger": "I am not free while any woman is unfree" (132), now reframed as circum-Atlantic Black feminist solidarity based on the shared environmental experience of living on an endangered earth.[4] When she reminds us of the connectedness between territory and mainland, Lorde emphasizes the labor involved in forging connections to other people and to nature. And she acknowledges that environmental disaster exacerbates vast inequities. She ends the letter in *Aché* with a request that her Bay Area friends stop making contributions to her and her partner Gloria—who three months after the storm have managed to rebuild partially, with a gas stove, temporary roof, and generator—and instead give to the St. Croix organization that originally brought Lorde to the island, "Sojourner Sisters," which worked to empower girls and women, in particular survivors of domestic abuse. In other words, she insisted that human flourishing was only possible through the rigorous maintenance of intersectional community.

---

[4] The connection I'm drawing might risk echoing an essentialist ecofeminism that was coterminous with Lorde's career. Lorde, however, calls upon an ecological commitment women must work to produce and maintain.

Feeling as Epistemology

While deemphasizing the individual psyche as the site of resilience, Lorde nonetheless represents poetry as a site of resistance because of the access it affords to affect. In her 1977 essay "Poetry Is Not a Luxury" she asserts that "women have survived. As poets" (39). Approaching this assertion as an example of ecological thought, I hope to highlight poetic feeling as a particularly vital and relational form of human flourishing.

In a 1979 conversation between Lorde and poet Adrienne Rich first published in *Signs* in 1981 and later collected in Lorde's book of essays *Sister Outsider*, Rich asks Lorde if they can talk about how the difference in their racial subject positions has informed the choices available to them. In response, Lorde revisits an earlier phone conversation in which Rich requested further evidence for Lorde's intuitions (103). Lorde reflects, "I will never forget that. Even at the same time that I understood what you meant, I felt a total wipeout of my modus, my way of perceiving and formulating" (103–4). What follows is their discussion of the possibilities and limitations of "documentation" as a "modus." "Documentation," Lorde (a former librarian) reminds her friend, "does not help one perceive. At best it only analyzes the perception. At worst, it provides a screen by which to avoid concentrating on the core revelation, following it down to how it feels. . . . So at certain stages that request for documentation is a blinder, a questioning of my perceptions. [. . .] I'm a poet, not a historian" (103–5). Lorde does not merely criticize the "documentary" ethos she associates with both whiteness and patriarchy but also refuses the long-standing expectation that Black writing must be evidentiary—of Black humanity, cultural continuity, and Africanist survival, and of the inhumanity of slavery, Jim Crow, and race-prejudice. To resist documentation may be to resist certain assumptions about the social function (or even sociological function) of Black art. As opposed to documentation, Lorde posits getting "down to how it feels" as an innovative formal practice.

Significantly, the poetics of feeling Lorde describes is not about individuation. Lorde dedicated herself not only to teaching and writing but also to activism and community organizing, in particular on behalf of women. Accordingly she insisted on poetry as a communal resource in political life.

For women, then, poetry is not a luxury. It is a vital necessity of our existence. It forms the quality of the light within which we predicate our hopes
and dreams toward survival and change, first made into language, then into
idea, then into more tangible action. Poetry is the way we help give name
to the nameless so it can be thought. (Lorde, "Poetry Is Not a Luxury," 37)

Lorde articulates the path from language to action as an essential political
theory. "Feeling" is a sanctuary for ideas that might otherwise be too threatening to the status quo, too difficult to conceptualize in other genres or disciplinary epistemologies. Lorde thinks of poetry as a form of what she calls
"disciplined attention" to feeling, an otherwise oft-neglected repository of
feminist knowledge (37).

Attending to "feeling" in Lorde's writings on Hugo (and more broadly), it
may be tempting to read her poems as lyrical accounts of individual survival.
The poem in which she most directly addresses the experience of surviving
Hurricane Hugo is titled "Hugo I," as if to highlight a singular subjective experience (Lorde, *The Collected Poems of Audre Lorde*, 461).[5] The poem at first
takes on the perspective of such a lyric speaker, opening with a catalog of environmental description:

> A coral stone at the edge of Bufano Road
> where the storm sat down
> but did not sleep
> the jack pine I used to curse
> for its ragged outline

In this opening scene all actions are in the past: "I used to curse," "the evening shadows walked," "quits perched all last summer." The hurricane has
stymied natural growth or flourishing. Against this scene of arrested growth,
the speaker cultivates beauty:

> A grey dog lay in the road
> pregnant with death
> as I planted new bougainvillea
> that fortnight Gloria went north.

---

[5] The "I" may also be a roman numeral "one," signifying the beginning of an unfinished series.

The speaker is alone, planting "new" flowers in an atmosphere of death and decay, but that which was green and growing remains mere memory: "this skeleton *was* an almond tree" (emphasis added). In the present, "All the rest is rubble."

But the final line of the poem shifts our focus from individual survival (or failure to thrive) by using an ecological trope for social relationships. Standing alone as a stanza, the line enacts a shift from first person singular to first person plural: "But the wind is our teacher." The possessive first person plural pronoun "our" crosses the natural context of the vehicle with the social world of the tenor, insofar as "our" includes all the human and nonhuman actors in the poem: the speaker, Gloria, the prickly pear cactus and almond tree, the gray dog "pregnant with death." While the imagery in the poem suggests death and decay, the structure of enjambments effects overflow or growth, suggesting the possibility of flourishing even in the context of the hurricane winds. Through natural metaphor, Lorde foregrounds not individual resilience but the socioeconomic, political ,and environmental contexts in and through which Black women (and Black women's feelings) survive.[6]

As we will recall, Lorde also echoes the image of nature as teacher in "A Letter from St. Croix" in which "the earth is telling us something about our conduct of living" (5). The repetition of this kind of metaphor and personification of earth and wind across Lorde's poetry and prose suggests that in the face of disaster the generic boundary between documentation and poetry, evidence and feeling, may be less rigid in practice than she had previously theorized. Or, put differently, Lorde strove to put the poetry of necessity in practice in all forms of writing. Her depiction of the relationship to nature as pedagogical is particularly important insofar as the teacher–student relationship is one that allows us to imagine continuity and preservation of knowledge outside of heteronormative, biological, linear models of genealogy.

---

[6] Taken together, Lorde's epistolary, experimental prose and poetic writings after Hugo likewise have implications for redefining the "positive" in positive psychology insofar as they direct us away from positivist methods of measurement and toward feeling as epistemology, while also insisting on the necessity of preservation and documentation in response to environmental and social catastrophe. Tamsin Shaw makes a persuasive case about the dangers of positivism in positive psychology in her article connecting the dots between Seligman's theory of "learned helplessness" and the CIA's "enhanced interrogation techniques" employed after September 11, 2001, although Seligman and other positive psychologists have refuted her claims (Shaw; Shaw et al.; Seligman's Response to Shaw's "The Psychologists Take Power").

Disaster and Survival: Hurricane

Indeed, for all of the skepticism Lorde expresses about the "evidentiary" work of documentation in her conversation with Rich, her prose writings on survival after Hurricane Hugo seem driven by a documentary impulse: preserving, organizing, and cataloging both human and environmental history. Rather than functioning as superfluous "evidence" of Black humanity, or subordination to Western notions of order, however, these writings, like Lorde's poetry and her organizing in feminist and lesbian community, reflect her investment in differently imagining Black futurity and community.

A few months after Hurricane Hugo, Lorde contributed to a volume edited by Hortense Rowe and by Gloria Joseph, who was Lorde's partner, and published by Winds of Change Press: *Hell Under God's Orders: Hurricane Hugo in St. Croix, Disaster and Survival*. Lorde's contribution is a letter, called "Of Generators and Survival—Hugo Letter 12/89," addressed to "Dear Friend"

> Dear Friend:
> Those who do not learn from history are doomed to repeat their mistakes. It is necessary to remember the nightmare experience and extraordinary heroisms of the hurricane. But it is also important that we remember those lessons, both immediate and long term, learned in the bleak days afterwards. (Lorde, "Hell Under God's Orders," 202)

Lorde's letter chronicles "The bleak days afterwards": "September 18. 1989. Day One. We venture forth, wet, trembling, exhausted, and relieved to be alive." She describes Day 3, Day 10, Day 15. And then, December 18, 1989 (12 weeks later). Here, three months after the hurricane, Lorde records the improvements in her own life and on the island more broadly, but she also asks,

> When the next hurricane season comes, will there still be unfortunate people displaced by Hugo still living under blue temporary tarpaulins that are decaying from overlong use in our tropical sun? We are a territory of the most powerful country on earth, supposed to be. Why are there almost 700 families still homeless? If we do not learn the lessons of Hurricane Hugo, we are doomed to repeat them. Because Hugo will not be the last hurricane in this area. (211)

Lorde, Joseph, and Rowe organized this volume as an effort of preservation, of the experiences and cultures of those who had survived the hurricane, an act of preservation of the earth itself:

"Our earth is healing herself. Again. And we pay a price for the violence we have done to her in the name of scientific progress."

Lorde thus posits her recollection in the context of the repeated assertion that "we are doomed to repeat" history if we do not read it, listen to it, learn it. Her piece is organized as a chronical (arguably, a documentary genre): a mundane, transparent recording of the everyday. The essay and the collection are intended as pedagogical—in that we should *learn* from them not to make the same mistakes.

But we also know that the answer to Lorde's question—"When the next hurricane season comes, will there still be unfortunate people?"—is most likely yes. The next hurricane season has come and will come again. I began work on this essay in the fall of 2017, as disaster struck St. Croix again in the form of Hurricane Maria. In 2017 as in 1989, federal and nongovernmental relief agencies were slow to extend support to US territories, including the US Virgin Islands and Puerto Rico. I complete this essay in September 2019, just as the United States turns away Bahamian survivors of Hurricane Dorian seeking refuge.

As much as Lorde depicts repetition as a "doom" we should avoid by recording history, repetition also *is*, *was*, and *is going to be* inevitable. We are doomed to repeat ourselves. Not because no one recorded, organized, or preserved the history. They did so, as evidenced by *Hell Under God's Orders*. But we are repeating ourselves anyway.

Repetition as a Figure of Black Feminist Culture

So what is the function of acts of cultural preservation and documentation when repetition is the inevitable action of the hurricane and the human? To some degree, Lorde, wittingly or unwittingly, seems to enact what in hindsight can only be read as a scene of pedagogical failure. But what could it mean, even though we are doomed to repeat ourselves, to think of the recording, publication, circulation, cataloging, and preservation in which Lorde engages (the collective work of writers, teachers, and librarians) as part of the work of human flourishing that Black feminism performs?

I have in mind as one possible response to this question James Snead's recovery of the positive value of "repetition" as a figure of Black culture, a value that has been repressed, denigrated, and "covered" in European cultural practice, but nonetheless constitutes the future of European aesthetics. "The separation between cultures was perhaps all along not one of nature," he concludes, "but of force" (Snead 153). Following Snead, how might we imagine human flourishing not in the mode of "accumulation and growth" but rather in a way that acknowledges "that the thing [culture] *circulates* (exactly in the manner of any flow, including capital flows) there in equilibrium" (149)? Dance scholar Kemi Adeyemi has more recently argued that repetition without accumulation might be the site where Black politics can be organized around the queer and the woman (Adeyemi). Lorde's responses to Hugo, indeed organized around queer and feminist politics,[7] thus not only represent repetition as destruction, but embody repetition as form.

Lorde's letter in *Hell Under God's Orders* closes three months after it begins, underscoring the iterability, the ongoingness of catastrophe and the struggle for survival. The genre of the letter describing the everyday bridges the singular friend addressed to a broader audience, situating its reader in the future through the creation of a literary network. This ethics of care, derived from Lorde's feminism, is Lorde's environmental ethics. The entry closes with an injunction and a wish,

> And remember Hurricane Hugo.
> My friend, I wish you were living down the road. Rocky as it may be, it is still also the most beautiful. Gloria and I would take our walking sticks after a long day's work, and the three little bluefish Curtis just brought by, and go clean them down on the beach, throwing the guts to the seabirds. We'd bring the fish over to your house and we'd all sit around and have a fish-fry over driftwood coals, swapping stories of how it was, and how it is, and how it is surely going to be. (212)

What strikes me is at once the familiarity of the discursive tropes of disaster recovery—the failure of the state to provide resources, the questions about belonging and citizenship, who sends bananas and who does not send emergency supplies, what Lorde calls "the man made ugliness" and the freshness,

---

[7] See Hume 2022 on "The Queer Restoration Poetics" of many of the same materials under discussion here.

specificity, and optimism of the world Lorde describes and makes. And then there is the mere fact of repetition evident in the annual circulation of hurricane winds through the Atlantic (most recently, the damage done to St. Croix by Hurricane Maria), and the repetitive social disaster of national and transnational care. In the Hugo letter, not only the hurricane repeats itself, but also the subjunctive mood of Lorde's "wish you were here" conclusion, in which "we would" constantly repeat the world-making of survival.

In this sense, environmental catastrophe reorders the linear chronical that would apparently catalog it, drawing our attention not to progress but to repetition. Hurricanes themselves borrow and repeat the circular and repetitive structure of the transatlantic slave trade (literally taking its power from the same winds), forming off the coast of West Africa and making landfall with greatest consequence in the Caribbean and the eastern coast of the United States.[8] To account for this environmental catastrophe requires forms of writing and community that, to borrow Lorde's words, allow feelings to survive even "within living structures defined by profit, by linear power, by institutional dehumanization" (Lorde, *Sister Outsider*, 39).

In her poetry and prose Lorde invites us to think of intergenerational continuity as a source of particular power in the face of intersecting spheres of social and environmental violence. I would draw attention, here, to what may or may not be a typo in the book *Hell Under God's Orders*, one that demonstrates a connection between Lorde's Black feminist vision of community her response to environmental disaster. The title of Lorde's letter in the edited volume on Hugo, in the table of contents and at its heading, is "Of Generators and Survival." The short title on the upper-right repeated page heading is, "of *generations* and survival" (emphasis added).

Based on this slip, shift, or revision from "generator" to "generations," from power to collective production, we can trace a connection between Lorde's writings on community in the wake of Hurricane Hugo and her earlier poetry about the place of women (and feminist pedagogy) in the movement for Black studies. In her 1973 poem "Blackstudies," for example, Lorde implicitly invites us to read "generations" not as biologically connected but as communities of women of different ages teaching and learning from one another (Lorde, *The Collected Poems of Audre Lorde*, 94–98). While on the surface "Blackstudies" would seem to have little to do with ecology, it exemplifies Lorde's thinking about survival through a nonreproductive model of relation

---

[8] For more on the formal consequences of this relationship see Posmentier 2017, especially the Introduction and Chapter 6.

and flourishing. Lorde overlaps an intimate narrative of childbearing with the more public space of the classroom "on the 17th floor," and the more public spaces still of institutional conflict and change. In the struggle to establish a Black Studies department at John Jay College, Lorde "saw the use and abuse of women, of Black people, saw how Black studies was being used by the university in a really cynical fashion" (Lorde, *Sister Outsider*, 98). Her poem describes and hopes for a different kind of "blackstudies" among women. In the first few sections of the poem, the speaker pictures herself on a high floor of a classroom building, dreading contact with her students, for fear she might be inadequate to the needs of this new generation. The poem's final section stages this confrontation:

> My searching students wait outside my doorsearching
>   condemning listening
> for what I am sworn to tell them
> for what they least want to hear
> clogging the only exit from the 17th floor
> begging in their garbled language
> beyond judgment or understanding
> "oh speak to us now mother for soon
> we will not need you
> only your memory
> teaching us questions." (*Collected Poems* 98)

Lorde describes intergenerational exchange of knowledge as painful and challenging. The ambiguous punctuation and lineation juxtapose the possibilities of pedagogy against its potential failure, or the fear of what really teaching might entail.

By the end of the poem Lorde has unlocked this fear, transformed the scene of the "young girls' assault[ing]" into the teacher's pedagogical death drive: "we will not need you," the students say, "only your memory / teaching us questions." Any of us who teach might recognize this fantasy that our students "will not need" us, that their questions will outlive and supersede us. In it, Lorde posits a model of black feminist intergenerational continuity (repetition) other than biological mothering. While Lorde often imagines biological maternity as both substance of and metaphor for empowering relationships, here she writes a queer futurity mobilized in the context of ecological survival. The concluding lines suggest that intergenerational feminist survival might yield a connection to the earth that is dangerous to the individual subject but radical in its imagination of community:

> Stepping into my self
> I open the door
> and leap groundward
> wondering
> what shall they carve for weapons
> what shall they grow for food

Without her, the students will face the question of how to flourish in the midst of catastrophe, the very question Lorde herself would later encounter when living with cancer and rebuilding her home after a hurricane: "what shall they grow for food." Through her later experience, in which *she* is the student and the wind "our teacher," Lorde writes a provisional answer worth repeating.

As we reread the final passage of Lorde's Hugo letter, it seems significant that she stages her late radical vision of community at the edge of the ocean. She describes that space—of middle passage, of rising sea levels—as a different kind of passage, formulating an example of life lived at an angle to the state, not unlike that which Fred Moten has more recently framed as the necessary remainder of the violence of the deep:

> The middle passage is and opens onto an alternative warp, enacting its own singular rupture of the space-time continuum, of a transcendental aesthetic that lays down the terms and conditions of possibility for the modern subject of knowledge and power. (Moten, *Stolen Life*, 209–11)

Lorde offers a relational structure of environmental flourishing that borrows the iterability of disaster itself. She recalls not only the damage to the island, and the various and violent failures of the state to repair that damage, but also the everyday networks of care, ritual, cooking over driftwood fire, the sharing of collard greens which are the only vegetable in the garden to have survived the storm, the cleaning and the writing attempted by, for, and with her community:

> And remember Hurricane Hugo.
> My friend, I wish you were living down the road. Rocky as it may be, it is
> still also the most beautiful. Gloria and I would take our walking sticks after

a long day's work, and the three little bluefish Curtis just brought by, and go clean them down on the beach, throwing the guts to the seabirds. We'd bring the fish over to your house and we'd all sit around and have a fish-fry over driftwood coals, swapping stories of how it was, and how it is, and how it is surely going to be. (Lorde, "Of Generations," 212)

Works Cited

Adeyemi, Kemi. "Gestures of Dissent." Panel Presentation. *Pedagogies of Dissent* Conference, American Studies Association, Chicago, IL, November 2017.

Haidt, Jonathan and Steven Pinker. "Moral Psychology: An Exchange." *New York Review of Books*, Apr 2016, https://www.nybooks.com/articles/2016/04/07/moral-psychology-an-exchange/.

Hume, Angela. "The Queer Restoration Poetics of Audre Lorde." *The Cambridge Companion to American Literature and the Environment*, edited by Sarah Ensor and Susan Scott Parrish, Cambridge University Press, 2022, pp. 204–21, https://doi.org/10.1017/9781108895118.016.

Lorde, Audre. *The Cancer Journals*. Special ed., Aunt Lute Books, 1980.

Lorde, Audre. *The Collected Poems of Audre Lorde*. Norton, 1997.

Lorde, Audre. "A Letter from St. Croix." *Aché: The Bay Area's Journal For Black Lesbians*, vol. 2, no. 1, Feb. 1990, pp. 4–5, 27.

Lorde, Audre. "Of Generations and Survival—Hugo Letter 12/89." *Hell Under God's Orders: Hurricane Hugo in St. Croix—Disaster and Survival*, edited by Gloria Joseph, Winds of Change Press, 1990, pp. 202–15.

Lorde, Audre. "An Interview: Audre Lorde and Adrienne Rich." *Sister Outsider: Essays and Speeches*, Crossing Press, 1984, pp. 81–109.

Lorde, Audre. "Poetry Is Not a Luxury." *Sister Outsider: Essays and Speeches*, pp. 36–39.

Lorde, Audre. "The Uses of Anger: Women Responding to Racism." *Sister Outsider: Essays and Speeches*, pp.124–33.

McKittrick, Katherine. "Plantation Futures." *Small Axe*, vol. 17, no. 42, Nov. 2013, pp. 1–15, doi:10.1215/07990537-2378892.

Moten, Fred. "Blackness and Nothingness (Mysticism in the Flesh)." *South Atlantic Quarterly*, vol. 112, no. 4, Fall 2013, pp. 737–80, EBSCOhost, https://doi.org/10.1215/00382876-2345261.

Moten, Fred. "Black Op." *PMLA: Publications of the Modern Language Association of America*, vol. 123, no. 5, Oct. 2008, pp. 1743–47.

Moten, Fred. *Stolen Life*. Duke UP, 2018, www.dukeupress.edu/stolen-life.

Pawelski, James O. "Defining the 'Positive' in Positive Psychology: Part I. A Descriptive Analysis." *Journal of Positive Psychology*, vol. 11, no. 4, July 2016, pp. 339–56, https://doi.org/10.1080/17439760.2015.1137627.

Posmentier, Sonya. *Cultivation and Catastrophe: The Lyric Ecology of Modern Black Literature*. Johns Hopkins UP, 2017.

Rowell, Charles H., and Audre Lorde. "Above the Wind: An Interview with Audre Lorde." *Callaloo*, vol. 23, no. 1, 2000, pp. 52–63, https://doi.org/10.1353/cal.2000.0062.

Seligman, M. E., and M. Csikszentmihalyi. "Positive Psychology: An Introduction." *American Psychologist*, vol. 55, no. 1, Jan. 2000, pp. 5–14.

Seligman, Martin. *Seligman's Response to Shaw's "The Psychologists Take Power."* 1 Apr. 2016, https://positivepsychologyprogram.com/seligmans-response-shaws-psychologists-take-power/.

Sexton, Jared. "People-of-Color-Blindness: Notes on the Afterlife of Slavery." *Social Text*, vol. 28, no. 2 (103), June 2010, pp. 31–56, https://doi.org/10.1215/01642472-2009-066.

Sexton, Jared. "The Social Life of Social Death: On Afro-Pessimism and Black Optimism." *InTensions*, no. 5, Fall/Winter 2011, https://doi.org/10.25071/1913-5874/37359.

Sharpe, Christina. *In the Wake: On Blackness and Being.*, Duke UP, 2016.

Shaw, Tamsin. "Moral Psychology: An Exchange (Reply by Tamsin Shaw)." *New York Review of Books*, Apr. 2016, https://www.nybooks.com/articles/2016/04/07/moral-psychology-an-exchange/.

Shaw, Tamsin. "The Psychologists Take Power." *New York Review of Books*, Feb. 2016, https://www.nybooks.com/articles/2016/02/25/the-psychologists-take-power/.

Snead, James A. "On Repetition in Black Culture." *Black American Literature Forum*, vol. 15, no. 4, 1981, pp. 146–54. *JSTOR*, https://doi.org/10.2307/2904326.

PART IV
NON-NORMATIVE FLOURISHING
Disability and Aging

7

Literary Study, the Hermeneutics
of Disability, and the Eudaimonic Turn

Janet Lyon

As literary teachers and scholars, we know how well human flourishing is supported by the foundational activities of our field. We see how classroom discussions of literary texts and memoirs can create new forms of collaborative understanding around human character, nonhuman forces, complex life events, and the many varieties of embodiment and mindedness, for example. This is especially vivid when the texts under study are concerned with disability, whether in an outright manner, through representations of nonnormative bodyminds, or linguistically, through disruptions of communicative norms, or ideologically, through the emanations of the grounding assumptions of ableism. The collective reading of disability literature in the classroom draws on the expansive properties of literary language and form to cultivate imaginative breadth and openness to meaning. It creates an interactive community in which ethics can be tested and enigmas honored. Rationality has its place in these discussions, but (as with all discussions of literature) so do the nonrational, the unreasonable, the affective, and the spiritual. Importantly, the various forms of disability knowledge that circulate in the literature classroom are highly portable: intrinsically suited to the social plane (since literature itself is fundamentally social), they provide all of us with apertures through which to perceive the otherness of the world that exists outside of local assumptions and beyond the influence of our wills. We might characterize this condition as an "openness to the unbidden,"[1] or else, in a less philosophical key, as a hedge against the strictures of doxa and the status quo. This condition of openness is part of the explicit domain of the

---

[1] The political philosopher Michael Sandel uses "openness to the unbidden" (a term he borrows from the theologian William F. May) to refer to the salutary experience of encountering that which has not been predicted or summoned in advance, and is therefore not under one's control (Sandel 57 and passim).

Janet Lyon, *Literary Study, the Hermeneutics of Disability, and the Eudaimonic Turn* In: *Literary Studies and Human Flourishing*. Edited by: James F. English and Heather Love, Oxford University Press. © Oxford University Press 2023. DOI: 10.1093/oso/9780197637227.003.0008

humanities. Flourishing that begins here on an individual intellectual or psychic level passes into the social domain, where it may enhance or become a condition of possibility for the flourishing of others.

I wish to argue three points in this chapter. First, that the positive psychology movement, with its laudable and revisionary focus on human flourishing and well-being, might extend its own flourishing as an enterprise by attending to the formations of knowledge cultivated in the field of literary studies—specifically, the efflorescent understanding of human and nonhuman life that occurs through reading, writing, and critical thinking. Second, that the lack of attention to disability in the foundational formulations of positive psychology is problematic and should be remedied. It seems to me that any programmatic discussion of the values associated with positive psychology—flourishing, well-being, eudaimonia—that doesn't explicitly acknowledge disability and ableism, risks being radically incomplete and ultimately self-undermining. And third, that close readings of disability literature, undertaken with the tools of literary study, can provide a window through which the multiple connections of disability, political value, and cultural depth may be perceived.

One of the milieus for the discussion of disability in the university setting is the field of Disability Studies (hereafter DS), an academic offshoot of the disability rights and disability justice movements, which crosses many academic fields of study, including the humanities, social sciences, arts, engineering, design, and the various branches of medical and clinical practice. The DS enterprise may be characterized as eudaimonic—that is, attuned to the conditions for a meaningful life—since one of its constitutive tenets holds disability to be neither de facto tragic nor inherently pathological. A related tenet emphasizes disability as something to be apperceived in the context of human variety, neurodiversity, bodymind plurality, existential capaciousness, and hierarchical social values and forces. DS centers the experiences, histories, and cultures of people with disabilities, and insists that disabled lives are not only fully legitimate and "worth living," but also valuable for and indeed central to all networks of human experience. Some philosophers of disability argue that disability is value-neutral, that it is mere difference, "something that makes you a minority—it is a way of having a *minority body*"—in contradistinction to Enlightenment models of harm/deficit which have been constructed by and around nondisabled assumptions about what constitutes "the good life" and "well-being" (Barnes 78).[2]

---

[2] In addition to Elizabeth Barnes, whom I quote here, other philosophers of disability include Stacy Clifford Simplican, Eva Feder Kittay, Stephen M. Campbell and Joseph Stramondo, Shelley Tremain, and Licia Carlson.

To emphasize this eudaimonic element of DS, however, is not to suggest that DS isn't firmly rooted in an understanding of the physical and /or psychic pain that often accompanies disability, whether that pain is intrinsic or imposed from without, by way of the pervasive forces of ableism. To the contrary, the evolution of the DS field has taken place precisely around questions of how to account for the lived experiences of disability in the face of pain, stigma, and privation.[3] And when within disability as the result of massive economic and environmental injustices—degraded water systems, exposure to industrial poisons, chronic warfare and displacement, employment segregation, or authoritarian violence (the list is endless). DS must ask not only about the systemic sources of those injustices but also the ways in which the conditions of possibility for well-being must be formulated and systematically maintained for affected disabled peoples. The fact that disability disproportionately intersects with minority racial identities and/or poverty and/or minority gender presentation or sexual identity means that DS must maintain a dual focus on disability as an individual lived experience and disability as a series of conditioned interactions in a world where ableism determines in advance the worth of bodies and minds. Thus DS is precisely *not* the study of disability/ies (in the manner of, say, "Abnormal Psychology,"

---

[3] Within DS scholarship, a variety of "models" of disability have been described and theorized, including the "moral" model, according to which disability signals an act of God, to be pitied or feared; the medical model, in which disability is approached as an individual problem of brokenness or functional deviance, to be fixed through the interventions of medicine or else abandoned as "hopeless"; and the social model (explicitly developed against the moral and medical models), in which a categorical distinction is made between impairment and disability—the former being the mere condition of an atypical body, and the latter being a product of inaccessible built environments (and the ideologies underpinning them). The social model was widely propagated in the years when disability activism (mostly) in North America and the United Kingdom gave rise to the formation of DS as a field of polemical scholarship; it insistently refutes the medical/social framing of disability as an individual's deviation from norms, and instead pursues a variety of critiques of systemic ableism. The social model's insistence that disability is a social creation (and a minority identity to be embraced) rather than an individual form of deviance is politically expedient, since it may avail itself of rights discourses and the energy of a pride movement, but it has had the damaging effect of erasing (and even censoring) lived experiences of disability, which often include pain, suffering, trauma, and isolation. Moreover, the social model's implicit universalism has had the effect of covering over or failing to acknowledge the intersectional nature of disability, and especially the significantly different experiences of disability that are determined by race, gender, sexuality, class, and geopolitical location. The phenomenological model, as it is sometimes called, explores and theorizes the bodymind as a site of alterity and also a valuable modality of knowing and being (sometimes through the assemblages of care that form around disability). Intersectional models emphasize the anti-Black or more generally racist underpinnings of ableism itself, and operate in tandem with antiuniversalist models of social justice. Cultural models foreground the ways that cultures are formed around or against disability, and also the vivid aesthetic and expressive modes opened up by disability art and activism. Global models mark the significant distinctions between the sociopolitical causes and experiences of disabled populations in the global north and south.

to take a cartoonish example); rather, it is a body of scholarship and cultural expression that relies on critique for its necessarily complex formulations of well-being. This is to say that the eudaimonic thrust of DS is dialectically dependent upon critical accounts of ableism in its many presentations, including not only eugenic ideologies of embodiment and mindedness but also the economic/racialized systems that generate debility and disability in tandem.

Given the complexity of eudaimonic well-being for those in disability communities, it's difficult to imagine how that mode of well-being could ever fit with positive psychology's stated aim of "making normal people stronger and more productive and making high human potential actual."[4] The ableism embedded in that mission statement borders on the eugenic, and convinces me that advocates of positive psychology could learn a lot from disability activists and DS more generally. It is true that positive psychology's efforts to "amplify strengths rather than repair . . . weaknesses" (Seligman and Csikszentmihalyi 8) run parallel to DS's repudiation of the deficit model of disability, according to which bodyminds are measured against "normal" and found wanting. And I recognize and admire James O. Pawelski's innovative, nuanced conception of "the positive" (in positive psychology) as "presence of the preferred" or "absence of the dispreferred" (Pawelski 359), which aligns with a central desideratum of self-advocacy in disability activism.(Since "preference" implies genuine options, the term presupposes a context of access, alternatives, and agency.[5] But for many people with disabilities, any contemplation of well-being is contingent upon a baseline of reliable medical support, safety from danger or violence, and protection from stigma, the effects of which run from the discriminatory to the murderous. Indeed, the possibility must always be entertained that, in Elizabeth Barnes's words, "negative effects on well-being could be largely or entirely determined by ableism, rather than by disability itself" (Barnes 55). Thus, before the currents of the so-called eudaimonic turn can be meaningfully absorbed by a humanities field like literary DS (or for that matter, any of

---

[4] Martin Seligman and Mihaly Csikszentmihalyi, "Positive Psychology," 8.
[5] Pawelski's well-developed definition of "the positive" (Pawelski 2016) extends beyond the mere absence or presence of the preferred, and includes relative preference, sustainability over time, sustainability across persons, sustainability across effects, and sustainability across structures, all of which are especially crucial components of well-being where disability is involv. Pawelski conceptualizes complexly sustainable flourishing as "fractal flourishing," by which he means to indicate a model that retains and reproduces the (preferred) conditions for flourishing on various scales and through various facets of an individual's life (Pawelski, "Defining the 'Positive'" 363).

the advocacy-related humanities fields that operate through the duality of eudaimonic affirmation and critique—including women's/gender/sexuality studies and critical race studies), two important questions must be posed. First, can the methods associated with the eudaimonic turn fully accommodate the forms of critique entailed in DS? And second, can those methods refrain from conflating "well-being" with normative models of health and embodiment?

Hermeneutics

What follows is a brief overview of some methods associated with literary study, undertaken in order to sketch the operations of the field. I assume these methods are of interest in this project—that is, I assume that the invitations extended to humanities scholars to participate in the new, pan-institutional sciences of well-being bespeak an interest in how we literary scholars delineate and approach our objects of study.

Literary study makes use of a variety of methods—historical, interpretive, genetic, digital, analytical, among others; the particular arrangements of these methods are governed by the methodological orientation of any given study. In literary study, "methodology" names the perspectival approach or theoretical underpinnings that guide a research question (e.g., feminist, psychoanalytic, materialist, formalist, and so forth); the methods determined by a given methodology or methodologies (usually more than one are in play) comprise the discreet means by which materials are amassed, arguments assembled, and questions answered. These methods include archival research, close readings, comparative studies, formal analysis, philosophical exegesis, digital assessment, and textual genetic investigations, among others. The "hermeneutics" referenced in my essay's title crosses method and methodology. In literary study, hermeneutics designates an approach to texts and other forms of cultural expression that aligns their linguistic and figural meanings with broader cultural concepts. Hermeneutics has always been a part of literary study, though within the past fifty years, a variety of (sometimes polemically) interrelated hermeneutic approaches have been formulated in order to light up specific patterns of thought, meaning, or aesthetic effect in literary texts; these patterns support different accounts of the human values embedded in literary texts. (At the risk of stating the obvious, I will note that one premise of the field of literary study is that literary texts can tell us things that can't be told—or at least not effectively told—in any other way.) For example, a "hermeneutics of suspicion," first named as such by Paul Ricoeur in the 1960s, reads against the grain of a text's apparent surface meanings in order to expose what Fredric Jameson called "a latent meaning behind a manifest one" (60);[6] it aims to detect coded or disguised meaning that is unacknowledged in the text itself. This is typically associated with practices of deep reading and persistent (one might say perseverative) maieutic inquiry in the service of ideological or discursive analysis—usually to unearth disruptive or contradictory forces at work. A "hermeneutics of affirmation," by contrast, emphasizes imaginative engagement with a text's world on its own aesthetic and narrative terms, and is typically associated with reading practices (sometimes misleadingly characterized as "surface reading") that explore the available, perceptible, evident meanings frankly offered by a text. This term, "hermeneutics of affirmation," has understandably held some appeal to advocates of the sciences of well-being, for whom it appears to signal a paradigm shift in literary study from negative suspicion to positive affirmation, from pessimistic criticism to appreciative enjoyment.[7] (Of course it is hardly the case that critique has disappeared from interpretive enterprises—which, in point of fact, require the grist of persistent inquiry for their operations.) A third general category of textual analysis, "reparative reading," was famously elaborated by Eve Kosofsky Sedgwick in a 1997 essay, and represents something like a dialectical extension (or perhaps an a priori deconstruction) of the suspicion/affirmation dyad: It acknowledges the presence and potentially destructive power of latent textual meanings—meanings that may rupture the seemingly complacent aesthetic surface of a text; but at the same time it engages affectively with the text, rents and all, finding there, through the engrossing pleasures of close reading, a site of complex joy offered by the text itself.[8]

---

[6] For citations of Jameson in relation to "symptomatic" reading, see, for example, Best and Marcus, "Surface Reading," and Jeffrey Williams, "The New Modesty."

[7] Pawelski (2016) acknowledges the affirmative role played by the humanities in lighting up the eudaimonic registers of culture, and notes that literary study often includes "identifying obstacles to well-being," and "understanding the nature of well-being itself and how it can be cultivated" ("Bringing Together" 209).

[8] As Amanda Anderson has noted, Sedgwick's use of the term "reparative" is indebted to Melanie Klein's object relations theory and its focus on the developmental value of psychic repair. Klein's theory, Anderson writes, offers one form of "psychological understanding that emphasize[s] healthy positive development, including healthy and positive relations with others" (62). Sedgwick makes use of Klein in her effort to "craft a reparative response" to suspicious reading (65).

The "hermeneutics of disability" that I am proposing hereentails aspects of all of these hermeneutic practices (and probably many more). I hope that it will act as an analog for the questions raised in this volume about positive psychology, eudaimonic pedagogy, and comprehensively conceived well-being. For my purposes, a hermeneutics of disability denotes a reading practice that looks for the multiple ways in which disability inhabits and affects a text's literary and contextual meanings. Such a practice includes the apprehension of disability's powerful reframings of aesthetic and communicative norms. Thus, I am less interested here in whether a text offers "good" or "bad" representations of disability (though I will never be uninterested in that question) than I am in demonstrating the stakes involved when critique and eudaimonic affirmation are held in different degrees of tension around the hermeneutical forces of disability.

To this end I will discuss three literary texts from varying interpretive angles. All three are written by US authors, and all feature intellectual disability (hereafter, ID).[9] One is a minor imagist poem by a major modernist; the second is a contemporary realist novel about a state-run institution for developmentally disabled adolescents; the third is an experimental novel published in 2018, in which a central character with Down syndrome is never named or described. A discussion of any one of these texts could take up dozens of pages, but in this limited space I'll simply try to demonstrate, through varying degrees of close reading, the complex entanglements of affirmation, critique, and reparation connected to disability in these texts.

"Even Idiots"

The first text is a short, untitled poem by the poet-physician William Carlos Williams. It is part of Williams's twenty-six-page collection of lyrics and prose, *The Descent of Winter*, derived from a daily writing journal kept during the second half of 1927. Williams's medical practice entailed home visits to

---

[9] "Intellectual disability" is part of a notoriously unstable lexicon designating a notoriously heterogeneous set of bodyminds. Fool, changeling, cretin, mongoloid, idiot, feebleminded, imbecile, moron—each term is a stake driven into the shifting sands of psychometric futility. When I am not using the historical term "idiot," I will use "intellectual disability," adopting Anna Hickey-Moody's powerful caveat that "intellectual disability is the only noun phrase available to characterise a broad spectrum of ontological conditions. Despite its limits, inadequacies, and the indisputable fact that the term intellectual disability is a medical coding that has perhaps unwisely been transferred into social and cultural contexts, the noun phrase retains some use value because it makes an ontological point: it articulates a state of being that is empirically very particular" (Hickey-Moody 2018, 141).

poor rural and immigrant patients in the borough of Rutherford, New Jersey; often the poetry and prose entries in the collection were composed in his car. The poem I am examining here appears toward the end of the published sequence, shortly after his prose meditation on "the difficulty of modern styles" (by which Williams means the experimental styles of modernist writing). He explains that modern styles are difficult because the writer must navigate "the fragmentary stupidity of modern life"; in the face of such fragmentation, "the only human value of anything, writing included, is intense vision of the facts" (Williams 312)—an imperative codified in his famous imagist credo, "No ideas but in things" (Williams 263). Given Williams's emphasis on "facts" here and throughout his oeuvre, it seems reasonable to approach the poem about an idiot with the poet's devotion to facticity in mind:

> Even idiots grow old
>   in a cap with the peak
>   over his right ear
>   cross-eyed
>   shamble-footed
>   minding the three goats
>   behind the firehouse
>   his face is deeper lined
>   than last year
>   and the rain comes down
>   in gusts suddenly (322)

We citizens of the twenty-first century might recoil at this casual sketch of a village "idiot," but the speaker's uninflected tone seems to work against recoil. It is Williams's cultivated tone of scientific detachment: assumed in the interest of protecting the material things of the world from object-destroying ideas, this tone characterizes all of the short lyrics in *Descent of Winter*.[10]
Like other poems in the sequence, this one opens with a "propositional declaration" (Keller 1987, 169)—"Even idiots grow old"—which establishes the theme of temporality and aging: everyone grows old, even idiots, even this village idiot. It also establishes the adverbial use of "even" as the fulcrum of the poem. "Even" trades on an apparent assumption—that idiots don't grow old—which the poem challenges by way of the facticity of observation: the

---

[10] This style is developed in Williams's previous collection, *Spring and All* (1923).

proof of the man's aging is offered by way of the lines on his face, which have grown deeper over the previous year. Hence, *even* idiots age, which is to say that in this respect, at least, they are like unto other mortals and even other human adults. That is what the surface of the poem tells us.

However, circulating beneath the poem's deadpan descriptive surface of the peaked cap and the firehouse and so forth we will find ideological currents, which is to say, ideas *not* in things. The year is 1927: six months before the poem's composition, the U.S. Supreme Court's decision in *Buck v. Bell* legalized the involuntary sterilization of "feebleminded" inmates in state asylums. That decision capped a decades-long effort, by eugenic social workers, medical superintendents, white supremacist zealots, and Progressive Era talking heads, to isolate the feebleminded in asylums and terminate their reproductive futurity.[11]) Williams's inoffensive idiot, quietly aging as he minds the goats behind the firehouse, is thus linked to the "menace" of feeblemindedness that threatens the nation's genetic stock. Also circulating beneath the poem's surface is another resonant idiot, the centuries-old literary-cultural *trope* of "the idiot." Until quite recently (thirty years or less), that trope operated as a multivalent emblem, which could stand in for comic or tragic opacity, or will-less inertia, or as the sine qua non of revolting inhuman difference, or as ironic foil, or as metaphor for incapacity, or as a "natural" innocent (as in Williams's poem). But it almost never denoted a person possessed of a life worth living.[12]

Now, given Williams's famous contempt for figurative tropes of any kind—in *Descent* he inveighs against "the bastardy of the simile" (302)—we might expect that part of the poem's work would involve the swapping out of this highly conventional figure of "the idiot" for the ordinary rural man embedded in the community. I mean, really, as a physician, Williams *surely knows* that idiots age. But even if, for the sake of his lyric proposition, he insists on suspending that knowledge, wouldn't the poem's "intense vision

---

[11] Adam Cohen (2016) reports that in the decision's immediate aftermath, "the number of sterilizations increased sharply, due both to new laws and to an increased willingness to use those that were already in place. In 1925 there were just 322 sterilizations of institutionalized people nationwide. In the two-year period from 1928 through 1929, there were 2,362" (Cohen 301). This figure would eventually rise to 70,000.

The vagueness of the term "feeble-minded" is acknowledged in a 1910 report by the American Association for the Study of the Feeble-Minded, which uses it "generically to include all degrees of mental defect due to arrested or imperfect development as a result of which the person so affected is incapable of competing on equal terms with his normal fellows or managing himself or his affairs with ordinary prudence" (Noll and Trent 2004, 87).

[12] For various expositions of this trope, see McDonagh et al. 2018, Halliwell 2004, Berger 2014, Valente, 2014; Lyon 2012.

of the facts"—the facts of this singular man's lined face, and the supporting facts of his cap and eyes and feet and the three goats and the firehouse and the rain— be sufficient to dissolve the allegorical fiction of the inorganic idiot?

Apparently not. For all his particularity, the figure in the poem remains an instance of the category "idiot"; the poem's "intense vision" has been overridden by the conventional stigmata of crossed eyes and shambling feet. The intensifying adverb "even" simply subsumes, intact, the minor categorical idiot into the major category of mortal aging. In some sense this subsuming is unsurprising, given "idiocy"'s history as a nosological concept tied to the metrics of developmental age—seen, for example, in a portmanteau like "man-child." Williams's figure of an aging idiot may disrupt that truism, but it doesn't displace it. And for this very reason, we can see how the surface of the poem—with its insistence on objective verity, its "no ideas but in things"—in fact relies for its intelligibility upon the submerged ideological connotations of idiocy. In other words, and despite Williams's intentions to the contrary, the surface of this poem simply does not and cannot tell the whole story, for that story requires readerly assumptions about idiocy. The poem's purchase on the everyday, and its insistence on a neutral redescription of the mundane material world of rural America, in other words, is actually secured through the murky cultural doxa surrounding ID; and that ideological doxa rises up to disrupt the surface poetics of objectivity.

However, we should also note that something of a chiasmic nature is simultaneously taking place: the surface of the poem is quietly, persistently disrupting its unreflective ideological grounding. This occurs by way of the *character* of the "idiot," and his emplacement in community. By speaking of character, I do not mean to invoke a conventional literary trope featuring action or individualism; it is quite obvious that the poem has no interest in building up a characterological portrait of the idiot-subject, and in any case the durable moniker "idiot" forecloses the very possibility of character development. But an aspect of the man's character is nevertheless patently available to us by way of surface relationality— specifically, by way of his relation to the three goats, which, it is implied, the man minds faithfully, year after year, even when the rain comes down suddenly in gusts. This character-revealing or character-creating relation of care, exemplified by the man's tending of the goats, is also implied in his enduring proximity to a central community building (the firehouse), and even in the speaker's (and likely, by extension, the community's) daily recognition of the man in the field. This feature of the man's character seems to encroach upon the doctor's gaze, which, though it picks out the man's static isolation, his synechdochal fragmentation (eyes, feet, face, cap) and his inert subordination to the vigorous weather, nevertheless registers his character through overlapping networks of attention and care. And those networks of care are right on the surface of the short poem, though they may be invisible to readers (and even authors) for whom ID is constitutionally opaque and definitively unlovable.

Surface and depth are dynamically inseparable in this poem, but the meaning that they produce in tandem is bound to mean differently for the doctor-poet than for, say, a reader who knows better.

Good Kings Bad Kings

One way to illustrate this surface-depth dynamic is through an example of its opposite, supplied by my second text, Susan Nussbaum's *Good Kings Bad Kings* (2013). This novel treats ID (and disability more generally) as a set of lived experiences made better or worse by institutional interventions. It is entirely narrated in the first person by multiple characters living in or employed at a bleak Chicago institution for disabled teens. These characters relay intersecting stories about care and harm, friendships and abusers, the devastating effects of neoliberal, for-profit disability "care," on the one hand, and the networks of care arising out of crip kinship, advocacy networks, and accessibility movements on the other. The passage I have in mind comes from one of the chapters narrated by Teddy, a twenty-year-old patient who is a great favorite of his peers, wears a rumpled suit every day, and is the boyfriend of a patient named Mia. This is Teddy's account of his own bodymind:

> They told my dad I'm retarded. They told him first at regular school and then when I moved in here. My dad said that's just a word they use that means I got a different way of learning stuff. That's the way I think of it because I sure don't feel retarded. My friend Ryan's retarded and I asked him if he feels retarded and he said no. So I guess I am but I don't notice it. And I look normal except for not walking and my arms not working perfect. (43)

Teddy frankly addresses the puzzling contradiction between his own experience of ordinary wholeness and the slur ("retarded") that is used to negate him. There is almost no question of surface or depth here—or anywhere in the novel for that matter. Like the other narrators, Teddy is forthright and reliable. Like the others, his language is literal, never enigmatic, and he speaks for himself. The disabled narrators are constructed in ways that foreground self-reflective experience rather than fantasies of disability projected by nondisabled authors. (Nussbaum, it should be said, was paralyzed in a bus accident and spent long months in a rehabilitation facility; she spent years researching the novel.) To note all of this is not to make the case that the novel is "good" because it gets representation right and accords its disabled characters the dimensions of authentic and valuable (if often punishing) experience. Rather, it is to observe that on its surface the novel does the work of dialogizing disability and exposing the illogic of stigma, and it does so through characters who not only self-create (through self-narration) but also mutually create (through recognition, care, and the intangibles shared by minority bodyminds in an institution defined by inflexible standards of normalcy). In the passage quoted above, Teddy's musings do the work of dismantling the neurotypical logic that undergirds psychometrics: "retarded" is a word that "they use," because "they" lack the ability to know what they can't measure, or to measure what they can't know. Moreover, "they" make the categorical error common to all psychometric accounts of ID: They reduce to a numerical code a wide range of ontological conditions, and then re-encode a general set of limits accordingly—limits to expectations, to experience, and yes, to well-being. But just as law bears little resemblance to justice, biomeasurement is almost comically ignorant of experience. When Teddy says that he doesn't "feel retarded," he is pointing out the aporia that inheres in psychometrics. Of course he doesn't feel "retarded." He feels like Teddy. Meanwhile the institution's foundational metrical dysfunction, intensified by a neoliberal model of operational efficiency, allows it to mistake its own watered-down clinical "science" for permission to underserve, to abuse, to incarcerate, to annihilate. In short, the pathologies of the novel's related institutions (jail, juvie, psychiatric warehouses, nursing homes) are fully on display across the intertwined stories.

But lest my discussion of *Good Kings Bad Kings* create the impression that it is merely an earnest, reformist novel (which it is), let me add that the novel is much more than that, not least because of its arresting portrayals of institutional life, and its renderings of teenagers crushed in the triple vice of poverty, race, and disability. I teach it regularly in my introductory DS course, and it does more work than all of the assigned critical and theoretical readings combined. Pedagogically, it is especially powerful on two fronts: first, it utterly de-exceptionalizes disability. Characters have sex, smoke cigarettes, run away; characters protect each other and converse with their demons; characters are hilarious and irritated and give zero fucks. They are, in other words, teenagers. And second, in its unfolding treatment of intersectional advocacy, the novel offers a comparative tableau of two kinds of institutions. The first kind—nursing homes, hospitals, warehouses, etc.—are protected by cynical and paternalistic fictions of "well-being." The second kind—growing out of disability advocacy networks and disability law support—make determinations about well-being from the ground zero of access, accommodation, and community. If we were to ask about the eudaimonic value of a novel like *Good Kings Bad Kings*, answers would be found along the twinned paths of affirmation and critique: affirmation of disabled lives, and of disability as a fiercely political, cultural, and phenomenological entity; and critique of the monstrous systems that flourish under the name of disability. Both paths are wrapped up in the hermeneutics of disability, which depends upon critical thinking, and especially upon thinking otherwise about disability and its power to reframe concepts. We (humanists) need to teach novels that do this. Medical and clinical professionals need to read novels that do this. In such an enterprise, we may wish to avail ourselves of The Fries Test, formulated by Kenny Fries as a counterpoint to Alison Bechdel's famous renunciation, in The Bechdel Test, of movies that don't feature at least two women characters who talk to each other about something besides a man/men. The Fries Test asks the following questions:

> Does a work have more than one disabled character? Do the disabled characters have their own narrative purpose other than the education and profit of a nondisabled character? Is the character's disability not eradicated either by curing or killing? (Fries)

Good Kings Bad Kings is on his list.

Census

Jesse Ball's novel *Census* probably wouldn't make Fries's list—it contains only one disabled character, whose direct speech is never recorded and whose activities are obliquely narrated by another character. His "disability" is never named, but his apparent ablebodiedness, coupled with the dehumanizing behavior directed toward him by some characters, suggests that he is neurodiverse in some way. This not-naming is of a piece with the style of the novel more generally, which is reminiscent of Kafka in its fable-like handling of people and places and expository narration. (This style characterizes most of Ball's previous six novels.) Within the textual world of *Census*, the generative powers of ID are accommodated precisely by way of this style. Whereas Williams's brush-like lines of surface description paradoxically lead to the ballast of "idiocy," and Nussbaum's self-disclosing characters discredit "idiocy" by their very existence, Ball's novel gives us a character almost entirely by way of the deliberative thoughts and actions that he produces in other characters, primarily the narrator.

This character is the adult son of the narrator, a retired physician, recently widowed, who has received a terminal medical diagnosis. The narrator decides that he and his son will spend his final days as census-takers, which, in the world of the novel, means traveling to all of the regions of the country (each region is designated by a letter of the alphabet), acquiring information about its inhabitants through home-visit interviews, and then marking each citizen with a small tattoo on a specific rib. They depart in an old car for their census tour. Chapters are divided by alphabetic letters/regions, and although the narrator hopes to survive all the way to Z, he knows that he probably won't. He has made plans to send his son by train back home and into the care of a neighbor when he feels his own death is near.

The author's preface to the novel plunges us directly into a readerly dilemma: Ball informs us that the character of the son is indebted to his own older brother Abram, who had Down syndrome, and died in 1998. In movingly plaintive language, Ball explains the novel's genesis and its central conceit:

> I felt, and feel, that people with Down syndrome are not really understood. What is in my heart when I consider him and his life is something so tremendous, so full of light, that I thought I must write a book that helps people to see what it is to know and love a Down syndrome boy or girl. [...] I didn't see exactly how it could be done, until I realized I would make a book that was hollow. I would place him in the middle of it, and write around him for the most part. He would be there in his effect. (viii)

Ball elaborates on this problem and its solution in an interview: "How would I manage to depict the fullness of the life of my brother, while not stepping on any of the fallacies and land mines of the English language that accompany disability and these lives that are not like the regular life?" The answer was to "constantly imagine a space in which he is present, and describe everything in the space except him, and eventually by doing that as a kind of a negative, he would appear" (Teicher 2018).

Here Ball recognizes Down syndrome (and, we may add, ID more generally) as both a formal problem and an epistemological problem. Ball knows that a textual identification of ID/Down syndrome will almost certainly crowd out the character, effectively "forfeit[ing] any possibility for a full portrait"; at the same time, the novel's project is to show how, in Ball's words, "the way of thinking and feeling that my brother utilized is fundamentally strong, and fundamentally worthwhile, and something that should be paid attention to" (Teicher 2018). The delicate textual space created for that portrait of thinking and feeling—his brother's epistemological realm—is spun by the characters of father and son in dialogue. And the spinning of the space depends upon the interdiction of the eugenic thinking that shadows Down syndrome. (As we have seen with Williams, the erroneous categorical conflation of signs with symptoms—that is, the presumption that mere signs, like "cross-eyed/shamble-footed," can be taken for symptoms of a totality of dysfunction—makes character impossible.) Thus the textual suppression of both diagnosis and physical description enables the narrative emergence of the son. But it also requires a preface that names his "condition." This disclosure thwarts in advance the (seemingly irresistible) hermeneutic game of diagnosis-guessing. Far more consequentially, it directs us to follow the narrator in taking seriously the son's "way of thinking and feeling." Here is an example of that kind of direction, from a conversation between father and son. The father is relating to his son the story of a woman who lived alone on an island and wore a dress made of cormorant feathers; after she was "rescued" from the island, she sang a song in an alien language, which the father relates to his son as they drive through the territory of E.[13] He tells us,

My son did not ask me what the song meant. The reason for this is: he doesn't ask that kind of question. The idea that someone could tell you the meaning of something that is before you—let us assume a thing is before

[13] Although the historical details are not explained in the novel, the story alluded to is that of "the lone woman of San Nicolas Island," a member of the Nicoleño tribe who was inadvertently left behind when missionaries "relocated" her tribe to the Santa Barbara mission in California. She survived alone from 1835 until her discovery and removal in 1853. She wore a dress made of cormorant feathers, and sang a song in her native language which became known as the Toki Toki song. For a journalistic account, see Robinson 2018.

you in its entirety and you do not know its meaning, and so you expect someone to give it to you—this is foreign to him. If there is something completely hidden, of which there is a small part—yes, he might ask. But, looking at a hare or a geode, he would not ask what it means. As well ask what a kaleidoscope means. What does it mean? (63)

The father understands and values his son's way of knowing, which he portrays as quite reasonable and as governed by an ethics of approach: the thing to be known is apprehended on its own terms, rather than categorically or analytically; its surface makes its meaning. (No ideas but in things.) The strange lyrics of the song that the father conveys to the son—"*Toki Toki yahamimena / Toki Toki yahamimena*"—are accepted by the son as sonic entities unto themselves, not as codes to be cracked open.[14] The son's indifference to meaning is different in kind from the stupidity presumed in the abiding (and surprisingly central) philosophical tropes of idiocy that reach historically from Locke's idiot-as-uninscribable-blank-slate to the uncomprehending, resisting idiot reified in some stripes of twentieth-century theory.[15] This son is an agent and a subject: he sings his own songs and arranges possible narratives of his life through the arrangement of family photographs; his conversations with his father (never directly given, but summarized by the father) are wide-ranging—concerning stories about the father's parents, for example, or entailing questions of judgment and expectation, as when he and his father argue about "whether people would be different" in the new territory of L. "Or rather," the father says, "we both agreed that they would be, but he thought they would be nothing like the ones before. I disagreed" (165).

Moreover, the father's recognition and valorization of his son's ways of knowing the world enriches his own life's practices, as a physician and now as a census-taker. (The two jobs come to resemble each other.) The son *affects* the father and is thereby known to us by those *effects*.[16] "I can say truly," the

---

[14] Ball's choice of a geode here is complex, since geodes must be cracked open in order to reveal the crystal formations within. Is the geode being adduced here already cracked open? Or is it a brown, dusty looking egg-like thing (an uncracked geode) whose undramatic appearance is being appreciated on its own terms?

[15] Consider the conceptual persona of "the idiot" formulated by Deleuze and Guattari 1994: they specify a "new idiot" (courtesy of Dostoyevsky's novel) who "wants to turn the absurd into the highest power of thought (62). In Seminar XX ("Encore"), Lacan speaks of "the jouissance of the idiot" (81; sometimes translated as "idiot pleasure"), by which he means phallic solitude that is incapable of "sexual rapport." Bakhtin's concept of carnival is presided over by the idiot and the madwoman (173ff).

[16] Ball explains his stylistic intentions in another interview: "Well, a thing can be known by its particular qualities. But it can also be—a thing can be known by its effect. And so if that's true, we could render a person simply through the effect that that person has on those around him. And that's

father tells us, that "I was a better doctor for having had my son, for it left me with a basic stance—that I should not expect anything in particular from anyone, nor should I underestimate anyone, a humility vested not so much in an appraisal of myself, as in a lack of confidence in valuation and prediction" (151). At the medical level the son has defied the vague, pessimistic prognoses concerning ability that are associated with his "condition" (in contrast to his father's "condition," which is unambiguously predictable, i.e., fatal). At the level of personhood, the son is stalwart and kind, and yet, paradoxically, his mere existence triggers gratuitous cruelty in random strangers. The father declines to relate any of the many incidents of cruelty because, he tells us, "none of them have any character. It is so easy for humans to be cruel, and they leap to it. They love to do it. It is an exercise of all their laughable powers" (41). In the face of this random cruelty, the son stands as an unwitting but highly accurate litmus test for human baseness. The father has learned to expect the manifestations of such baseness, and also manifestations of kindness and respect, but not from anyone in particular.

That the father and son are mutually imbricated in the textuality of the novel—each attached fully to the other, each shadowing and inflecting the reported experiences of the other—illustrates a vibrant material element that is central to any evaluation of well-being and personhood: relations of attachment and care with others.[17] The relations of care that structure this novel—and that we saw from different angles in Williams's poem and in Nussbaum's novel—are central to the lived experience of disability. Michael Davidson nicely sums up this relationality:

> For persons with disabilities, personhood is relational, subject to varying
> criteria of ability and agency. Against restricted versions of embodied

what I decided to try to do. And the reason is that I wanted to avoid all of the cruel and caricatured language that surrounds disability. A word like 'retarded'—people constantly say it, and for years and years I corrected them. But I thought, in this book I'll just show why that word is a fallacy in and of itself" (Gonyea 2018).

[17] Although I have not touched on it in this discussion, the role of the narrator's wife/son's mother is central to the novel's sensitive development of family love/storgē. She is dead when the novel opens, but appears everywhere in the text. A brilliantly creative and successful performance artist, her unconventional genius suits her to parenting their new son. The narrator explains that "No one really knew how to deal with him, how to teach him, in what way to help him. There was a common wisdom that he should be left to his own devices, in essence, ignored. This approach is practically criminal. Luckily . . . my wife was a peculiar individual with a thousand odd thoughts," and she had learned in her performance training the art of patience. "In order to affect another person you perform some action. Then, you must be patient enough to wait for its effect" (150). The wife is never far from the thoughts of the narrator or his son.

personhood, a disability perspective considers the individuals as part of a network of family members, friends, care-givers, and community that troubles the location of impairment in a single individual. (Davidson 2019, viii)

In *Census*, the parent-kin-son network of care is an engine for flourishing and well-being in all of its members. In fact, I would describe one facet of the novel as a narrative elaboration of *storgē*, the least-explored of the many varieties of love typologized by Aristotle. *Storgē* is familial love, love that is inextricably linked to an expectation for care, but I would insist that "family" is a more expansive term than its mere suggestion of progeny. (Like queer kinship, disability kinship moves well beyond the purview of nuclear families, especially when nuclear families are absent or simply cannot be sources of flourishing or support.) Davidson's network components listed above may stand in as a sketch of what "family" might mean. But it is important to note that *storgē*-love, at least according to Aristotle's translators, carries within it a force that is "irrational but moral."[18] Irrational *and* moral, perhaps, in the face of systemic ableism that equates disability with failure. This *storgē*, these networks of care-love, must be taken into account as the creative efflorescences of disability: although they may at times entail pain or sorrow or frustration, they are a great good, a bulwark against contemporary corrosive forces that value productivity, independence, genius, and profit over more nuanced and less ableist signs of flourishing.

Literary texts can show us these signs; a disability hermeneutic not only reveals them in their (fictionalized) contexts, but in doing so it demonstrates the textual power of disability. In texts where disability is present but maligned or exceptionalized/sentimentalized (this latter effect is often referred to as "disability porn"), it invites critical attention to the specious contradictions that inhere in ableism. In texts where disability appears as mere difference, or, more dramatically, through depictions of alternative epistemologies and sensoria, a disability hermeneutic can take the measure of disability's distance from the ablebodied hysteria that produces stigma. In texts where disability is apparently absent, a disability hermeneutic urges us toward an examination of habitual reading practices and communicative norms. We notice disability's unnatural absence, in the first case: we

---

[18] "στβγή [στοργή] is the natural and instinctive affection that subsists between parent and child; irrational, but moral" (Cope 292).

ask, where is disability in all of this? (And then usually discover, as Michael Bérubé has argued, that it is right in front of us, embedded in aesthetics or morals.) In the second case, we begin to notice how communicative norms themselves depend unreflectively on qualities like clarity, balance, and persuasive logic (for example, when exposition or argument are the modes in play). By contrast, we may notice how, in writing deemed literary, language and imagery and aesthetic modes more generally reach again and again toward affect, embodiment, gesture, proximity, inexplicable networks, and complex emotions like *storgē*.

The late disability theorist Tobin Siebers memorably declared that "aesthetics is the science of discerning how some bodies make other bodies feel" (Siebers 2010, 10). If we take on this unconventional meaning—which I am glad to do here—we may wish to include its implications in any attempt to evaluate or promote eudemonia. People with disabilities are not hobbled versions of a normate ideal; nor are they to be disqualified in advance (whether through ignorance or neglect) from considerations of well-being.[19] And those considerations must acknowledge the centrality of care-networks to the cultivation of well-being for all members of the networks—the mutuality of the many co-carers and friends, the cared for, and the society that cultivates their particular conditions of well-being.[20]

Works Cited

Anderson, Amanda. *Psyche and Eros: Moral Life after Psychology*. Oxford, 2018.

Ball, Jesse. *Census*. Ecco, an imprint of Harper Collins, 2018.

Bakhtin, Mikhail. *Problems of Dostoyevsky's Poetics*. Edited and translated by Caryl Emerson, U Minnesota P, 1984.

Barnes, Elizabeth. *The Minority Body: A Theory of Disability*. Oxford, 2016.

Berger, James. *The Disarticulate: Language, Disability, and the Narratives of Modernity*. New York UP, 2014.

[19] Similarly, and as Scott Herring argues in his essay in this collection, those who do not conform to an ideal model of "successful" development—in the case of Herring's study, "successful aging"—may in fact be flourishing under the sign of aberrancy. Hering's reading of the work of A. R. Ammon demonstrates how effectively literary study may help to recover what is lost under the prevalent gerontological assumption that wisdom (and the related properties of sagacity and sapience) is the desirable outcome of aging. Our literary heritage is replete with aged fools who grasp at life with immoderation (W. B. Yeats's "Wild Old Wicked Man" comes to mind) and bumbling elders who, in Hering's words, "revel" in the "vices of senescence."

[20] For a tour de force account of the constitutive relations between disability and care, see Piepzna-Samarasinha 2018, *Care Work*; also see Kittay 2019, *Learning from My Daughter*.

Bérubé, Michael. *The Secret Life of Stories: From Don Quixote to Harry Potter, How Understanding Intellectual Disability Transforms the Way We Read*. New York UP, 2016.

Best, Stephen T., and Sharon Marcus. "Surface Reading: An Introduction." *Representations*, vol. 108, no. 1, 2009, pp. 1–21.

Campbell, Stephen M., and Joseph Stramondo. "The Complicated Relationship of Disability and Well-Being." *Kennedy Institute of Ethics Journal*, vol. 27, no. 2, 2017, pp. 151–84.

Carlson, Licia. *The Faces of Intellectual Disability: Philosophical Reflections*. Indiana UP, 2009.

Cohen, Adam. *Imbeciles: The Supreme Court, American Eugenics, and the Sterilization of Carrie Buck*. Penguin, 2016.

Cope, Edward Meredith. *The Rhetoric of Aristotle*, vol. 1. Cambridge UP, 1877.

Davidson, Michael. *Invalid Modernism: Disability and the Missing Body of the Aesthetic*. Oxford UP, 2019.

Deleuze, Gilles, and Félix Guattari. *What Is Philosophy?* Columbia UP, 1994.

Fries, Kenny. "The Fries Test." https://medium.com/@kennyfries/the-fries-test-on-dis ability-representation-in-our-culture-9d1bad72cc00. Accessed 1 June 2018.

Gonyea, Don. "One Final Road Trip Takes a 'Census' of the Hurt in the World." NPR Weekend Edition, 10 Mar. 2018, https://www.npr.org/2018/03/10/592073879/one-final-road-trip-takes-a-census-of-the-hurt-in-the-world. Accessed 1 June 2018.

Hickey-Moody, Anna. "Slow Life and the Ecologies of Sensation." *Feminist Review*, no. 111, 2018, pp. 140–48.

Halliwell, Martin. *Images of Idiocy: The Idiot Figure in Modern Fiction and Film*. Routledge, 2004.

Jameson, Fredric. *The Political Unconscious: Narrative as a Socially Symbolic Act*. Cornell UP, 1981.

Keller, Lynn. *Re-Making It New: Contemporary Modernist Poetry and the Modernist Tradition*. Cambridge UP, 1987.

Kittay, Eva Feder. *Learning from My Daughter: The Value and Care of Disabled Minds*. Oxford UP, 2019.

Kittay, Eva Feder. *Love's Labor: Essays on Women, Equality, and Dependency*. Routledge, 1999.

Lacan, Jacques. *The Seminar of Jacques Lacan*. Book XX, "Encore: On Feminine Sexuality, The Limits of Love and Knowledge, 1972–1973." Translated by Bruce Fink, Norton, 1998.

Lyon, Janet. "On the Asylum Road with Woolf and Mew." *Modernism/Modernity*, vol. 18, no. 3, 2012, pp. 551–74.

McDonagh, Patrick. *Idiocy: A Cultural History*. Liverpool UP, 2008.

McDonagh, Patrick, et, C. F. Goodey, and Tim Stinton, editors. *Intellectual Disability: A Conceptual History, 1200–1900*. Manchester UP, 2018.

Noll, Steven, and James W. Trent Jr., editors. *Mental Retardation in America: A Historical Reader*. New York UP, 2004.

Nussbaum, Susan. *Good Kings Bad Kings*. Algonquin Books of Chapel Hill, 2013.

Pawelski, James O. "Bringing Together the Humanities and the Science of Well-Being to Advance Human Flourishing." *Well-Being and Higher Education: A Strategy for Change and the Realization of Education's Greater Purpose*, edited by Donald Howard, Association of American Colleges and Universities, 2016, pp. 207–16.

Pawelski, James O. "Defining the 'Positive' in Positive Psychology: Part II, A Normative Analysis." *Journal of Positive Psychology*, vol. 11, no. 4, 2016, pp. 357–65.

Piepzna-Samarasinha, Leah Lakshmi. *Care Work: Dreaming Disability Justice.* Arsenal Pulp Press, 2018.

Robinson, Joe. "Marooned." *Los Angeles Times*, 15 June 2004, https://www.latimes.com/style/la-os-island15jun15-story.html. Accessed 1 June 2018.

Sandel, Michael. "The Case against Perfection," *The Atlantic*, April 2004, https://www.theatlantic.com/magazine/archive/2004/04/the-case-against-erfection/302927/. Accessed 1 June 2018.

Seligman, Martin E. P., and Mihaly Csikszentmihalyi. "Positive Psychology: An Introduction." *American Psychologist*, vol. 55, no. 1, 2000, pp. 5–14.

Siebers, Tobin. *Disability Aesthetics.* U Michigan P, 2010.

Simplican, Stacy Clifford. *The Capacity Contract: Intellectual Disability and the Question of Citizenship.* U Minnesota P, 2015.

Teicher, Craig Morgan. "Interview with Jesse Ball." *Publishers Weekly*, Feb. 2018, https://www.publishersweekly.com/pw/by-topic/authors/profiles/article/75970-jesse-ball-s-next-novel-pays-a-loving-brotherly-tribute.html. Accessed 1 June 2018.

Tremain, Shelley. *Foucault and Feminist Philosophy of Disability* (Corporealities: Discourses of Disability). U Michigan P, 2017.

Valente, Joseph. "The Accidental Autist: Neurosensory Disorder in *The Secret Agent*." *Journal of Modern Literature*, vol. 38, no. 1, 2014, pp. 20–37.

Williams, Jeffrey. "The New Modesty in Literary Studies." *Chronicle of Higher Education*, January 5, 2015.

Williams, William Carlos. *The Collected Poems of William Carlos Williams, Vol. I, 1909–1939.* Edited by A. Walton Litz and Christopher MacGowan, New Directions, 1991.

8

Wise Old Fools

Positive Geropsychology and the Poetics of Later-Life Floundering

Scott Herring

For all of its attention to the mind, positive psychology remains preoccupied with the body, and the aging body at that. In its initial throes, the movement distinguished itself from abnormal psychology by accentuating not only happiness in human consciousness but the human body's capacity to maximize positive states of flourishing. Before and after its institutionalization, such aims bolstered what the Positive Psychology Manifesto referenced as "the scientific study of optimal human functioning" (n.p.). A founder of positive psychology and a coauthor of this statement, Mihaly Csikszentmihalyi, noted in *Flow: The Psychology of Optimal Experience* (1990) that anyone could tap "unlimited powers of the mind" at the same time that "the joy of surpassing the limits of the body is open to all" (25, 97). In the introduction to their special issue of *American Psychologist* (2000), Csikszentmihalyi and Martin E. P. Seligman prophesied a decade later that positive psychology "may make the lives of clients physically healthier, given all that psychologists are learning about the effects of mental well-being on the body" (8). Other advocates then went further to suggest that positive flow could lead to life extension. As a fellow Manifesto drafter proclaimed in an *American Scientist* article: "there are benefits to personal health, development and longevity, as well as evolutionary reasons why human beings experience positive emotions" (Fredrickson 331).[1] Whether or not you now encounter its popularized ethos at a bookstore or at a senior center, one can see why such claims

---

[1] Fredrickson makes a similar claim in an interview with Angela Winter (2010), pointing to "stunning correlations between expressing more positive emotions and living longer" (Winter n.p.). See, also, Horowitz's critique, which summarizes that "happier people were [felt to be] more productive, creative, and effective; not only were they healthier, but they also lived longer" (166).

Scott Herring, *Wise Old Fools* In: *Literary Studies and Human Flourishing*. Edited by: James F. English and Heather Love, Oxford University Press. © Oxford University Press 2023. DOI: 10.1093/oso/9780197637227.003.0009

garner an international following: Do it for your life, the story goes, and you prolong the one life you got. What's to lose but years of living in our era of "new longevity" (Carstensen 10)?

A personal investment in positive psychology's outlooks can, indeed, compound during later life. With longevity but one outcome of its wellness programs, its founders esteem the wisdom that these aging bodies can amass. Csikszentmihalyi and Seligman find, for example, that "individual strengths unfold over an entire life span" and that "wisdom is one of the most prized traits in all cultures" (8, 11). Referencing prominent American gerontologists such as G. Stanley Hall and Bernice Neugarten as well as German psychologist Paul Baltes, the two present positive psychology as finishing what Hall started with his *Senescence*, "a model of wisdom in aging as far back as 1922" (11). Baltes—an advocate for "successful aging" discourses—likewise casts wisdom in the aged as a pillar of positive psychology and describes it in *Flow*-like terms as the "search for a perfect synergy of mind and character" (Baltes and Staudinger 132). Seen in this light, positive psychology unlocks the fullest moral and intellectual potential of the aging body's aging mind.

That wisdom is a desired outcome for aging well has become commonplace within what some shorthand as *positive geropsychology* or *positive aging*.[2] It has also infused literary studies of well-being. I have in mind philosopher James O. Pawelski and literary scholar D. J. Moores's *The Eudaimonic Turn: Well-Being in Literary Studies* (2013) and the edited collection *On Human Flourishing: A Poetry Anthology* (2015). The former considers wisdom "among the things we value most in life" (9). With Pawelski and Moores serving as two of its six coeditors, the latter gives wisdom pride of place by situating it first in a litany of positive character traits embodied in poems by William Wordsworth, Emily Dickinson, Alexander Pushkin, and others. Interestingly, *On Human Flourishing*'s selection from Pushkin— "God, Don't Let Me Lose My Mind" (1833)—promotes wise reasoning not for mental benefits alone but for fear of social stigma and incarceration: "But here's the rub: lose your mind, / And you will be frightening like the plague, / You will be locked up straight away, / They will chain and brand you, a fool" (31). Written before psychology's advent in the later nineteenth century, Pushkin's poem presciently diagnoses how mental states often go hand in

---

[2] See Fernández-Ballesteros et al.; and Freund and Baltes.

hand with moral dictates. Threats of social shackle (looking like "a fool") match threats of imprisonment with no clarity about which is the greater punishment.

Such lines also hint at a more intricate social system than positive psychology's proponents suggest when they value—overvalue, I argue— wisdom as a late-life virtue. As a humanist working part-time in literary studies of aging, I fully share their commitment to elderly bodies all too often scoffed at in contemporary cultures. But numerous critics remain chary of age norms to which positive psychology weds itself, and I am curious what literary gerontology brings to the table as both a critique of—and a compeer to—what one historian refers to as "wisdom traditions" (McMahon).[3] More than four decades of literary gerontology has, in fact, wondered what amounts to proper or improper aging in the first place. Following their lead, I ask: what does positive geropsychology's emphasis on aging-as-expertise oversimplify? What does its focus on wisdom as late-life flourishing foreclose that literary studies of aging might reinstall?

By answering these two queries this chapter conjures a peaceable kingdom for the subfields of literary gerontology and positive geropsychology. It details how literary aging invites creative forms of ignorance and nonmastery often dismissed as unfortunate foolishness or lamentable decline. With wisdom seen as optimal flourishing, such traits may deter normative aging, but floundering can also sponsor startling forms of resilience. I detail a wise old fool who confirms this last claim later in my piece. First, I further review how positive psychology's advocates frequently favor wisdom as the gold standard for a long life and downgrade other character traits. I next turn to literary age critics who advance models of geriatric flourishing that champion blunder alongside sagacity. I conclude with a brief reading of a deceased American poet who, in his seventies, confirms theories in literary gerontology. Written in 1996 and posthumously published almost a decade later, A. R. Ammons's lines of wise foolishness blur distinctions between flourishing and floundering in the time of optimized aging. Nowhere near perfect, this septuagenarian managed to age just well enough, even as "wisdom and catatonia appear to / exchange places occasionally" (64).

---

[3] For critiques of successful aging, see Holstein and Minkler 2003; Lamb et al. 2017; and Ehrenreich 2018.

The Wisdom/Foolishness Binary

Around the same time that Csikszentmihalyi published *Flow*, protopositive iterations of psychology identified "wisdom as a key component of resilience in old age" (Clark et al. 53). Baltes and his colleagues took the lead here by asserting in a series of 1991 lectures that wisdom was inextricable from "mastering old age" and clarified it as "expert knowledge in the fundamental pragmatics of life permitting exceptional insight and judgment involving complex and uncertain matters of the human condition" (Baltes et al. 1992: 124, 136). A year prior to this publication, Baltes coauthored a companion piece with Jacqui Smith in intelligence theorist Robert J. Sternberg's *Wisdom: Its Nature, Origins, and Development*. Proposing the exact same definition, the two acknowledged that, hypothetically, anyone could acquire wisdom at any point along the human lifespan but agreed that "among wise persons there may be a disproportionately large number of older individuals" (112–13).[4]

Long-standing associations between elderly individuals and hard-earned knowledge in modern Western cultures are not uncommon, but I draw attention to how connections between extraordinary knowledge and later life became "a viable topic for scientific psychological research" as well as one of positive psychology's chief objectives for older persons (Baltes and Smith 113). Researchers not only found wisdom to be demonstrably more prevalent in aging populations. They also sought to show how it might be cultivated for individual and societal improvement. Psychological studies of wisdom were thus thought to enrich late life as well as foster the transmission of expert knowledge to subsequent generations—presumably a win-win proposition for the young, the old, and those reaching what Louise Glück once referred to as "that time of life / people prefer to allude to in others / but not in themselves" (22).

Subsequent iterations of these claims saturated books aimed at specialists and nonspecialists alike.[5] In step with Baltes's and his fellow researchers' use of superlatives, hyperbolized adjectives suggesting unequaled performance crop up across these publications: "exceptional understanding, superior judgment, general competence in decision making, excellent communication skills, and social ease" (Hill 69). A faith in perfectibility, or what two

[4] See also Birren and Fisher. For a rejoinder to these findings in the same volume, see Meacham.
[5] A sampling includes Hill; Edmondson; Zacher and Staudinger; Lavretsky; and Haidt.

European psychologists reference as "the notion of a perfect integration of mind and virtue that presupposes many years of life," often stands out (Moraitou and Efklides 189). Wisdom as perfected knowledge was thus endorsed as an apex of psychological development. Its acquisition signaled a hallmark of *mature* individuals in both senses of that adjective: those entering older age (conventionally defined as 65+) and those maximizing their mental capacities (*gerotranscendence* is the neologism describing such positive aging).

I respect the wish for better days in later years behind these writings. I do not want to broad-brush their often nuanced claims. Yet once wisdom figures as perfectible proficiency, traits that fall outside this schema can depreciate. A distilled visualization of this scenario appears in the late Christopher Peterson's essay "The Values in Action (VIA) Classification of Strengths," an elaboration of a collaboration with Seligman titled the "Manual of the Sanities" (qtd. in Peterson and Seligman 4). In his piece Peterson includes an influential document, a table titled "Classification of Psychological Disorders," that unintentionally codifies a virtue/vice binary with wisdom/foolishness included in the mix (Figure 8.1). I write *unintentionally* because Peterson originally meant these classifications to function "along a continuum" (38), and he noted that "these disorders (and the corresponding strengths) exist in degrees" as his table outlined twenty-four strengths and virtues juxtaposed with their "absence," "opposite," and "exaggeration" (38, 39).

Given that the table itself presents a column of virtues as, well, virtuous and other characteristics as "disorders," one can see how the Classification of Psychological Disorders could unwittingly tip over into moralistic pathologization (39). Even Peterson intuited this possibility. In the chapter from which I quote, he finds that

> the labels I have chosen are unambiguously moral in flavor, yet as noted, this is only an apparent shortcoming of my classification. After all, people with psychological disorders are annoying, alarming, or offensive. Essentially, every linguistic analysis of "abnormality" arrives at this conclusion (e.g., Peterson, 1996). Rather than arguing in vain that my classification is value-neutral, I prefer to say that it is value-informed and to suggest that more productive lines of inquiry would ask who is annoyed, alarmed, or offended by these ways of behaving and why. (40)

Table 2.2. Classification of Psychological Disorders

Strength	Absence	Opposite	Exaggeration
	Disorders of Wisdom and Knowledge		
Creativity	Conformity	Triteness	Eccentricity
Curiosity/Interest	Disinterest	Boredom	Morbid curiosity/ Nosiness
Judgment/Critical thinking	Unreflectiveness	Gullibility	Cynicism
Love of learning	Complacency	Orthodoxy	Know-it-all-ism
Perspective	Shallowness	Foolishness	None*
	Disorders of Courage		
Bravery	Fright/Chicken Little-ism	Cowardice	Foolhardiness
Persistence	Laziness	Helplessness	Obsessiveness
Authenticity/Honesty	Phoniness	Deceipt	Righteousness
Vitality	Restraint	Lifelessness	Hyperactivity
	Disorders of Love		
Intimacy	Isolation/Autism	Loneliness/Avoidance of commitment	Emotional promiscuity
Kindness	Indifference	Cruelty/Mean-spiritedness	Intrusiveness
Social intelligence	Obtuseness/ Cluelessness	Self-deception	Psychobabble
	Disorders of Justice		
Citizenship	Selfishness	Narcissism	Chauvinism
Fairness	Partisanship	Prejudice	Detachment
Leadership	Compliance	Disruptiveness/ Sabotage	Despotism
	Disorders of Temperance		
Forgiveness/Mercy	Mercilessness	Vengefulness	Permissiveness
Humility/Modesty	Footless Self-esteem	Arrogance	Self-deprecation
Prudence	Sensation seeking	Recklessness	Prudishness/ Stuffiness
Self-regulation	Self-indulgence	Impulsivity	Inhibition
	Disorders of Transcendence		
Appreciation of beauty/Excellence	Oblivion	*Schadenfreude*-ism	Snobbery
Gratitude	Rugged individualism	Entitlement	Ingratiation
Hope	Present orientation	Pessimism/Despair	Pollyannaism
Humor	Humorlessness	Dourness	Buffoonery
Spirituality	Anomie	Alienation	Fanaticism

*I am willing to be convinced otherwise, but I think it is impossible to have too much perspective.

Figure 8.1 Christopher Peterson, "Table 2.2. Classification of Psychological Disorders," in *A Life Worth Living: Contributions to Positive Psychology*, edited by Mihaly Csikszentmihalyi and Isabella Selega Csikszentmihalyi (Oxford UP, 2006), 39.

I am on the same page with the second half of this observation regarding societal considerations of non-normative behavior. But I still worry that this "value-informed" table resumes what positive psychology imagined it supplemented—classifications of abnormal mental states that guide *DSM* thinking as well as Peterson's own *Psychology of Abnormality* (1996). I also fret that its subsequent adopters fail to consider that some opposites of its listed strengths might be strengths in and of themselves. Once we approach Peterson's table as "24 strengths, that generates 72 (3 x 24) pathologies," I mean to say, we can slip into oversimplification (Seligman 4).

There is also, I sense, a tension between the table's "systematic" format, which flattens into an easily digestible and easily reproducible document, and Peterson's more nuanced elaborations in the essay itself (38). Take the table's delineation of "Disorders of Wisdom and Knowledge." Embracing character strengths such as "creativity," "love of learning," and "perspective," it labels other traits such as "boredom," "eccentricity," "unreflectiveness," and "foolishness" as deviations (39). From one interpretive vantage point, these latter states of mind can appear as personality flaws or even mental disorders. When condensed into a table, a continuum of characterological traits thus potentially reproduces an abnormality/normality binary under a different guise: a virtue/vice dualism whereby the foolish, the weird ("eccentricity"), the blasé ("boredom"), the rubberneckers ("morbid curiosity/nosiness"), and the mimickers ("triteness") find themselves on the wrong side of the tracks (39).[6]

While aging goes unmentioned in Peterson's table, we nonetheless witness how a wisdom/expertise and foolishness/ignorance dualism can graft onto other binaries: moral/immoral; strength/weakness; normal/abnormal; good/bad; well/unwell; optimal/suboptimal; positive/negative. Considering wisdom as a virtue paints other alternatives of knowing like boredom or cynicism as a vice—or as evidence of a mental disorder. Considering wisdom as expertise likewise casts a long shadow on those late-lifers who have to keep learning the same lesson over and over again. If you agree that the table should be read in terms of virtues and pathologies, then a good late life appears inseparable from being a normal, right-minded late-lifer. Yet we need to remember that these successfully aged seniors (as I elsewhere argued

---

[6] Horowitz usefully charts a social history of these shifts in positive psychology, especially when he delineates how "character, as a key to a meaningful life, was prominent among the issues present as a relatively minor note before and that now came to the fore among positive psychologists" (189).

in analyses of *DSM-5*'s new mental disorders such as Hoarding Disorder) rely upon societal age norms that stigmatize their inverse: the thoughtlessly aged; the subpar coper; the buffoon. I happily grant that some geropsychologists propose "selective optimization with compensation" to loosen these hierarchized binaries and that Peterson intended a flexible schema, but it is not hard to see how traits that positive psychology associates with optimal aging can feel like cruel optimization to some (Baltes and Baltes 21).[7] As it explicitly and implicitly addresses longevity, age consciousness, and ageism, the field's perceived wisdom about wisdom as a positive character trait raises a question: What, if any, are the hidden benefits to over-the-hill folly?

The Prospects of Literary Age Studies

In one form or another literary studies of aging asks a version of my last question. A component of critical age studies (a multidisciplinary inquiry into how cultures represent human life spans), literary gerontology or literary aging is a decades-long enterprise initiated in the 1970s. Traditionally, it works against platitudes that mischaracterize later life as a chronological period best spent mastering the art of social and psychic disengagement. It shares positive geropsychology's desire to facilitate flourishing within and beyond middle age, but several of its thinkers complicate a positive/negative binary in terms of fitting traits for mature well-being. None of its foundational voices (Margaret Morganroth Gullette, Linda Hutcheon and Michael Hutcheon, Kathleen Woodward, Eve Kosofsky Sedgwick, Wayne Booth) assume aging to be a walk in the park. They instead offer guideposts to later life that support emotional and epistemological registers within and beyond age norms that push primarily, if not exclusively, for lifelong expertise or incomparable knowledge.

Foremost in these undertakings is feminist literary and cultural critic Kathleen Woodward. Woodward initially launched her career in literary aging with somewhat idealized interpretations of "a new hero, the wise old man, in a society that worships youth" in her monograph *At Last, the Real Distinguished Thing: The Late Poems of Eliot, Pound, Stevens, and Williams* (1980) (6). She originally dwelled on this figure to shed light on how

---

[7] As my allusion to their work testifies, this chapter's findings owe much to Berlant.

modernist poetics faced off against evolving norms of twentieth-century ageism. Over subsequent decades her scholarship moved beyond this patriarchal sage with writings such as her edited collection *Figuring Age: Women, Bodies, Generations* (1999) and *Statistical Panic: Cultural Politics and Poetics of the Emotions* (2009). Nowhere is this shift more apparent than in an understudied chapter, "Against Wisdom: Anger and Aging," in the latter work. Anchored in close readings of Hall's *Senescence* and Betty Friedan's *The Fountain of Age* (1993), her chapter straightforwardly states that "it is time to declare a moratorium on wisdom" and contends that "wisdom should not be advocated as an emotional (or unemotional) standard or ideal" (74). In her desire for more ire in the aged—for not canceling out what my thesaurus lists as *annoyance, irritation, infuriation, antagonism,* and *resentment* in later life—Woodward also challenges "wisdom as a developmental capacity" and its "connotation of dignified behavior" (74, 75). She maintains that default wisdom cultivation precludes "a new way of thinking (and thus being in the world), a new mode of cognition, [which] may emerge in old age" (*At Last* xii).

Writing as a midlifer, I take from Woodward that as we age we need not know best, even though I do not want to completely toss out wisdom. Pushing her argument further, I am curious about modes of late-life being that fall under classifications of unwisdom and obliquity. Simpatico with Woodward, the writings of another literary critic, Eve Kosofsky Sedgwick, help with this task given that Sedgwick theorized "a senile sublime" in the last decade of her life: "more or less intelligible performances by old brilliant people, whether artists, scientists, or intellectuals, where the bare outlines of a creative idiom seem finally to emerge from what had been the obscuring puppy fat of personableness, timeliness, or sometimes even of coherent sense" (24). In this cross-disciplinary model of aging, heightened intellect or what Woodward sees as heightened "developmental capacity" are far from the end goal: four sentences after she defines "a senile sublime," Sedgwick affirms "cognitive frustration" (*Statistical* 74, 24).

Several years prior to promoting such senility, Sedgwick presented herself as a queer lifespan theorist and asked fellow literary critics to think beyond standardized life narratives. In her 1997 reading of Proust's *In Search of Lost Time*, she extrapolates that longevity is often unviable for individuals such as her middle-aged self "living with advanced breast cancer" (148). She then casts doubt on the idea that aging wisely should assist both the self and subsequent generations by instead embracing "the present fullness of a becoming whose arc may extend no further" (149). "Arc" here is synonymous with life-span, and at the time she published these words Sedgwick tried to trouble "the regular schedule of the generations" affirmed by late-twentieth-century heteronormativity (149).

Like Woodward's comments on wisdom, Sedgwick's remarks are valuable counterweights to the counterweight that positive psychology thinks itself. In this same piece that discusses Proust, Sedgwick also refuses to dichotomize too strictly between aging wisely and aging foolishly. Two paragraphs prior to her citation of how Proust's narrator " 'began to understand what old age was,' " she shares correspondence with Joseph Litvak, a Victorianist who also works in queer studies and Jewish studies, on what he refers to as "the importance of 'mistakes' in queer reading and writing" (qtd. on 148, 147). These blunders are, for Litvak, part and parcel of many a queer lifespan. Affirming that what Peterson devalues as "know-it-all-ism" is often a survival strategy for queer youth (39), Litvak then asserts that, "later on," some queers get good at "practices aimed at taking the terror out of error, at making the making of mistakes sexy, creative, even cognitively powerful" (147).

Sedgwick reprints Litvak's remarks to give her readers a taste of reading practices that enable "queer possibility," but his words also apply to age matters. Embedded in Litvak's literary theory of reading is, I believe, a queer theory of aging and maturation that advocates for what gerontologists would dub diverse adult developmental paths. Such paths are fundamentally mistake-prone and mistake-laden ways of flourishing in the world across whatever counts for a lifetime. Highly variable, they refute the perfectibility of knowledge as they entertain what Litvak terms "the traumatic, inevitable-seeming connection between mistakes and humiliation" (147). To follow them out is to look a fool, but for those of us getting on they can be lifesavers.

In line with Sedgwick's subsequent endorsement of "cognitive frustration," then, what happens when we approach foolishness as a "more or less" positive trait for senior well-being, or if we entertain nonexpert, nonstandardized ways of growing older that shirk wise mastery as a terminal objective? Floundering, for some, is a form of semioptimal flourishing, and a lifetime full of repeated mistakes may be a psychic good. While many understandably find comfort in the unlimited potential that positive geropsychology promises, Sedgwick and Litvak remind us that there are sustainable possibilities that do not culminate in utmost insight; that are open-ended rather than finalized; that wind up right back at square one. Like Woodward's refusal to venerate calm, Sedgwick invites less severe readings of those who err, goof, stumble, and flounder, or those who keep at it and keep getting it wrong. Their mental states or moral characters should not be pathologized, and a similar logic also applies to their aging selves. Rather than amplifying functional or cognitive mastery, a recognition that bones, ligaments, teeth, hearts, and headspaces break down over time may take the edge off optimization ideals. Some may achieve what counts for wise thinking and I wish them the best, but does this necessarily entail that we penalize others for "cognitive frustration"—for voluntarily or involuntarily inhabiting this state in their later life?

What these literary gerontologists together share, I sense, is an allegiance to senescent variation in all of its supposed flaws.[8] Cast in this light, the "confusions, tensions, and inconsistencies" that positive geropsychology strives to purge may enable "good rather than bad surprises" (Pawelski, "Part II," 359; Sedgwick 147). If we accept Pawelski's observation that it is "paradoxically difficult to separate the two completely," we might train our sights on those who straddle the binary of wisdom/foolishness rather than stamp out half of it ("Part I" 347). Having allowed for an imperfect world of unwisdom, we may well contest the surety of the cliché that there's no fool like an old fool.

A. R. Aamons: A Case Study

After charting how literary aging conceivably amends the wisdom traditions of positive geropsychology, I note that gerontological literatures themselves—as much as criticism in literary gerontology—schematize those faltering through late life's unknowns. Fools, Folly, and Vice are, of course, mocked and beloved figures across centuries of non-Western and Western literature. One of the most exhaustive records of these individuals, Enid Welsford's *The Fool: His Social and Literary History* (1935), begins, for instance, with fourth-century Persian oral traditions, all the while confirming that "the fool's resilience" facilitates "a birth of new joy and freedom" (319).[9] My chapter cannot do full justice to this ongoing global tradition of "fool-literature," but as a

---

[8] I echo a point made by Linda Hutcheon, a literary critic, and Michael Hutcheon, a physician, who jointly find that "no generalized late-style discourse can encompass all the variety of individual artists' careers, creative work, and reception" (55).

[9] Welsford's treasure trove of literary fools matches any contemporary age theorist as she repeatedly considers "the paradoxical reversal of wisdom and folly" (263–64).

scholar versed in modern American literature I spotlight post–World War II works such as lesbian feminist Adrienne Rich's "Contradictions: Tracking Poems," which acknowledges "badly-done exercises / acts of the heart forced to question / its presumptions in this world" (Welsford 241, 172). Or an unnamed persona in Gwendolyn Brooks's "weaponed woman" who finds that "life has been a baffled vehicle / And baffling" but manages to do "Rather Well" with "the stiff / Frost of her face" (125).[10]

These two poets appear in Wayne Booth's *The Art of Growing Older: Writers on Living and Aging* (1992), a moving anthology of literature, visual culture, criticism, and personal reflection which testifies to the intricacies of later life from Sappho to May Sarton. Canvassing ancient Roman satirists such as Juvenal, Harlem Renaissance avant-gardists like Langston Hughes, and psychologists such as B. F. Skinner, Booth's collection considers those who have not yet figured it out by reviewing well-known writers who often flounder through later life. In a rather Sedgwickian observation, Booth cautions that we "must tread lightly" when esteeming aged wisdom, and his collection overflows with artists who may not have expert knowledge but still exhibit "ironic complexities that . . . risk downright inconsistency or incoherence" (237, 254).

With his posthumous publication *Bosh and Flapdoodle* (2005) released thirteen years after Booth's *The Art of Growing Older*, it is hard to find a better promoter for this particular "art of growing older" than poet A. R. Ammons (1926–2001). Writing lines that turn floundering at age seventy into an art form rather than a disgrace, this formerly rural working-class white male who became one of America's more lauded poets during his thirty-four-year tenure at Cornell University agrees with the literary gerontologists I cited above. Ammons, it turns out, is quite wise about being quite dumb, and the title of his poetry collection is itself a giveaway. Largely synonymous with each other, *bosh* and *flapdoodle* denote nonsense while the latter term can also mean "foolish talk" and "a fool" (*Collins*, "Flapdoodle"; *Oxford*, "Flapdoodle"). With this clever title, we find Ammons lyrically performing the fool in a departure from earlier masterworks such as *Corsons Inlet* (1965). Super-sharp about how we lose sharpness, his gerontological literature is nonsense poetry whereby aged mastery may be hard for some to extract but

---

[10] Another poem by Brooks, "The Crazy Woman," reverberates in my head: "I'll wait until November. / That is the time for me. / I'll go out in the frosty dark / And sing most terribly" (99). To further augment this genealogy of Black literary aging and vernacular foolishness, see the folk tale "A Flying Fool," in which the titular character figures as elderly.

resilience is still there for the taking—even if such resilience means barely getting out of bed in the morning.

Set in and around Ithaca, New York, near the close of a calendar year, *Bosh and Flapdoodle* would seem to offer negative examples to many a geropsychologist. Its sixty-eight poems literally and figuratively thematize the final seasons of life as the collection passes through the winter solstice. Permit me citational indulgence to give you a taste of its not-so-nonsensical foolishness. "Wetter Beather": "but my talent is so expired / that I need not trouble myself with digital // advances, I merely amuse myself in the comfort / of my own surrounding ignorance" (89). "Focal Lengths": "I'm largely a big joke: if somebody else / doesn't make a crack about me, I do" (39). "Mouvance": "I myself have never / known what to do about anything: as I look // back, I see not even a clown but a clown's / clothes flapping on the clothesline of some // tizzy" (65).[11] "Widespread Implications": "how like a sail set out from harbor // hitting the winds I flounder this way and that" (109). Still other poems do the same as Ammons self-identifies as one of the "old fools" who "can't tell where they are / sometimes" (106). While the English Renaissance jester Tom Fool (Tom Skelton) is long thought to haunt Muncaster Castle in Cumbria, he and his balderdash frequent these pages too. "Tom Fool" is, in fact, the title of one of the last poems in this collection.

Situating themselves in this lineage, Ammons's doddering personae tussle with late modern age norms and their accompanying longevity promises. Toying with the genre's emphasis on daybreak, his "Aubade" centers on random thoughts about his aged well-being while sitting down to break-fast: "They say, lose weight, change your lifestyle: / that's, take the life out of your style and // the style out of your life: give up fats, / give up sweets, chew rabbit greens, raw: and // how about carrots: raw: also, wear your / hipbones out walking" (21). Uninterested in eat-your-vegetables instructions, he sees the unnamed "they" of wellness routines as subtractive rather than additive, decreasing esprit even as they purport to extend biological existence a wee bit further.

Observing that "one's / own body molds away or flakes off in pasty / chunks," Ammons does not long for more improvement as he embodies de-clension (120). With the Fountain of Youth nowhere in sight, he finds good company. Others like him are aging okay, all things considered, and rather than correct amputees with Type 2 diabetes, those with forgetfulness, and

---

[11] See Fogel for more on Ammons's clown persona.

those who need assisted living—all mentioned in "In View of the Fact"—
he finds that they may all be fading but not so fast. Far from reaching their
peaks, Ammons is "hanging on with a grip" as others like him are "not giving
up on the / congestive heart failure or brain tumors" (30). Intentionally or
no, these individuals collectively disappoint the modern ideals that advance
long-lasting well-being: "we never // thought we would live forever (although
we did) / and now it looks like we won't" (29).

Recognizing that "great sayers" often "say nothing," the cumulative effect of *Bosh and Flapdoodle*'s poetic meanderings is to confirm without
pathologizing "our ignorance with the world," to dissolve distinctions between serene insight and stupor as "wisdom and catatonia appear to / exchange places occasionally," and to withhold judgment on those seniors
who acquire little judgment (64). Clowning around upstate New York in a
personal winter during the last decade of the twentieth century, Ammons
refutes any superiority of perspective: "this way of // seeing things is just a
way of seeing things" (52).[12] In so doing this laughingstock embeds himself
in a genealogy of old fools which starts not only with Tom Fool but the dawn
of mankind. "We're all so / recent," he marvels five years before he died of
cancer on February 25, 2001 (52).

It is worth mentioning that *Bosh and Flapdoodle*'s stylistics buttress the
volume's late-life perspective. In early middle age Ammons theorized that his
postmodern poetics had psyches and somata. "A poem is not simply a mental
activity," he claimed in 1968. "It has body, rhythm, feeling, sound, and mind,
conscious and subconscious" ("Poem" 16). Implicitly repeating this thesis
again in 1996, his creaky craft mirrors his worn-out hips. Embracing both
corporeal and aesthetic deficiency with all the accompanying cognates (frustration, limitation, imperfection), he admits that "I / confess now to some
interest in good bad // writing"—*Bosh and Flapdoodle* included (151). Like
their creator, his poems each have an aging body with a not-exactly-positive
geropsychology.

None the wiser and unconcerned about any mistake-making, this poetic flailing is also a precondition for something that starts to look like loopy
grace as "the disjunctiveness of my // recent verse cracks up the dark cloud"

---

[12] As such, Ammons exhibits what anthropologist Jason Danely, in a discussion of aging and contemporary Japan, characterizes as "foolish vitality," or "the playful, unashamed, acceptance of old
age, wrinkles and all. It brings together the joy, creativity, and liberation found when one no longer
resists the signs of aging, and even comes to embrace them in ways that are silly and saucy but not
self-deprecatory or ageist" (157). I appreciate Danely's humane vision, but I am also interested in
foolishness as unwisdom. I grant, however, that Ammons's poetics blur these distinctions.

(51–52). *Bosh and Flapdoodle*'s closing poem bears out this claim with an invocation—"make room for the great presence of nothing"—that ends with capitalized gibberish: "DRAB POT" (158, 159). True to the collection's title, "drab pot" is nonsense. But with Ammons as a self-styled clown it is also a gut punch of a last line. From one perspective, "DRAB POT" describes Ammons mired in less desirable states of aging with pot meaning "the pit of hell" (*Oxford English*, "Pot"). From another it signals an ambivalence about growing older, a process which can be dull/"drab" as well as a treasure/"pot." Or it could refer to Ammons's pot belly at age seventy. Or "DRAB POT" could be his refusal to end up TOP BARD. While blatherskite, "DRAB POT" is also a semordnilap. Reversing the highest recognition—or the highest possible achievement—of his chosen profession as an elderly poet and claiming instead an imperfect, dulled paunchiness for *Bosh and Flapdoodle*'s final words, this phrase adds up to something "wonderful" even if it's not exactly clear what that wonderful something is (152).

How is this not an old brilliant performance made possible thanks to Ammons's tomfoolery? Dumbfounded by where his late life has brought him, he differs with George Vaillant, who claims in *The Wisdom of the Ego* that "fulfilling the role of keeper of the meaning is an objective indication of wisdom in older adults" (158). Ammons instead revels in what geropsychology sees as the vices of senescence. As a poeticized body, his verse eats too many calories, doesn't regularly exercise, barely walks, learns little, wavers at the level of the line. Positive geropsychology spends its energies postponing this particular body with this particular state of mind.[13] Yet in Ammons's poems there is no refinement of a life. "I arise and thank God I can get up" is another aubade through which he extols his singular yet shared senescence (77). Such states offer novelty if not the wisdom of supreme insight: "what summary learning is one // to take from all this: why, that it is some / of the world's oldest baggage, incredibly new" (139). This floundering is not necessarily pejorative. It's just aging with "room to // breathe and stretch and not give a shit" (52).

By focusing on the wisdom/foolishness binary I hoped to pry open the dualism to further comprehend what counts as late-life flourishing. Positive psychologies unquestionably offer us compelling models for growing older, and I admire their attentiveness to the lifespan amid ageism's ongoing wake.

---

[13] See, for instance, Hill's claim that "wisdom is linked to positive aging and coping mechanisms that are accessed through positive aging to maximize well-being and life satisfaction in old age are at the basis of cultivating a 'wisdom skill set'" (71).

As it develops, this relatively "new science of strength and resilience" may further help individuals nurture novel outlooks on decades of living that too many deride as anything but golden years (Seligman and Csikszentmihalyi 8). With its overarching commitment to thinking with and alongside pathological models of human subjectivity, the field can potentially welcome better modes of late-life flexibility that other disciplines also cultivate. As I earlier observed, the shorthand for these necessary late-life skills falls under the phrase "selective optimization with compensation."

Yet we need to keep in mind that what is optimal for one may not be for another. If and when foolishness or ignorance have been objects of empirical study—Sternberg's collection *Why Smart People Can Be So Stupid* comes to my mind—psychology's intent has often been to eradicate mistake-making as "a defect" (Sternberg 233). The same may be said for other traits featured in Peterson's table such as boredom, eccentricity, and hyperactivity. Whether in a subfield such as literary age studies or poetics such as Ammons's last collection, however, "old age imaginaries" steeped in literature adroitly postpone such foreclosures (Gullette, *Aged*, 184). These artworks of growing older invite confusion, ambivalence, foiling, dissatisfaction, incoherence, fret, and ignorance as much as marvel, buoyancy, and knowing your next step.

I am the first to admit that some of these feelings and ways of unknowing are not everyone's cup of tea, but that is precisely the point of such gerontological variation. Once decompartmentalized, these humanistic traits nevertheless amount to a different kind of *geroresilience*, a nonsense word that makes more and more sense to me as I get up in years. Positive geropsychology well knows, but sometimes underreports, that "human development consists of grays, not blacks and whites" (Vaillant, *Aging*, 58).[14] So with the aid of literary aging, here's to welcoming ever more gray areas. Avowedly "over and done with," works such as *Bosh and Flapdoodle* ask us "TO GO WITH IT," to carry on error-ridden until one cannot (78, 146). Full of clueless insights and insightful cluelessness, Ammons demonstrates how to relate otherwise to life's prolonging within and alongside its optimal idioms.[15] His poems amount to a selective compensation without optimization, a wondering wonder amid "a lifetime's // worth of getting on with life" (54–55). There's something to be said for such poetics that rehearse the lurching through longinquity many will

---

[14] Carstensen and Charles offer a parallel claim to this assessment.

[15] Framed as such, Ammons again finds an ally in age critics such as Gullette, who states that "even if a person's triumph is bare survival, we can salute that as a feat of resilience and interdependence" ("Our Best" 34).

undertake. With no small amount of imagination and struggle—in the end, what's the difference?—these persons will flourish by floundering, however foolish this logic seems. Their lives may not look like expert achievements to some, but to them they will still be worth living.

Works Cited

Ammons, A. R. *Bosh and Flapdoodle*. Norton, 2005.

Ammons, A. R. "A Poem Is a Walk." *Set in Motion: Essays, Interviews, and Dialogues*, by A. R. Ammons, edited by Zofia Burr, U Michigan P, 1996, pp. 12–20.

Baltes, Paul B., and Margret M. Baltes. "Psychological Perspectives on Successful Aging: The Model of Selective Optimization with Compensation." *Successful Aging: Perspectives from the Behavioral Sciences*, edited by Paul B. Baltes and Margret M. Baltes, Cambridge UP, 1990, pp. 1–34.

Baltes, Paul B., and Jacqui Smith. "Toward a Psychology of Wisdom and Its Ontogenesis." *Wisdom: Its Nature, Origins, and Development*, edited by Robert J. Sternberg, Cambridge UP, 1990, pp. 87–120.

Baltes, Paul B., et al. "Wisdom and Successful Aging." *Nebraska Symposium on Motivation*, vol. 39, 1992, pp. 123–67.

Baltes, Paul B., and Ursula M. Staudinger. "Wisdom: A Metaheuristic (Pragmatic) to Orchestrate Mind and Virtue Toward Excellence." *American Psychologist*, vol. 55, no. 1, 2000, pp. 122–36.

Berlant, Lauren. *Cruel Optimism*. Duke UP, 2011.

Birren, James E., and Laurel M. Fisher. "The Elements of Wisdom: Overview and Integration." Sternberg, *Wisdom*, pp. 317–32.

Booth, Wayne. *The Art of Growing Older: Writers on Living and Aging*. Poseidon, 1992.

Brooks, Gwendolyn. "The Crazy Woman." *Selected Poems*, Harper & Row, 1963, p. 99.

Brooks, Gwendolyn. "weaponed woman." *Selected Poems*, p. 125.

Carstensen, Laura L. *A Long Bright Future: Happiness, Health, and Financial Security in an Age of Increased Longevity*. PublicAffairs, 2009.

Carstensen, Laura L., and Susan T. Charles. "Human Aging: Why Is Even Good News Taken as Bad?" *A Psychology of Human Strengths: Fundamental Questions and Future Directions for a Positive Psychology*, edited by Lisa G. Aspinwall and Ursula M. Staudinger, American Psychological Association, 2003, pp. 75–86.

Clark, Phillip G., et al. "What Do We Know about Resilience in Older Adults? An Exploration of Some Facts, Factors, and Facets." *Resilience in Aging: Concepts, Research, and Outcomes*, edited by Barbara Resnick et al., Springer, 2011, pp. 51–66.

Csikszentmihalyi, Mihaly. *Flow: The Psychology of Optimal Experience*. Harper Perennial, 1990.

Danely, Jason. "Foolish Vitality: Humor, Risk, and Success in Japan." Lamb, pp. 154–67.

Edmondson, Ricca. *Ageing, Insight, and Wisdom: Meaning and Practice across the Lifecourse*. Policy, 2015.

Ehrenreich, Barbara. *Natural Causes: An Epidemic of Wellness, the Certainty of Dying, and Killing Ourselves to Live Longer*. Twelve, 2018.

Fernández-Ballesteros, Rocío, et al. "Introduction: GeroPsychology: Demographic, Sociopolitical, and Historical Background." *GeroPsychology: European Perspectives for an Aging World*, edited by Rocío Fernández-Ballesteros, Hogrefe and Huber, 2007, pp. 1–14.

"Flapdoodle." *Collins Dictionary*. Web, 7 Aug. 2018.

"Flapdoodle." *The Oxford Pocket Dictionary of Current English*. Web, 7 Aug. 2018.

"A Flying Fool." *African American Folktales: Stories from Black Traditions in the New World*. Selected and edited by Roger D. Abrahams, Pantheon, 1985, pp. 280–81.

Fogel, Daniel Mark. "The Humor of A. R. Ammons: The Clown and the Seer." *Considering the Radiance: Essays on the Poetry of A. R. Ammons*, edited by David Burak and Roger Gilbert, Norton, 2005, pp. 150–59.

Fredrickson, Barbara L. "The Value of Positive Emotions." *American Scientist*, vol. 91, no. 4, 2003, pp. 330–35.

Freund, Alexandra M., and Paul B. Baltes. "Toward a Theory of Successful Aging: Selection, Optimization, and Compensation." Fernández-Ballesteros, pp. 239–54.

Glück, Louise. "Visitors from Abroad." *Faithful and Virtuous Night*, Farrar, Straus and Giroux, 2014, pp. 22–23.

Gullette, Margaret Morganroth. *Aged by Culture*. U Chicago P, 2004.

Gullette, Margaret Morganroth. "Our Best and Longest Running Story: Why Is Telling Progress Narrative So Necessary, and So Difficult?" *Narratives of Life: Mediating Age*, edited by Heike Hartung and Roberta Maierhofer, Lit, 2009, pp. 21–36.

Haidt, Jonathan. *The Happiness Hypothesis: Finding Modern Truth in Ancient Wisdom*. Basic Books, 2006.

Hill, Robert D. *Positive Aging: A Guide for Mental Health Professionals and Consumers*. Norton, 2005.

Holstein, Martha B., and Meredith Minkler. "Self, Society, and the 'New Gerontology.'" *Gerontologist*, vol. 43, no. 6, 2003, pp. 787–96.

Horowitz, Daniel. *Happier? The History of a Cultural Movement That Aspired to Transform America*. Oxford UP, 2018.

Hutcheon, Linda, and Michael Hutcheon. "Historicizing Late Style as a Discourse of Reception." *Late Style and Its Discontents: Essays in Art, Literature, and Music*, edited by Gordon McMullan and Sam Smiles, Oxford UP, 2016, pp. 51–68.

Lamb, Sarah, et al. "Introduction: Successful Aging as a Twenty-first-Century Obsession." *Successful Aging as a Contemporary Obsession: Global Perspectives*, edited by Sarah Lamb, Rutgers UP, 2017, pp. 1–23.

Lavretsky, Helen. *Resilience and Aging: Research and Practice*. Johns Hopkins UP, 2014.

McMahon, Darrin M. "From the Paleolithic to the Present: Three Revolutions in the Global History of Happiness." *Handbook of Well-Being*, edited by Ed Diener et al., DEF, 2018, web, 13 Feb. 2019.

Meacham, John A. "The Loss of Wisdom." Sternberg, *Wisdom*, pp. 181–211.

Moraitou, Despina, and Anastasia Efklides. "Wise Thinking, Hopeful Thinking, and Positive Aging: Reciprocal Relations of Wisdom, Hope, Memory, and Affect in Young, Middle-Aged, and Older Adults." *A Positive Psychology Perspective on Quality of Life*, edited by Anastasia Efklides and Despina Moraitou, Springer, 2013, pp. 189–218.

Pawelski, James O. "Defining the 'Positive' in Positive Psychology: Part I. A Descriptive Analysis." *Journal of Positive Psychology*, vol. 11, no. 4, 2016, pp. 339–56.

Pawelski, James O. "Defining the 'Positive' in Positive Psychology: Part II. A Normative Analysis." *Journal of Positive Psychology*, vol. 11, no. 4, 2016, pp. 357–65.

Pawelski, James O., and D. J. Moores. "Introduction: What Is the Eudaimonic Turn? *and* The Eudaimonic Turn in Literary Studies." *The Eudaimonic Turn: Well-Being in Literary Studies*, edited by James O. Pawelski and D. J. Moores, Fairleigh Dickinson UP, 2013, pp. 1–63.

Peterson, Christopher. "The Values in Action (VIA) Classification of Strengths." *A Life Worth Living: Contributions to Positive Psychology*, edited by Mihaly Csikszentmihalyi and Isabella Selega Csikszentmihalyi, Oxford UP, 2006, pp. 29–48,

Peterson, Christopher, and Martin E. P. Seligman. *Character Strengths and Virtues: A Handbook and Classification*. American Psychological Association and Oxford UP, 2004.

"Pot." *Oxford English Dictionary*. Web, 23 June 2018.

Pushkin, Alexander S. "God, Don't Let Me Lose My Mind," translated by Tatsiana DeRosa. *On Human Flourishing: A Poetry Anthology*, edited by D. J. Moores et al., McFarland, 2015, pp. 31–32.

Rich, Adrienne. "Contradictions: Tracking Poems." *Later Poems: Selected and New: 1971–2012*, Norton, 2013, pp. 164–79.

Sedgwick, Eve Kosofsky. *Touching Feeling: Affect, Pedagogy, Performativity*. Duke UP, 2003.

Seligman, Martin E. P. "Chris Peterson's Unfinished Masterwork: The Real Mental Illnesses." *Journal of Positive Psychology*, vol. 10, no. 1, 2015, pp. 3–6.

Seligman, Martin E. P., and Mihaly Csikszentmihalyi. "Positive Psychology: An Introduction." *American Psychologist*, vol. 55, no. 1, 2000, pp. 5–14.

Sheldon, Ken, et al. "Positive Psychology (Akumal) Manifesto." 1999/2000. *Positive Psychology Center*. Web, 11 Feb. 2019.

Sternberg, Robert J. "Smart People Are Not Stupid, But They Can Be Foolish: The Imbalance Theory of Foolishness." *Why Smart People Can Be So Stupid*, edited by Robert J. Sternberg, Yale UP, 2002, pp. 232–42.

Vaillant, George E. *Aging Well: Surprising Guideposts to a Happier Life from the Landmark Harvard Study of Adult Development*. Little, Brown, 2002.

Vaillant, George E. *The Wisdom of the Ego*. Harvard UP, 1993.

Welsford, Enid. *The Fool: His Social and Literary History*. Faber and Faber, 1935.

Winter, Angela. "The Science of Happiness: Barbara Fredrickson on Cultivating Positive Emotions." *The Sun* May 2009, n.p. Web. 11 Feb. 2019.

Woodward, Kathleen. *At Last, the Real Distinguished Thing: The Late Poems of Eliot, Pound, Stevens, and Williams*. Ohio State UP, 1980.

Woodward, Kathleen. *Statistical Panic: Cultural Politics and Poetics of the Emotions*. Duke UP, 2009.

Zacher, Hannes, and Ursula M. Staudinger. "Wisdom and Well-Being," *Handbook of Well-Being*, edited by Ed Diener et al., web, DEF Publishers, 2018, https://www.nobascholar.com/books/1.

PART V
POSITIVE AFFECT
Redescription and Repair

9

Therapeutic Redescription

Beth Blum

What if our happiness depended not on income, health, or popularity but on something as internal and prosaic as our aptitude for description? This was the contention of the ancient Greco-Roman Stoics (c. 300 BCE–AD 200), who attributed to description the power to determine the equanimity and even morality of a life. The Stoics knew that a single act could have a multitude of different descriptions. Epictetus, for instance, describes two different ways of thinking about attending an event with a large crowd. In response to the man who dreads being caught amid the "turmoil" of the masses, he advises he learn to redescribe the crowd as a "festival" (*Discourses* 326; 4.4). Or, in the more extreme case of the death of a child: "Never say about anything, I have lost it, but say I have restored it. Is your child dead? It has been restored" (for the child was never really "yours" to begin with) (*Encheiridion* xi). The philosophy is particularly germane to authors and literary critics, for it allots language a tremendously important role in determining how we anticipate and cope with events.

A corollary of this Stoical investment in description is their technique of therapeutic redescription, which developed as a form of volitional training meant to emancipate individuals from the false "impressions" that govern their lives. Individuals must examine their impressions, whether desires (e.g., for wealth, love, and fame) or fears (e.g., of death, loss and poverty), and redescribe them until they are evacuated of the power to seduce or terrorize.[1] Marcus Aurelius used what Michel Foucault calls "reductive description" and "description that aims to discredit" to remind himself that the finery he coveted is "dyed sheep's wool" and nothing more, or that the melody that so entranced him was merely a series of discontinuous notes. This practice of "looking down on things from above"—the spatial metaphor is key—was

---

[1] The converse of this practice might be the Roman rhetorical device of "paradiastole," or the reframing of vice as virtue, with thanks to the volume's anonymous reader for this insight.

Beth Blum, *Therapeutic Redescription* In: *Literary Studies and Human Flourishing*. Edited by: James F. English and Heather Love, Oxford University Press. © Oxford University Press 2023. DOI: 10.1093/oso/9780197637227.003.0010

meant to be applied to all spheres of life: sex, identity, and mortality (Foucault 305). Aurelius explains:

> Surely it is an excellent plan, when you are seated before delicacies and choice foods, to impress upon your imagination that this is the dead body of a fish, that the dead body of a bird or a pig; and again, that the Falernian wine is grape juice and that robe of purple a lamb's fleece dipped in shellfish's blood; and in matters of sex intercourse, that it is attrition of an entrail and a convulsive expulsion of mere mucus. Surely these are excellent imaginations, going to the heart of actual facts and penetrating them so as to see the kind of things they really are. (*Meditations* 36; 6.13)

This strategy of discursive reframing has proven strikingly durable; it has been adopted by Cognitive-behavioral therapy (CBT), with its technique of cognitive restructuring, and by Gestalt psychology's emphasis on modifying language for therapeutic benefit (for instance, emphasizing a shift from third to first person as a means of encouraging the transformation from helplessness to agency) (Tallis 36). "We are the unwitting victims of our own internal rhetoric run amok," asserts Donald Robertson in his riveting Stoical genealogy of CBT (155). The point is not lost on the new wave of self-help authors who wield Stoicism as another "life hack," or as "an operating system for thriving in high stress environments," as celebrity life-hacker Timothy Ferriss puts it ("Why").

Whether through direct exposure to Stoicism, or indirectly, via the philosophy's considerable therapeutic influence, the practice of therapeutic redescription has become a significant aesthetic method informing contemporary autofiction (novels that blend fiction and autobiography), such as Karl Ove Knausgaard's *My Struggle* (2009–2011) and Sheila Heti's *Motherhood* (2018), in which the authors use the technique to liberate themselves from the bewitching ideas of death and motherhood, respectively. Heti in particular makes visible how redescription brings together the therapeutic and neorealist investments of the contemporary novel, both of which are driven by impatience to get at the core or essence of life. But the contemporary literary practice is part of an older genealogy, stretching back through the recursive feminist fictions of Doris Lessing and the mnemonic reconstructions of Marcel Proust. Finally, the Stoical precedent can shed insight into the "descriptive turn" taking place in literary criticism, as Heather Love calls it ("Close But Not Deep"), from Rita Felski's ambition to "redescribe" critique rather than "refute" it (9), to the project of "Building a Better Description" advanced by Love, Stephen Best, and Sharon Marcus (1), to Dora Zhang's recent reassessment of the "heterogeneity" of literary description (4). The turn to description may, as some of these scholars suggest, be a culmination of the intensifying suspicion of charisma that has underwritten the practice of literary criticism since the Cold War, but its deeper origins lie with the ascetic exercises of the Stoics.

The therapeutic tends to be lumped on the side of the fuzzy and subjective, self-centered and naïve, but this is not the therapeutic vision the Stoics advance. Conversely, description may be variously associated with science and facts, or with inaction and digression, but it is less commonly appreciated for its autotherapeutic utility. Its use emerges, above all, during periods of self-reappraisal, when the individual—whether author or literary critic—is trying to separate the wheat from the chaff, to come to grips with the reality of things, and to decide where to invest her care. Analytical thinking and individual well-being don't always seem compatible, but they converge in the Stoical exercise of therapeutic redescription.

The Reality of the Egg

It is not so surprising that the Stoics would be experiencing a revival today, when the future looks bleak, the economy precarious, and our power to avert disaster limited. Zadie Smith opens her essay collection *Intimations*, a real-time meditation on the unfolding pandemic, with an epigraph from Marcus Aurelius, relating that she turned to the Stoic for "practical assistance" (xi). And the words that come to Mira, the protagonist of Sheila Heti's latest novel *Pure Color* (2022) at her dying father's bedside are from *Hamlet*'s channeling of Epictetus: "for there is nothing either good or bad, but thinking makes it so" (63). It is not exactly a progressive philosophy, for as even Henry James noted, the idea of Stoicism is largely incompatible with the idea of rights or social progress (7). One of its greatest teachers, Epictetus, was a disabled former slave who was adamant about the necessity of accepting one's fate. Its focus is less on improving conditions than on helping people cope and endure (which could, arguably, be said to improve conditions). Toussaint L'Ouverture, who was also born enslaved, was said to have treasured his volume of Epictetus (Worth 25). Nietzsche, in contrast, cuttingly criticized the movement for imagining "*indifference* as a power" (5). However, Stoicism does not condone resigning oneself to the future but rather advises learning to constructively cooperate with whatever may arise, a distinction that goes much deeper than word choice.[2]

For the newest generation of humanities scholars, Stoicism may seem redolent of a stodgy Western canon they are working to revise or even supplant, but in the contemporary self-help and life-optimization movement it has become cutting-edge. There are "Stoicon" meetings, podcasts, online communities, and TED talks. An extension of the broader interest in the classics among "red pill" enthusiasts (see Zuckerberg), Stoicism is a favorite resource of the "podcast bros," as a 2018 New York Times piece calls the newest generation of male wellness gurus for whom it offers an alternative to the feminized, softer, New-Age strands of self-help (Worthen). Numerous publications tout Stoicism's relevance to modern times, but perhaps the most influential of these are the books of Ryan Holiday, the former director of marketing for American Apparel turned life-hacker and self-help coach, who helped to popularize Stoicism in *The Obstacle Is the Way: The Timeless Art of Turning Trials into Triumph* (2014) and *The Daily Stoic: 366 Meditations on Wisdom, Perseverance, and the Art of Living* (2016).

The contradictions of a former PR strategist for a trendy clothing store embracing the antimaterialist dogma of Stoicism, and one who had previously published such a venerable tome as *Trust Me, I'm Lying: Confessions of a Media Manipulator* (2012), are hard to ignore. But this may be less contradictory than it seems, for Holiday's exposé of media manipulation and his Stoicism converge in their suspicion of charismatic language and their advocacy of rhetorical detachment. In Holiday, the line between Stoic and spin doctor becomes revealingly blurred. As he explains, the modern media system "rests on exploiting the difference between perception and reality" (*Trust Me* xiii). *Trust Me, I'm Lying* actually is somewhat prescient in detailing the rising power of fake news and alternative facts. Echoing the Stoical insistence on the power of impressions, Holiday confesses that during his early career, "I created false impressions through blogs, which led to bad conclusions and wrong decisions—real decisions in the real world that had consequences for real people" (5). This convergence between Holiday's forays into media manipulation and his later advocacy of Stoicism might offer a clue to the philosophy's contemporary appeal, besides the seeming

---

[2] See Pierre Hadot (194).

advocacy of radical individualism that right-wing pundits seek to exploit. Stoicism's relevance for both Holiday and contemporary novelists and literary critics has to do with its aim to lay bare the real-world consequences of rhetorical framing. Moreover, life-hacking is driven by a suspicion of power and the establishment, by the promise that underground, personalized life-management systems could liberate us from dependence on authorities (even, of course, as it produces new celebrity-authorities). Stoicism, too, posits its rationalized life-management system as an antidote to the false values that govern public life.

The revival of Stoicism might also reflect dissatisfaction with the omissions of self-help triumphalism. Discussing the resurgence of interest in the Greco-Roman art of living, Elizabeth Lasch-Quinn maintains that what is missing from modern versions of self-cultivation is "a sense of human limits, and the humility it can inspire" (74). Stoicism supplies this sense of humility or perspective (Holiday's fourth book is called *Ego Is the Enemy*), in addition to offering protection against the manipulations of internal and external talk.

Beyond its recent popularity among life-hackers, Stoicism has long been a life-management resource for cognitive-behavioral therapists. Ever since the psychologist Albert Ellis was inspired in the 1960s by Epictetus to argue that our interpretations are more powerful than events, therapeutic redescription—also known as cognitive reframing or "cognitive reappraisal"—has been a core principle of his rational emotive behavior therapy (Wiener 29). CBT encourages individuals to become more aware of their "attributional style" (Laird and Metalsky 133) (the valences of their internal rhetoric) and asks them to learn to reformulate fears or obsessions in less emotive and irrational terms. For example, The *CBT-Practitioner's Guide* warns that "we often confuse descriptions and evaluations" and offers the exercise pictured in Figure 9.1 as demonstration.

The exercise asks readers to come to grips with the reality of the egg, apart from their ideas or impressions of it. This might be straightforward enough when it concerns a basket of eggs, but it is much more difficult when the object becomes more abstract and complex, or when applied to our own self-talk. Following the egg exercise, readers are asked to write down a situation they are struggling with and then attempt to sift their evaluations from their descriptions: "We think evaluations are as solid as prison bars or as dangerous as real threats. We often let ourselves be bullied by our evaluations" (Ciarrochi and Bailey 35). The Stoical name for this volitional struggle is

Part A: We would like you to consider the eggs in the picture. When you are ready, please circle the best response—D for a description or E for an evaluation.

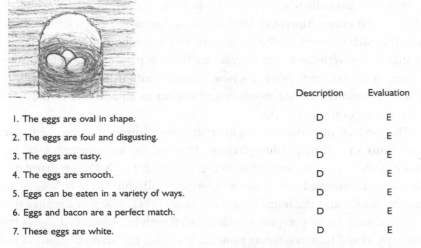

	Description	Evaluation
1. The eggs are oval in shape.	D	E
2. The eggs are foul and disgusting.	D	E
3. The eggs are tasty.	D	E
4. The eggs are smooth.	D	E
5. Eggs can be eaten in a variety of ways.	D	E
6. Eggs and bacon are a perfect match.	D	E
7. These eggs are white.	D	E

Figure 9.1 From Joseph V. Ciarrochi and Ann Bailey, *A CBT Practitioner's Guide to ACT* (New Harbinger Publications, 2008), 35.

"prohairesis" ("choice" or "decision"); it designates the choice of giving into or withholding assent to one's impressions (Graver).

CBT developed in the early twentieth century in competition with Freudian psychoanalysis, with now largely forgotten antecedents such as Paul Dubois and Émile Coué preferring to focus on the client's present, conscious coping strategies, rather than past, invisible drives and causes, and aiming largely to eliminate painful thoughts and habits instead of approaching them as revealing indexes to deeper, more primal preoccupations. CBT and Stoicism share this privileging of the present over the past. Dubois, for instance, a CBT predecessor who was influenced by Seneca and the Stoics, advocated in 1907 "educating [the client] about the effect of the mind on the body, and teaching him to adopt remedial 'philosophical' attitudes.'" When he argued that "the treatment should go to root," he was not referring to the primal scene or original repression but to "the erroneous idea that the patient has allowed to creep into his mind" (qtd. in Robertson 20).

Despite their differences, there are of course points where the redescriptive techniques of psychoanalysis and behavioral therapy converge. Adam Phillips writes that "the most useful general way of formulating what psychoanalysis is, is simply to say that it is an art of redescription" (131).[3] In his terms, which echo the Stoical aim of deflating or discrediting, the analyst becomes a "translator": "the analyst translates to diminish the power of the repetition—where compulsion was, something like choice might be—and so to make something disappear. And here translation means redescription: in the service of dissolution" (136). Phillips acknowledges that the experience of being "translated" can be off-putting for the patient; that it can feel like "being second guessed by someone more powerful" (139). Roy Schafer supports this account of the analytic situation when he observes that it is the job of the analyst to "retell" the stories people offer about themselves: "In the retelling, certain features are accentuated while others are placed in paren-theses. . . . The analyst's retellings progressively influence the what and how of the stories told by analysands" (35–36). Autofiction strives to subvert this psychoanalytic reliance on an external authority to serve as the mediator for one's redescriptions. In the narratives I will discuss, the author becomes her own translator or interlocutor in a way that enables her to focus on imme-diate coping strategies rather than the more remote pleasures of diagnosis or demystification. In his chapter on "Sage Writing," David Russel notes the con-temporary backlash in the form of "surface reading" and other movements against the "diagnostic vision" that has been seen as ascendant in literary criticism (XX). In this spirit, the practice of therapeutic redescription strives to democratize the interpretive hierarchy upon which so much of Western hermeneutics—including psychoanalysis—traditionally depends.

Word Power

Like the CBT practitioners, Sheila Heti desperately wants to get at the re-ality of the egg (or embryo). Her "novel" *Motherhood* doubles as a work of autotherapy as she dilates on the subject of whether or not to have a child. As she comments, "What I need is so small: to eradicate any sentimentality from my feelings and to look at what is. Today I defined *sentimental* to myself as *a feeling about the idea of a feeling*. And it seemed to be that my inclinations towards motherhood had a lot to do with *the idea of a feeling* about mother-hood" (41). What has frustrated some reviewers by seeming like lot of cir-cular dithering over the question of whether or not to have a child adopts a

---

[3] My thanks to David Russell for this useful reference.

different valence as a reanimating of the Stoical exercise of therapeutic redescription. We could say that Heti's book is trying to deconstruct the impression of motherhood in order to separate the reality of the experience from its status as ideal, social expectation, or fear.

In so doing, Heti extends a longer tradition of novelists using redescription to emancipate themselves from the power of imposed language and impressions, whose early practitioners include Marcel Proust and Doris Lessing. Speaking of this tendency in Proust, Richard Rorty argues that Proust used redescription "simply to free himself from the descriptions of himself offered by the people he had met. . . . His method of freeing himself from those people—of becoming autonomous—was to redescribe the people who had described him" (102). To put it in Stoical terms, a tradition Rorty's book does not mention, Proust sought to liberate himself from the false impression of others' authority. Indeed, though Rorty identifies Proust as an "ironist" rather than a "metaphysician" (99), the Stoical correspondences are striking, from the mistrust of common impressions to the belief in redescription as a key to autonomy.

But what is most striking about Rorty's discussion of Proust is his contention that redescription is above all "a literary skill" (rather than a philosophical or argumentative one), and one that draws on strengths that authors and literary critics already have—namely, their attunement to rhetorical contingency and framing—which he reveals to be a very practical, ethical, even spiritual skill (78). Because they can indulge in perspectivism without feeling obliged to settle on a "final word," he writes, "novels are a safer medium than theory for expressing one's recognition of the relativity and contingency of authority figures" (107). In the land of redescribers, the literary wordsmith is king.

Proust likely absorbed some Stoicism through his engagement with the early CBT of this day. His ailments led him to read the Swiss psychologist and CBT forefather Paul Dubois's 1904 *Psychic Treatment of Nervous Disorders* and to recommend, in a 1905 letter, the work to his friend Madame Straus: "I wanted so much to talk to you about Dubois. Perhaps he could do something for you." (*Letters* 161). And he elsewhere elaborates, "Doctors said not long ago (and the tardy still repeat it) that a pessimist is a man with a bad stomach. Today Dr. Dubois says in print unmistakably that a man with a bad stomach is a pessimist. And it is no longer his stomach that must be cured if his philosophy is to change, it is his philosophy that must be changed if his stomach is to be cured" (*Sésame* 106). Dubois's method of what he called "rational persuasion" had an explicitly Stoical bent; he argued for the relevance of Epictetus, Aurelius, and Seneca to modern life: "We must turn here towards the ancients in order to recover the idea of patience towards disease, that stoical philosophy which not only helps to support us in evils, but diminishes or cures them" (qtd. in Robertson 23). Intrigued though wary of Dubois's approach, Proust nevertheless shared with his version of updated Stoicism a sense of the social and physical consequence of our impressions.

Proust is a fitting entry into this discussion as an early practitioner of the genre of autofiction so popular today. As an article for *The Guardian* recently inquired, "Why have novelists stopped making things up"? While Wittgenstein insisted that philosophers "ought to describe, but never explain" (524), many contemporary novelists writing in this Proustian tradition are choosing to describe rather than invent. This does not mean that there is an overwhelming amount of ornamental detail in their narratives. In some cases, as in Heti's, there is actually very little; the object of the description is not setting or character but life itself. Though authors who are dispensing with the contrivances of character and plot—from Alison Bechdel to Ben Lerner, Teju Cole, Brenda Lozano, Chris Kraus, Rachel Cusk, Knausgaard, and Heti—have garnered a great deal of attention, the therapeutic or psychoeducational motives of their methods remain underdiscussed.

Perhaps this is because it seems increasingly redundant to point out that writing is a form of autotherapy or working through. Following the psychoanalytic revelation that "it is the task of the literary work to control [the] anxiety" that underwrites fantasy (Holland 189), the therapeutic work that writing performs for an author has seemed at once too facile and too self-evident to warrant serious attention. As David James points out in his contribution to this volume, literature of uplift, branded as "Up Lit," is even more explicitly premised on "the promise of writing as a vehicle for rehabilitation," and suffers from the stigma associated with this practice (Chapter 5). The difference between a psychoanalytical reading of a text and an ameliorative one consists in part in the degree of self-awareness attributed to the author's therapeutic practice. Maybe, too, critics have preferred this therapeutic work of the author to remain repressed because it gives them something to find and to do.

Like Proust, Heti is also writing against received ideas and internalized authorities: "the feeling of not wanting children is the feeling of not wanting to be someone's idea of me" (22). As she explains in an interview for the *Paris Review*, "I felt that there was something wrong with the word mother." And she elaborates, "When people would tell me they wanted to be mothers, I would think, What are you even talking about? What is it you want to be? How do you even know what that is, a mother?" ("The Child Thing"). The challenge she presents herself in her novel is to formulate not being a mother as something active, rather than passive, something other than a negation. Her quest is to find her "authentic or original desire" in regard to motherhood (41).

In pursuit of this end, her redescriptions of motherhood run the gamut. Motherhood is "egoism/colonialism" (84); endless worry (128); an enemy of art (35); a substitute for idealism (184); a "fantasy" (135); "letting another child come through you, whose life is entirely its own" (43). She comes closest to the deflationary description of the Stoics when she observes, "I know a woman who refuses to mother, refuses to do the most important thing, and therefore becomes the least important woman. Yet the mothers aren't important, either. None of us are important" (134). Though reviews of the novel have been mixed, in terms of exorcizing her fixation on motherhood, the exercise was a success. Heti stated that, as a result of writing *Motherhood*, "I don't ever have to think about this book or this question again—specifically the child thing. . . . I'm so glad I don't have to think about that anymore. It's such a relief" ("The Child Thing"?).

Seneca advised that "the happy life is one that is in harmony with its own nature" ("On the Happy Life," 87), an idea Heti has internalized, even if unwittingly. Her Stoical proclivities reach their peak when she muses, "I don't know why I don't do the obvious thing—instead of fantasizing about other lives, why not try to imagine what it's like to be me, and live the life I'm living now—fantasize into the life that's actually mine?" (125). The book tracks this process of fantasizing into the life she has, of bringing her will into harmony with her circumstance—which may be why some parts read a bit like self-convincing—and this is its most Stoical aspect. "I made a resolution this year that I would be happy, I so wanted to be happy, sort of at the expense of everything else, but I did not know what happiness consisted of. Now that I know, I will focus on that. Happiness and joy are feeling like you belong to the world, and are at home in the world, at the level of nature, humanity and time" (79). Epictetus would agree.

To be sure, on some level most writing can be subsumed under this rubric of therapeutic redescription, in so far as it dilates on a nagging problem or theme. But therapeutic redescription is distinguished from more familiar and less controlled instances of aesthetic obsession or repetition by its blurring of the line between author and character in a way that makes explicit the text's ambition to resolve a particular, governing impression. It is not neurotic replaying, or what Jennifer Fleissner has called the "compulsion to describe"—a misguided assertion of control that ends up reinforcing one's "frozenness" (68)—but an attempt, through reformulation rather than invention or contrivance, at neutralizing an idea to which the author is in thrall. What such works share is not just their blending of author and character, life and plot, but the candor with which they lay bare the effort and struggle of working on the self.

In addition to Proust, Doris Lessing's writings also offer a prime early example of how the aims of therapeutic redescription and autofiction converge. Considered as a precedent for Heti, it is notable that Lessing is the author who first inspired the term "matrophobia," even before Adrienne Rich's discussion of it as the "fear of becoming the victim in ourselves, the unfree woman, the martyr" (Sukenick 519; Rich 235).[4] Once describing herself as "aggressively rational," Lessing is even more stringent than Heti about the need to eliminate sentimentality from her work (see Sukenick 518). Like Heti, Lessing is interested in the neglected aspects of female experience that have been omitted from the conventional novel, from the social experiences of unmarried, "free" women to the more mundane circumstances of, for instance, meal preparation and workplace menstruation. If Proust wanted to use redescription to transcend society's impressions and accounts of him, Lessing describes the struggle to emancipate herself from masculinist definitions.

In particular, *The Golden Notebook* details the four different notebooks of Lessing's alter-ego Anna Wulf, in which she records and revisits events from her life: her youth in South Africa and early loves, her subsequent romantic encounters, collaborations with the communist party, female friendships, and the routines of motherhood. It culminates in the purchasing of a "golden notebook" in which Anna hopes to combine all of the different threads of her personality into one overarching text. Protesting the artifice of narrative convention in a way that prefigures Heti's "novel[s] from life," she wonders "why did I not write an account of what had happened, instead of shaping a "story" which had nothing to do with the material that fueled it."[5] And she continues, "I am not talking now of that game writers play with themselves when

---

[4] Rich's use of the term was inspired by Lynn Sukenick.
[5] Heti's novel *How Should a Person Be?* is subtitled *A Novel from Life.*

writing, the psychological game—that written incident came from that real incident, that character was transposed from that one in life, this relationship was the psychological twin of that. I am simply asking myself: Why a story at all. . . . Why not, simply, the truth?" (61). The examples of Lessing, Heti, and Proust suggest a convergence between the therapeutic practice of redescription and its status as a formal vehicle for genre renewal. The autofictional and therapeutic motives of these works are linked by the desire to gain independence from inherited narrative paradigms.

The formal conceit of Lessing's novel's division into different notebooks and narrative threads mirrors her protagonist's ongoing self-analysis, whether through writing, informal conversation, or, as in the following passage, therapy sessions. An exchange between Anna and her therapist Mrs. Marks (or "Mother Sugar" as she is sometimes dubbed parodically for her saccharine take on art and identity) makes plain the importance of redescription to this project:

> "Describe yourself." "How?" "Describe yourself as if you were describing someone else." "Anna Wulf is a small dark thin spiky woman, over-critical and on the defensive. She is thirty-three years old. She was married for a year to a man she didn't care for and has a small daughter. She is a communist." She smiled. I said, "No good?" "Try again: for one thing, Anna Wulf wrote a novel which was praised by the critics and did so well she is still in fact living on the money it earned." I was full of hostility. "Very well: Anna Wulf is sitting in a chair in front of a soul-doctor. She is there because she cannot deeply feel about anything. She is frozen. She has a great many friends and acquaintances. People are pleased to see her. But she only cares about one person in the world, her daughter, Janet. "Why is she frozen?" "She is afraid." "What of?" "Of death." (223)

Anna is patently dissatisfied with Mrs. Marks's "retellings," which only inspire "hostility" in response (or, what psychoanalysts would call "defense"). Throughout the text, as in the above passage, Anna's narrative redescription takes off where her therapist's schematic diagnoses fail. The book charts this antagonism between the self-reliant redescriptions enacted in the notebooks and her therapist's counter-takes.

Identifying herself as a "latter-day stoic" (258), Anna claims to live in an era where, she says, "detachment" is the ideal: "something we need very badly in this time, but that very few people had" (570), as "people everywhere are trying not to feel" (520). As Lynn Sukenick argues, this embrace of Stoicism (despite Anna's contradictory complaint of feeling anhedonic to her therapist) was a product of Lessing's resistance to "the feminine tradition of sensibility" in the culture and the novel genre (516). Recoiling against the compulsory emotion and sensitivity associated with women, Anna develops what Sukenick describes as a form of watchful intelligence in response: "She could . . . feel that intelligence there at work, defensive and efficient—a machine. And she thought: this intelligence, it's the only barrier between me and . . . cracking up" (Lessing 378; qtd. in Sukenick 521).[6] Part of this intelligent watchfulness involves the use of the practice of "naming" as way of coping with the incursion of overwhelming or irrational thoughts: "I have to hold fast to this—that Anna, the thinking Anna, can look at what Anna feels and 'name' it" (Lessing 459). During a panic attack she finds that "'Naming' the state I am in as an anxiety state lessened it for a while" (530), a practice she began as a child when, "before I slept each night I lay awake, remembering everything in the day that had a quality of fear hidden in it; which might become part of a nightmare. I had to 'name' the frightening things, over and over, in a terrible litany; like a sort of disinfection by the conscious mind before I slept" (588). If Anna is attuned to the ameliorative power of naming, it is also because she has noticed its strategic deployment by men; her lodger and lover Saul Green, for example, lectures her, like a "fair-minded pedant, on the dangers and pitfalls and rewards of a woman living alone." "I was," she laughs, "being 'named' on such a high level" (526). In Lessing, therapeutic redescription assumes a different cast from the one it dons as a life-hacking strategy of the "podcast bros." Tied to the feminist project of historical revisionism, "naming" and renaming in Lessing have the aim of wresting the descriptive, rationalist script from the experts and the men. Feminist scholars have long seen redescription as part of their mission, like the historian Donna Haraway, who related that "if one were going to characterize my way of theorizing, it would be to redescribe, to redescribe something so that it becomes thicker than it first seems' (108). The feminist philosopher Alison Jaggar likewise maintains that "those who construct the standpoint of women must begin from women's experience as women describe it, but they must go beyond that experience theoretically, and ultimately may require that women's experience be redescribed" (384).

---

[6] Sekenick discusses how Lessing invokes "watchfulness" and "intelligence" as defenses against irrationality (519, 521).

Toward *The Golden Notebook*'s conclusion, Anna confesses: "What's my strongest need—being with one man, love, all that. I've a real talent for it" (596).This is one of the pressing fixations her narrative aims to unsettle through its documentation of Anna's sequence of unsatisfying encounters with men, which, like Heti's parsing of the word "mother," uses narrative retellings to strip away the sentimentalism and to "distinguish between what I had invented and what I had known" (591).

Just as Lessing—via Anna—confesses to feeling "sick" at the contrivances of plot (61), and Heti refuses to abide by the pretense of character and fiction, Karl Ove Knausgaard has commented that the idea of inventing fiction makes him want to vomit (Kunzru). Volume 1 of *My Struggle* also follows a redescriptive arc. Like Anna, who cites the "fear of death" as the ultimate and most oppressive impression (223), Knausgaard begins his opus by obsessively detailing our complex cultural strategies of death-repression. However, he concludes by deconstructing death into material units, precisely in the manner of the deflationary description modeled by Aurelius and Epictetus. In the book's final sentences, Knausgaard comes to realize that "death, which I have always regarded as the greatest dimension of life, dark, compelling, was no more than a pipe that springs a leak, a branch that cracks in the wind, a jacket that slips off a clothes hanger and falls to the floor" (441). This is precisely the kind of deflationary description that the Stoics recommend as a means of transcending oppressive anxieties or fears. For the Stoics, the use of metaphor is not incongruous with the seemingly literalist act of redescription but a tool in the service of it. For instance, writing before the days of the global industrial agricultural complex, Epictetus says that wishing for your loved ones to be around forever is like wishing to be able to eat figs all year round, even in winter (*Discourses* 278; 3.24).

As these writings collectively suggest, death is the supreme impression from which individuals need emancipation. A great deal of Stoical practice revolves around the problem of death and grieving; redescription is above all about reminding oneself of the true, mortal, transient nature of each thing. However, the deflationary redescriptions of death that the Stoics recommend do not preclude attachment to one's intimates or this world, although they are often erroneously read in this way. The anticipation of death is not meant to breed callous indifference but to increase our appreciation for the present and those we love. Seneca says, "Let us greedily enjoy our friends, because we do not know how long this privilege will be ours" ("Grief" 433; 63.8). Love for the Stoics is more precious precisely because it is not a romantic illusion but a relation that demands a tremendous amount of courage and forbearance. Moreover, coming to terms with the transient nature of our love objects was for Seneca not a cause for eradicating our attachments but an incentive to distribute our affections more fulsomely so that we will not be entirely destroyed by one particular loss. In attempting to preserve a space for love and attachment despite their insistence on descriptive autonomy and rationality, the Stoics model one way to reconcile the impulses toward critique and cathexis in literature and also literary criticism.

Redescribing in Times of Crisis

The use of therapeutic redescription seems clear enough as a way to work through the fixation on death, authority, or motherhood, but what happens when the influence from which we seek emancipation is literary (or academic) language itself? This conflict between enchantment and detachment lies at the heart of debates over method in the discipline, in which description, tellingly, plays a central role. Rita Felski's aim in *The Limits of Critique* is "not just to describe but to *redescribe* this [suspicious] style of thinking: to offer a fresh slant on a familiar practice in the hope of getting a clearer sense of how and why critics read" (2). For Heather Love, description is a tool of what Erving Goffman called "role-distance," or of detaching oneself from sacralized disciplinary norms (381). In his argument for "weak modernism," which draws on Silvan Tomkins's account of "weak theory" as "little better than a mere description of the phenomena it purports to explain" (Tomkins 433–34), Paul Saint-Amour explains his project as "finally descriptive rather than laudatory, hortatory, or polemical" (Saint-Amour 451). Description mediates the conflicting demands of the profession—for magnetism, persuasion, individualism, polemics, but also humility, communal spirit, specialization.

In this way, the embrace of description among literary critics is connected to broader ambivalence toward the ideology of charisma pervading the discipline and our culture-at-large, from the rise of computational modeling to geek chic, infrastructure studies to #MeToo.[7] Understandably, given the

---

[7] In *Enumerations* (2018) Andrew Piper argues that "models replace charisma as the guiding vehicle for generalization" in the field of cultural analytics (10). For an interesting discussion of Piper's and DH's anti-charismatic energies, see Laura B McGrath, "Charisma (Embodiment): A Response to Tess McNulty."

lessons of recent political history, literary scholars are linked by their aversion to charismatic master discourses, particularly those associated with literary theory's golden age. For Love, the appeal of "descriptive reading" has to do in part with the way that it "undermines the ethical charisma of the critic" (387), while Best and Marcus argue that surface reading offers a rebuttal against "professional criticism as a strenuous and heroic endeavor" (5–6). As it did for the Stoics, description supplies a means of disciplining desire, and a way of tempering the formidable sway of "His Majesty the [academic] Ego."[8]

Charisma, then, and the loss of rationalist self-possession it inspires, is the governing illusion from which these disparate disciplinary manifestos seek autonomy, with their shared conviction that productive scholarship resists the temptation to beguile readers with risky hypotheses, magnetic personalities, and grand claims. It is an open question whether this abnegation of charisma is a good thing for the discipline (the perspective of enrollment suggests it may not be, for the 1980s–90s heyday of critique was a golden era for English studies, while the decade of descriptive method has been one of alarming decline, although there are crucial institutional and socioeconomic causes for this descent). However, we can ask whether they are really the renunciations of charisma that they appear. For the proliferation of prodescription arguments, and attendant embrace of critical self-effacement, reflects the paradox that the anticharismatic manifesto has itself become charismatic—witness the enormous popularity of the descriptive turn, the renewed interest in the scholarly humility championed by theorists such as Tomkins and Eve Sedgwick, and the rising prestige of what Thom Dancer terms "critical modesty." Of course, the opposition between humble description and heroic interpretation is a tenuous one at best; as Zhang notes, "description is always already bound up with interpretive commitments that immediately foil any attempt to posit it as an alternative" (24). What is clear is that both scholarly and literary production renovate themselves through a series of successive appeals to redescription as an antidote for the misprisions of the previous generation.

In a related though divergent strain, scholars such as Deidre Lynch, Felski, and Lisa Ruddick have argued that we need to counterbalance academia's deflationary tendencies—its posture of Stoical detachment—and to restore the neglected import of "attachment" to the humanities and literary studies. Lynch, for example, writes of the inhibitory effects of "the reluctance

---

[8] See Sigmund Freud, "Creative Writers and Day-dreaming," *Selected Essays*, 1908, 150.

to engage the affective attachments that have connected readers to the institutions of English" (11), while Ruddick claims that "it is clear that our profession ... has a bias against one-on-one attachment" ("When Nothing Is Cool"). Felski objects to ideology critics and surface readers alike for the way that "both guard against any risk of deep involvement, absorption, or immersion in their object, priding themselves on their stoicism and lack of susceptibility to a text's address" (9, 54). David James likewise argues in this volume that "we need to take a second look ... at affirmative structures of feeling that critique has traditionally earmarked as unsound" (pp. 117–18).

It is impossible to avoid reference to the erotic (and antierotic) subtext of this trend. If the Stoics are more relevant than ever, in other words, it might be because today nobody wants to be seduced.[9] For the Stoics, erotic and aesthetic activity were linked by the threat they posed to the individual's self-possession (recall Aurelius's account of sex as "attrition of an entrail and a convulsive expulsion of mere mucus"). Here is Foucault describing the way Aurelius's clinical descriptions applied to a dance or a musical composition:

> if we look at a dance in the continuity of its movements, or if we hear a melody in its unity, we will be carried away by the beauty of the dance or the charm of the melody. We will be weaker than it. If we want to be stronger than the melody or the dance, if we want to prevail over it—that is to say, to remain master of our self with regard to the enchantment, flattery, and pleasure they arouse ... it will be by dissecting it instant by instant, note by note, movement by movement. (302)

Ours are not sexy times, for a variety of reasons, and this may be another reason why Stoicism resonates, in literary theory as in the popular sphere. Foucault's account of this passage was partly inspired by Pierre Hadot's treatment of such spiritual exercises in the 1976 article that would form the basis of his book *Philosophy as a Way of Life*, where he delves into this Stoical practice of *phantasia kataleptike*, which he defines as a "method of objective representation" (187; 189). As Hadot explains there, "Marcus' seemingly pessimistic declarations are not expressions of his disgust or disillusion at the spectacle of life; rather, they are a means he employs in order to change his way of evaluating the events and objects which go to make up human existence" (186).

---

[9] See, e.g., Julian, "Why are Young People Having So Little Sex?"

Part of this Stoical reevaluation involves learning to resist "anthropocentric prejudice" by deconstructing the constituent parts of the self, just as one would a melody or sumptuous dish. Addressing the lure of fame and posterity, Aurelius cautions "Soon you'll be ashes, or bones. A mere name at most—and even that is just a sound, an echo" (63). Redescription "teaches us to relocate human existence within the immeasurable dimensions of the cosmos" (Hadot 245), a process that entails an inevitable dislodging of the self's centrality. Ecocritical long before the invention of the term, the Stoics insisted on the individual's status as mere part of the cosmic whole, and upheld living in agreement with nature (understood as the divine order of the universe) as the very purpose of life. (In this important respect, Foucault's use of the Stoics in service of his celebration of "practices of the self" is for Hadot a deviation from their original focus on unity with nature through virtue) (206–213). They invoked spatial metaphors to reinforce this cosmic lesson, and in particular the aerial view; as Aurelius models, we need to step back from our impressions, to look down at our fixations from above: "When you are reasoning about mankind, look upon earthly things below as if from some vantage point above them" (qtd. in Hadot 224), he counsels himself. The aerial vantage has once again become important amid our own disciplinary search for a less anthropocentric, less self-aggrandizing perspective; whether in terms of "distant" "surface" "close" or "deep" readings, "spatial metaphors are now front and center in literary debates," as Felski observes (52).

To a degree, literary criticism has always been premised on taking a step back from the bewitchment of the text in order to neutralize it and unpack how it signifies; this has long been the implicit difference between the professional and amateur reader.[10] Amid periods of propaganda or autocratic rule, the recoil against charisma becomes more pronounced. During the height of Cold War anxieties over political manipulation, the job of the literary critic became to reverse-engineer the charisma of the literary text, to understand how it works and to guard against its seductions. As Tobin Siebers recounts, for critics working during this period, whether deconstructionists or new historicists, the best way "to avoid charismatic leadership" was to "learn how to read" (53). As with our contemporary disciplinary manifestos, these deconstructions of the literary text often ended up producing their own charismatic discourse (see, for example, John Guillory on Paul de

---

[10] In addition to Lynch and Felski, some scholars productively challenging this distinction include Carolyn Dinshaw, *How Soon Is Now? Medieval Texts, Amateur Readers, and the Queerness of Time* and Aarthi Vadde and Saikat Majumdar, *The Critic as Amateur*.

Man). Nevertheless, the project of repositioning the self that links Proust's *Recherche* and Holiday's *The Ego Is the Enemy* also finds expression in literary scholars' adoption of redescription as a way of reckoning with their role-ambivalence.

The contention that description can liberate us from naïve fascination and blind, anthropocentric egotism is at the core not only of the disciplinary manifestoes explicitly celebrating description, but implicitly of a great quantity of contemporary scholarship. Redescription has become a rallying cry in the field of archival science, where a widespread "auditing "of archival description for instances of bias is taking place (see, e.g. Heslin). For many scholars, wariness toward former descriptions and established attachments are coterminous. Lauren Berlant has written that "all attachment is optimistic," and therefore potentially cruel (1). "Cruel optimism" designates for Berlant our dependence on objects, people, and institutions which promise to bring happiness but in reality only stand in its way. Though Berlant does not dwell on remedial measures for this situation, her book itself extends the Stoical practice of "convinc[ing] ourselves of the worthlessness of the objects [in her case, optimism, love, or "the good life"] toward which passion was leading us astray" (Badouin & Lestchinsky qtd. in Robertson 34). There are of course legitimate political motives for this embrace of detachment. In the fields of identity politics and feminist criticism, descriptive deflation is seen as a pressing, political task: "Identity politics starts from analyses of oppression to recommend, variously, the reclaiming, redescription, or transformation of previously stigmatized accounts of group membership. Rather than accepting the negative scripts offered by a dominant culture about one's own inferiority, one transforms one's own sense of self and community, often through consciousness-raising" (Heyes). Scholars are faced with the challenge of how to reconcile the standards of rigorous, politically informed exegesis with the investment in enacting, preserving, and inspiring literary attachment and transformation.

For the Stoics, though, critique and attachment can coexist. Contrary to its reputation, Stoicism does not strive to deny one's attachments but to make them poignant by bringing their risky fragility into full view. And Stoical critique is less about putting down than about exercising vigilance over the ideas we accept and reject. One version of the "agency of description" that Zhang emphasizes in her study may consist in this realization that every description contains an assent, and that these minor acts of linguistic assent have profound spiritual and existential consequences; they can prepare us for life or be the source of tremendous grief and disappointment. Contemporary therapy takes from Stoicism the principle that in recalibrating our sentences, we recalibrate our lives. The point for the Stoics is not to discard the aesthetic but to be more conscientious about the wording we invite into our heads, for "it is not enough merely to repeat some rational principle to oneself, everything depends on how you formulate it" (Hadot 201). "Everything depends on how you formulate it": one would be hard pressed to come up with a better answer to the question of why language, and literature, matter.

Works Cited

Aurelius, Marcus. *Meditations*. Translated by Gregory Hays, Everyman's Library, 1992.

Berlant, Lauren. *Cruel Optimism*. Duke UP, 2011.

Best, Stephen, and Sharon Marcus. "Surface Reading: An Introduction." *Representations*, vol. 108, no. 1, 2009, pp. 1–21.

Burke, Kenneth. "Literature as Equipment for Living." *The Philosophy of Literary Form: Studies in Symbolic Action*, U California P, 1941, pp. 293–304.

Ciarrochi, Joseph V., and Ann Bailey. *A CBT Practitioner's Guide to ACT*. New Harbinger Publications, 2008.

Clark, Alex. "Drawn from Life: Why Have Novelists Stopped Making Things Up?" *Guardian*, 23 June 2018, https://www.theguardian.com/books/2018/jun/23/drawn-from-life-why-have-novelists-stopped-making-things-up.

Cognitive Behavioral Therapy Los Angeles. "Improve Your Perspective Using Cognitive Reappraisal." *Cognitive Behavioral Therapy, Los Angeles*, May 4, 2014, http://cogbtherapy.com/cbt-blog/2014/5/4/hhy104os08dekc537dlw7nvopzyi44.

Dancer, Thom. *Critical Modesty in Contemporary Fiction*. Oxford UP, 2021.

Dinshaw, Carolyn. *How Soon Is Now? Medieval Texts, Amateur Readers, and the Queerness of Time*. Duke UP, 2012.

Epictetus. *Discourses*. Translated by George Long, D. Appleton & Co., 1904.

Epictetus. *The Encheiridion (The Handbook)*. Translated by Nicholas P. White, Hackett Publishing, 1983.

Felski, Rita. *The Limits of Critique*. U Chicago P, 2015.

Ferriss, Tim. "Why You Should Define Your Fears Instead of Your Goals." *TED: Ideas Worth Spreading*, Apr. 2017, https://www.ted.com/talks/tim_ferriss_why_you_should_define_your_fears_instead_of_your_goals.

Fleissner, Jennifer. *Women, Compulsion, Modernity: The Moment of American Naturalism*. U Chicago P, 2004.

Foucault, Michel. *Hermeneutics of the Subject: Lectures at the Collège de France 1981–82*. Edited by Frédéric Gros, translated by Graham Burchell, Palgrave Macmillan, 2005.

Frye, Northrop. "Literature as Therapy." 23 Nov. 1989. *The Secular Scripture and Other Writings on Critical Theory 1976–1991*, edited by Joseph Adamson and Jean Wilson, U of Toronto P, 2006, pp. 463–534.

Graver, Margaret. "Epictetus." *Stanford Encyclopedia of Philosophy*, edited by Edward N. Zalta, Fall 2018 ed., https://plato.stanford.edu/archives/fall2018/entries/epictetus.

Gruender, David. "Wittgenstein on Explanation and Description." *Journal of Philosophy*, vol. 59, no. 19, Sept. 1962, pp. 523–30.

Guillory, John. *Cultural Capital: The Problem of Literary Canon Formation.* U Chicago P, 1993.

Hadot, Pierre. *Philosophy as a Way of Life.* Blackwell Publishing, 1995.

Haraway, Donna. Interview with Thyrza Nichols Goodeve, *How Like a Leaf: An Interview with Donna Haraway.* Routledge Press, 1998.

Heslin, Kayla. "Redescription as Liberatory Memory Work: Revisiting the Case of Auditing Description for Bias and Oppressive Language." March 2, 2021, https://kayl aheslin.com/redescription-as-liberatory-memory-work-revisiting-the-case-of-audit ing-archival-description-for-bias-and-oppressive-language/.

Heti, Sheila. *How Should a Person Be? A Novel From Life.* Picador, 2012.

Heti, Sheila. Interview with Claudia Dey, "The Child Thing: An Interview with Sheila Heti." *Paris Review*, 26 Apr. 2018, https://www.theparisreview.org/blog/2018/04/26/ the-child-thing-an-interview-with-sheila-heti/.

Heti, Sheila. *Motherhood: A Novel.* Henry Holt and Company, 2018.

Heti, Sheila. *Pure Color: A Novel.* Farrar, Straus and Giroux, 2022.

Heyes, Cressida. "Identity Politics." *Stanford Encyclopedia of* Philosophy, edited by Edward N. Zalta, Fall 2018 ed., https://plato.stanford.edu/archives/fall2018/entries/ identity-politics.

Holiday, Ryan. *Ego Is the Enemy.* Portfolio Books, 2016.

Holiday, Ryan. *The Obstacle Is the Way: The Timeless Art of Turning Trials into Triumph.* Portfolio Books, 2014.

Holiday, Ryan. *Trust Me, I'm Lying: Confessions of a Media Manipulator.* Portfolio Books, 2012.

Holiday, Ryan, and Stephen Hanselman. *The Daily Stoic: 366 Meditations on Wisdom, Perseverance.* Portfolio Books, 2016.

Holland, Norman. *The Dynamics of Literary Response.* Oxford UP, 1968.

Jaggar, Alison. *Feminist Politics and Human Nature.* Rowman and Allanheld, 1983.

James, Henry. "The Works of Epictetus." *Literary Criticism: Essays on Literature, American Writers, English Writers*, The Library of America, edited by Leon Edel, 1984, pp. 5–14.

Julian, Kate. "Why Are Young People Having So Little Sex?" *The Atlantic*, Dec. 2018, https://www.theatlantic.com/magazine/archive/2018/12/the-sex-recession/573949/.

Knausgaard, Karl Ove. *My Struggle, Book 1.* Translated by Don Bartlett, Farrar, Straus and Giroux, 2009.

Kunzru, Hari. "Karl Ove Knausgaard: The Latest Literary Sensation." *Guardian*, 7 Mar. 2014, https://www.theguardian.com/books/2014/mar/07/karl-ove-knausgaard-my- struggle-hari-kunzru.

Laird, Rebecca S., and Gerald I. Metalsky. "Attribution Change." *General Principles and Empirically Supported Techniques of Cognitive Behavioral Therapy*, edited by William T. O'Donohue and Jane E. Fisher, John Wiley and Sons, 2009, pp. 133–37.

Lasch-Quinn, Elizabeth. "The New Old Ways of Self-Help." *Hedgehog Review*, vol. 19, no. 1, 2017, https://hedgehogreview.com/issues/the-post-modern-self/articles/ the-new-old-ways-of-self-help

Lessing, Doris. *The Golden Notebook: A Novel.* HarperCollins, 1990.

Love, Heather. "Close But Not Deep: Literary Ethics and the Descriptive Turn." *New Literary History*, vol. 41, no. 2, 2010, pp. 371–91.

Lynch, Deidre. *Loving Literature: A Cultural History.* U Chicago P, 2014.

McGrath, Laura B. "Charisma (Embodiment): A Response to Tess McNulty." *Post45*, 7 May 2019, https://post45.org/2019/05/charisma-embodiment-a-response-to-tess-mcnulty/.

Nietzsche, Friedrich. *Beyond Good and Evil: Prelude to a Philosophy of the Future*. Dover Thrift Editions, 1997.

Phillips, Adam. "On Translating a Person." *Promises, Promises: Essays on Literature and Psychoanalysis*, Basic Books, 2001, pp. 125–47.

Piper, Andrew. *Enumerations: Data and Literary Study*. U Chicago P, 2018.

Proust, Marcel. "Letter to Madame Straus. November 9, 1905." *The Letters of Marcel Proust*, edited and translated by Mina Curtis, Helen Marx Books, Books & Co., 2006.

Proust, Marcel. Note to translation of John Ruskin. *Sésame et les Lys*, Paris, 1906.

Rich, Adrienne. *Of Women Born: Motherhood as Experience and Institution*. W.W. Norton, 1995.

Robertson, Donald. *The Philosophy of Cognitive Behavioral Therapy: Stoic Philosophy as Rational and Cognitive Psychotherapy*. Karnac Books, 2010.

Rorty, Richard. *Contingency, Irony, and Solidarity*. Cambridge UP, 1989.

Ruddick, Lisa. "When Nothing Is Cool." *The Point Magazine*, vol. 10, 2015, https://thepointmag.com/2015/criticism/when-nothing-is-cool.

Saint-Amour, Paul. "Weak Theory, Weak Modernism." *Modernism/Modernity*, vol. 24, no. 3, August 25, 2018, pp. 437–59.

Schafer, Roy. "Narration in the Psychoanalytic Dialogue." *Critical Inquiry*, vol. 7, no. 1, On Narrative, 1980, pp. 29–53.

Seneca. "On the Happy Life." *Dialogues and Essays*, translated by John Davie, Oxford UP, 2007, pp. 85–111.

Seneca. "Grief for Lost Friends." *Epistles*, vol. 1., translated by Richard M. Gunmere, Loeb Classical Library 75, Harvard University Press, 1917, pp. 428–37.

Siebers, Tobin. *Cold War Criticism and the Politics of Skepticism*. Oxford UP, 1993.

Smith, Zadie. *Intimations*. Penguin, 2020.

Sukenick, Lynn. "Feeling and Reason in Doris Lessing's Fiction." *Contemporary Literature*, vol. 14, 1973, pp. 515–35.

Tallis, Frank. *The Act of Living: What the Great Psychologists Can Tell Us about Finding Fulfillment*. Basic Books, 2020.

Tomkins, Silvan S. *Affect Imagery Consciousness*, vol. 2, *The Negative Affects*. Springer, 1962.

Vadde, Aarthi, and Saikat Majumdar. *The Critic as Amateur*. Bloomsbury, 2019.

Wiener, Daniel Norman. *Albert Ellis: Passionate Skeptic*. U Michigan P, 1988.

Worth, Richard. *Toussaint L'Ouverture: Fighting for Haitian Independence*. Enslow Publishing, 2018.

Worthen, Molly. "The Podcast Bros Want to Optimize Your Life." *New York Times*, 3 Aug. 2018, https://www.nytimes.com/2018/08/03/opinion/sunday/podcast-bros-rogan-ferriss-junger.html.

Zhang, Dora. *Strange Likeness: Description and the Modernist Novel*. U Chicago P, 2020.

Zuckerberg, Donna. *Not All Dead White Men: Classics and Misogyny in the Digital Age*. Harvard UP, 2018.

10

Merely Ameliorative

Reading, Critical Affect, and the Project of Repair

Heather Love

In the late twentieth century, literary criticism took up many of the prerogatives of philosophy, commenting via textual readings on matters of epistemology, ethics, and value. As a discipline within the modern professional university, however, literary criticism did little to cultivate the love of wisdom, in the sense of an erotic drive to approach the truth and to live by its dictates. It has rather been the burden of critical theory to question the foundations of such an idea, to question the equation of truth with beauty, and to undermine the idea that there is a single truth that all could live by. Despite such resistance, the dream of a transformative criticism, one that would aim to do more than critique what is given, continues to resurface. One of its most recent appearances is in the field of affect studies, which aims to cross the blood-brain barrier through an address to living substance.

One of the foremost figures in the field of affect studies is the literary critic and queer theorist Eve Kosofsky Sedgwick. In a series of essays published in the 1990s and early 2000s, she approached questions of feeling, embodiment, and truth through the framework of reading, and through an extended meditation on the ethics of interpretation. In her essay "Paranoid Reading and Reparative Reading" (1996/1997/2003),[1] Sedgwick describes the limits of what she understands as the paranoid complexion of contemporary criticism, drawing on Paul Ricoeur's analysis of the "hermeneutics of suspicion." She suggests that the critical tradition associated with Freud, Marx, and Nietzsche, and, more recently, with Foucault, has reached a dead end.

---

[1] The essay was published in two earlier versions before its final appearance in Sedgwick's 2002 book. I refer to the 2002 version throughout this essay. Robyn Wiegman offers a careful and clarifying account of the evolution of the essay in "The Times We're In" (2014).

Heather Love, *Merely Ameliorative* In: *Literary Studies and Human Flourishing*. Edited by: James F. English and Heather Love, Oxford University Press. © Oxford University Press 2023. DOI: 10.1093/oso/9780197637227.003.0011

Sedgwick argues that like paranoia itself, paranoid criticism tends to discover the same truth everywhere, and she sees diminishing returns in the project of exposing hidden violence. Drawing on the work of Melanie Klein, Sedgwick imagines another critical approach which she calls reparative reading. More a disposition than a method, reparative reading is responsive rather than rigid; approaches its objects with loving attention and care rather than with wariness or skepticism; and is oriented to positive rather than negative affect. Through this elaboration of a methodological ethics, Sedgwick suggests a novel aim for criticism: subjective repair.

Sedgwick's turn to affect and the link she proposes between reading and psychic healing makes her work an important touchstone for discussions of flourishing and well-being in the humanities. "Paranoid Reading and Reparative Reading" is especially important in this regard because it marks a shift in Sedgwick's thinking to a focus on positive affect. While Sedgwick's earlier work addressed the feelings associated with the conditions of the closet (shame, paranoia, jealousy), this essay ties the project of repair to the experience of joy and to aesthetic pleasure. Sedgwick is aware of the prestige that attaches to negative feelings in both literary studies and critical theory; she acknowledges the vulnerability of her call for a more loving and less defensive criticism to charges of self-indulgence and quietism. As she puts it: "The vocabulary for articulating any reader's reparative motive toward a text or a culture has long been so sappy, aestheticizing, defensive, anti-intellectual, or reactionary that it's no wonder few critics are willing to describe their acquaintance with such motives" (150).

Sedgwick's aim in the essay is to outflank such maneuvers by casting doubt on the association between suffering and moral and political seriousness. Sedgwick characterizes paranoid reading as "monopolistic." She suggests that paranoid reading practices tend to crush alternatives, thus "impoverish[ing] the gene pool of literary critical perspectives and skills" (144). As Sedgwick writes,

The monopolistic program of paranoid knowing systematically disallows any explicit recourse to reparative motives, no sooner to be articulated than subject to methodological uprooting. Reparative motives, once they become explicit, are inadmissible in paranoid theory both because they are about pleasure ("merely aesthetic") and because they are frankly ameliorative ("merely reformist"). What makes pleasure and amelioration so "mere"? (144)

To be concerned with pleasure and with amelioration can be understood as a kind of shirking—a refusal to confront a pervasive and fundamental horror. But if pleasure and amelioration are dismissed as trivial or self-indulgent, Sedgwick characterizes paranoid criticism as both callous and ineffective: "Only the exclusiveness of paranoia's faith in demystifying expo-sure: only its cruel and contemptuous assumption that the one thing lacking for global revolution, explosion of gender roles, or whatever, is people's (that is, other people's) having the painful effects of their oppression, poverty, or deludedness sufficiently exacerbated to make the pain conscious (as if other-wise it wouldn't have been) and intolerable (as if intolerable situations were famous for generating excellent solutions)" (144).

Sedgwick's argument in "Paranoid Reading and Reparative Reading" skirts both hedonism and tautology: she does not argue that pleasure is good just because it is pleasurable, however she does suggest that it constitutes a kind of truth. But she wants to have it both ways: Sedgwick defends amelioration on the grounds that happiness is hard to come by and that it provides its own justification; at the same time, she stakes out more familiar ground, suggesting that turning aside from paranoia may open novel solutions to persistent injustice and violence. While Sedgwick acknowledges that pleasure and amelioration may be irrelevant to poli-tics, and suggests that's ok, she also looks to pleasure to open new pathways in political life. This ambivalence regarding the uses of pleasure—and whether it makes sense to talk about it in terms of use—makes the essay important in any discussion of aesthetics and well-being. But it also points to significant tensions in such discussions between the aims of individual and collective flourishing.

I address these questions by reading Sedgwick's defense of positive affect alongside the work of the critic who is perhaps most closely identified with practices of painful demystification: Theodor Adorno. More than any other twentieth-century thinker, Adorno is associated with a position of thorough-going negativity. In *Minima Moralia*, written during and in the immediate aftermath of World War II, Adorno locates ethical value in the ability and willingness to face terrible facts. The epigraph to Part Two of the book, by the philosopher F. H. Bradley, is fitting: "Where everything is bad it must be good to know the worst" (Adorno 1974, 83). Knowing the worst, bearing witness to the horrors of modernity, and refusing consolation: this is the program of critical askesis that Adorno undertakes in *Minima Moralia*. But he stipulates that even given the most adamant stance of refusal, there is no way to escape the general doom: "Wrong life cannot be lived rightly" (39). In contrast to Sedgwick's interest in repair as a motive for criticism, Adorno embraces an ethics of subjective damage: the suffering of the critic should reflect the suffering of the world at large. Despite their diametrically opposed stances, there are surprising resonances between Sedgwick and Adorno—most notably the fact that they make affect and in particular the affective response of the critic central. Furthermore, despite the scouring negativity of Adorno's writing, images of happiness recur throughout his work. In the Dedication to *Minima Moralia*, Adorno identifies the book with the philosophical pursuit of "the good life" (15): although he suggests that this project is impossible in a moment in which "there is life no longer" (15), he nonetheless turns to personal experience, arguing that the life of the individual becomes meaningful "in the period of his decay" (17). In this essay, I consider the paradoxes that arise in the pursuit of affective criticism and weigh the value of pleasure and pain as critical affects.

* * *

Sedgwick's most radical suggestion in "Paranoid and Reparative Reading" is that the pursuit of happiness might displace the search for truth in literary criticism. Sedgwick's disdain for the usual scholarly protocols, and her frank embrace of pleasure, are meant to provoke. They mark a radical departure from the attitude of paranoia. In characterizing paranoia, Sedgwick draws on the work of the midcentury psychologist Silvan Tomkins, and in particular his taxonomy of positive and negative affects. For Tomkins, Sedgwick writes, paranoia is "a strong theory of a negative affect" (136). A strong theory, in Tomkins's account, overorganizes the territory it surveys. It is characterized by "wide reach and rigorous exclusiveness" (Sedgwick 135), and finds evidence of what it is looking for everywhere—in the case of paranoia, what it looks for is threat, or harm, thus its link to negative affect. For Tomkins, the successful avoidance of pain can lead to a weakening of this "monopolistic" theory and eventually to the ability to seek out pleasure rather than simply to avoid pain.[2] Sedgwick contrasts Tomkins's interest in possibilities for maximizing positive affect with Freud's account of the pleasure principle—and his "silent installing [of] the anxious paranoid imperative ... as 'reality'" (137).

[2] Sedgwick sees the potential to seek pleasure as an ethical achievement also in the work of Melanie Klein and in the late work of Michel Foucault, both of whom she mentions in this context.

Still, neither Tomkins nor Freud offers a theory of pleasure that is adequate to Sedgwick's aims.[3] Ultimately, she turns away from psychology to literature—and specifically to Proust—for a suggestion of how the experience of joy might serve as a criterion of truth.

There is "no room," she writes, in Freud's account for

> the Proustian epistemology whereby the narrator of À la recherche, who feels in the last volume "jostling each other within me a whole host of truths concerning human passions and character and conduct"—recognizes them as truths insofar as "*the perception of [them] caused me joy.*" In the paranoid Freudian epistemology, it is implausible enough to suppose that truth could be an even accidental occasion of joy, inconceivable to imagine joy as a guarantor of truth. Indeed, from any point of view it is circular, or something, to suppose that one's pleasure at knowing something could be taken as evidence of the truth of the knowledge. (137–38, Sedgwick's emphasis)

Sedgwick takes seriously Proust's suggestion that the value and indeed the truth of a statement might be confirmed by its ability to give pleasure. She suggests that although the self-confirming Proustian epistemology might be circular, it is no more so than a paranoid epistemology which looks out for painful and threatening experiences, and, finding them, repeatedly confirms its worst fears.

Demonstrating some of the hypervigilance characteristic of the paranoid position, Sedgwick is keenly aware of potential objections to her argument. Her turn to affect was, from the start, ringed with provisos. Her "Queer Performativity" essay, published in 1993, introduced affect as a central concern for the first time. Discussing the uses of shame in Henry James's Prefaces to the New York Edition of his novels, Sedgwick includes a paragraph responding to imagined doubts about the psychological or even pop-psychological turn of her writing. "Readers who have paid attention to the recent, meteoric rise of shame to its present housewife-megastar status in the firmament of self-help and popular psychology—along with that of its ingenue sidekick the Inner Child—may be feeling a bit uneasy at this point" (8). Sedgwick distances herself from the domain of self-help, suggesting

---

[3] Sedgwick's objections to Freud are that he naturalizes the pleasure principle, and that he grants too much authority to reality as he frames it in his elaboration of the reality principle. See Sedgwick 2002, 137.

that shame in this context has become part of the "bifurcated moralisms" that Foucault identified with the "repressive hypothesis" (8). But the separation is not total: "Am I really going to talk about Henry James's inner child?" Sedgwick continues. "My sense of the force and interest of the affect shame is clearly very different from what is to be found in the self-help literature, but there it is: Henry James and the inner child it must be" (8). Sedgwick is aware of the risks she is running in turning to feeling, and she anticipates objections with both wit and direct argument. She defends shame on the grounds that it is irreducibly relational and therefore incipiently social; she also pursues its relation to stigma and to the social history of non-normative gender and sexuality. For these reasons, and because of its negative cast, shame has more gravity than joy. In this context, it is not the affect itself but rather Sedgwick's desire to repair—to repair Henry James, to repair herself—that raises the specter of self-help.

To avow psychic healing as an explicit goal in criticism raises difficult questions.

There is something inimical to theory, to concept, and arguably to thought itself in turning aside from the project of truth-telling. Criticism—and academic discourse generally—might be defined by its willingness to play by the rules of truth: to presuppose that statements can describe an existing and verifiable state of affairs. Particularly in the context of Left criticism, the task is not only to discover the truth, but to face hard truths—the stubborn facts of violence, inequality, and social exclusion. Given that confrontation with these facts tends to be not healing but hurtful, focusing on subjective repair might mean blocking out the world, or at least what is most painful in it. Further, the repair sought or achieved by any individual reader is in tension with the aim of *collective* reparation that constitutes the ultimate horizon of progressive thought. What makes amelioration so inadequate is that its target is only one person. In a field in which general social transformation is the highest goal, how to reckon with the aim of merely personal happiness?

At the individual level, reparation *can* be understood as a worthwhile project if it is necessary for survival. That is to say, Left critics sidestep the question of pleasure by justifying repair and positive affect more generally as a response to trauma. But Sedgwick raises the stakes of this discussion by linking repair not just to survival but also to pleasure—to flourishing. Rather than focusing on the fate of vulnerable subjects, Sedgwick names joy as a value in itself, without tying it to states of injury. She thus risks an association with feelings widely understood as self-indulgent, unworldly, and feminized.

But this discussion also brings her into the ambit of the field of positive psychology, which takes good feeling as an end in itself. Sedgwick's insistence on pleasure recalls the distinction between the hedonic—closely tied to positive affect—and eudaimonic—indicating broader-spectrum thriving and growth—in the literature on well-being. The distinction between well-being as a matter of sensation versus well-being as a matter of capacity building is moralized. However, Sedgwick does not describe reading as a route to self-realization, or as a way of increasing empathy or even cultivating attention. Instead she invokes joy—a feeling that is useless, and without justification—or which provides its own justification in the form of a quantum of pleasure. The question of pleasure, so fundamental to the experience of the aesthetic, is often an embarrassment to fields like literary studies in which it is central. The pleasures of absorption and fantasy are not separable from the experience of reading. But how does dreaming by the book help us to change the world?

* * *

Sedgwick's suggestion that pleasure might serve as a criterion of truth is answered in *Minima Moralia* via a citation of Nietzsche. In a section titled "*Court of appeal*," Adorno writes,

> Nietzsche in the *Antichrist* voiced the strongest argument not merely against theology but against metaphysics, that hope is mistaken for truth; that the impossibility of living happily, or even living at all, without the thought of an absolute, does not vouch for the legitimacy of that thought. He refutes the Christian "proof by efficacy," that faith is true because it brings felicity. For "could happiness—or, more technically speaking, pleasure—ever be a proof of truth? So far from this, it almost proves the converse, at any rate it gives the strongest grounds for suspecting 'truth' whenever feelings of pleasure have had a say in the matter. The proof of pleasure is proof of pleasure: nothing more. (97)

For Nietzsche, not only is happiness not a proof of truth, it is not a proof of anything. Pleasure is self-justifying, but in a tautological way; the feeling of pleasure does not suggest the presence of truth but rather delusion and fantasy. There are many moments in Adorno's writing (and in his collaboration with Max Horkheimer) in which pleasure is cast as an enemy of truth. In his writing on the culture industry, pleasure appears as a scourge, an empty spectacle which, in seeking to distract people from their real conditions of existence, reproduces them. For Adorno, only the most stringent critique is adequate to the historical disaster he identified simply as "Auschwitz." In this context, it might be said that it is suffering rather than pleasure that signals that you are in the vicinity of truth.

It is for this reason that Peter Sloterdijk understands Adorno's criticism as characterized by "*a priori pain*" in the Preface to *The Critique of Cynical Reason* (xxxiii). The stringency and negativity of Adorno's thought identifies him, in this context, with the dead end of critique. In his account of "enlightened false consciousness," Sloterdijk argues that the voiding of pleasure is the signature of post-Enlightenment modernity. As a result of the rigorous negations of critical theory, philosophy is "lying on its deathbed" (xxvi). What was once an "erotic theory—the love of truth and the truth through love" (xxvii)—has been destroyed by the binding together of knowledge and power. Sloterdijk calls for a reanimation of philosophy through the cultivation of its bodily, affective, and erotic dimensions. One might see Adorno in Sloterdijk's description of those critics who, succumbing to a "sour temperament," have become "more morose than precise" (xxxii). Adorno's melancholy philosophy can certainly tend to gloom, and he often strikes a sour note, whether he is excoriating the "monstrous machinery of amusement" (139), the "arty-crafty" poses of intellectuals (134), or lamenting the decline of casement windows (40). Yet this is not Sloterdijk's final word on Adorno: he does not count him among the bloodless philosophers (or, worse, the sociologists). Although Adorno's cultural criticism often sounds a note of bitter contempt, Sloterdijk sees him not as a distant observer but as a hypersensitive instrument. Even contempt in Adorno has the affective charge of curdled hope rather than simple renunciation. There is an erotics in his work. Although it is not pleasure-seeking, but rather masochistic, and can take the form of "nausea toward everything and anything" (Sloterdijk xxxiv), it is nonetheless an erotics of a kind, and therefore in touch with truth. For, as Sloterdijk writes, "to discover the living body as a sensor of the world is to secure a realistic foundation for philosophical knowledge of the world" (xxxiii).

Because, as Sloterdijk suggests, truth in *Minima Moralia* is tied to the vagaries of feeling, memory, and desire, the book cannot be said to be in any real sense *against* happiness. Focused on the cancelation of happiness, *Minima Moralia* is nonetheless filled with images of satiety and security, of repleteness and repose. Many of these images are taken from the realm of childhood and family life; they recall a world of bourgeois intimacy, the experience of "privacy" before it gave way "to the privation it always secretly was" (14). Adorno's images of happiness are "waste products and . . . blind spots"—they represent the "cross-grained, opaque, unassimilated material" (151) that survives through irrelevance. It is not happiness itself but rather instrumental happiness that Adorno opposes. He writes, "To happiness the same applies as to truth: one does not have it, but is in it. Indeed, happiness is nothing other than being encompassed, an after-image of the original shelter within the mother. But for this reason no-one who is happy can know that he is so. . . . He who says he is happy lies, and invoking happiness, sins against it" (112).[4] Happiness that is unknown, that is lost, that is in the past tense, is the only possible happiness. To identify it in the present and to attempt to hold it fast destroys it, turning it from quality into quantity. But it is also a betrayal of the possibility of happiness to project it into the future. Sloterdijk links Adorno's barring of future happiness to what he sees as the utopian aspect of his sensitive criticism: "To remain sensitive was, as it were, a utopian stance—to keep the senses sharpened for a happiness that will not come, a stance that nevertheless, by being prepared for happiness, protects us from the worst kinds of brutalizations" (xxxiv).

The most degraded images of happiness in *Minima Moralia* are the stereotyped forms of enjoyment purveyed by the culture industry. But as hellish as these images of mass cheerfulness are, Adorno reserves his most pointed critiques not for empty entertainment but for the instrumentalization of pleasure. If for Nietzsche it is the collapse of pleasure and truth that is the scandal, Adorno's objection is to the conflation of pleasure and ethics. This conflation is objectionable not only because suffering reflects the state of the world more fully. But, for Adorno, any attempt to ground a vision of the good life in the ephemeral and useless experience of happiness is a betrayal. Happiness founds no program; to count on it is to destroy it. The main culprit in this warping of happiness is not the culture industry but the human sciences, and in particular those curative sciences that aim to restore health to modernity's ailing individuals.

Minima Moralia features many diatribes against both happiness and health: the prescription of happiness is a prime target for Adorno, perhaps because of its insistently individual focus (as opposed to, say, mass entertainment for the workers). Like Sedgwick, Adorno opposes the naturalization

---

[4] Cf. Sloterdijk's point about critical theory as focused on the "utopia of the feminine" (xxxv).

of a "pleasure principle" in psychoanalysis: the fact that it is understood as timeless and universal, and that it is enforced as an aspiration, drains any real pleasure out of the concept. He writes,

> Psycho-analysis prides itself on restoring the capacity for pleasure, which is impaired by neurotic illness. As if the mere concept of capacity for pleasure did not suffice gravely to devalue such a thing, if it exists. As if a happiness gained through speculation on happiness were not the opposite. . . . What a state the dominant consciousness must have reached, when the resolution proclamation of compulsive extravagance and champagne jollity, formerly reserved to attachés in Hungarian operettas, is elevated in deadly earnest to a maxim of right living. (38)

The reproach of Adorno's words to the regime of compulsory well-being still resonates today—arguably even more in a moment when the health consequences of happiness are regularly used to encourage a positive attitude.[5] His equation of happiness with the "champagne jollities" of light opera is enough to satisfy the critical impulses of any enemy of positive psychology. It is such moments, alongside his melancholic indictments of life that does not live, that have justified Adorno's reputation as the king of pain. But Adorno's violent denunciations of happiness are in the service of a form of happiness that would evade both commodification and instrumentalization.

Glimmers of such happiness appear in a section of *Minima Moralia* titled "Regressions," in which Adorno describes his love of lullabies by Brahms and Taubert, and of a popular song, "Between the Mountain and the Deep, Deep Vale." The song tells the story of two rabbits who are shot by a hunter, fall down, then realize they are alive and run off. Commenting on the necessity of "absurdity," Adorno writes,

> One ought to follow the example of the two rabbits; when the shot comes, fall down giddily, half-dead with fright, collect one's wits and then, if one still has breath, show a clean pair of heels. The capacity for fear and for happiness are the same, the unrestricted openness to experience amounting to self-abandonment in which the vanquished rediscovers himself. What would happiness be that was not measured by the immeasurable grief at what is? For this world is deeply ailing.

---

[5] I wrote about this double bind in Love 2007/2008.

He who cautiously adapts to it by this very act shares in its madness, while the eccentric alone would stand his ground and bid it rave no more. He alone could pause to think on the illusoriness of disaster, the "unreality of despair," and realize not merely that he is still alive but that there is still life. (200)

The fact that Adorno's image of a life that could still be lived is taken from a childhood lexicon—and that it falls under the heading "regressions"—suggests strongly that happiness is a receding horizon, more mirage than oasis. There is, in any case, no direct way to access it.[6] Rather, it can only be approached obliquely, beyond all rational calculation. Adorno stipulates too that it can be achieved only in the midst of suffering: it is through a confrontation with "absolute despair," with death, that the unreality of despair can be grasped.

Sedgwick's embrace of joy as a criterion of truth and her frank embrace of pleasure as an end in itself set her at some distance from Adorno's melancholy aphorisms on the end of the world. But this is not everything *Minima Moralia* is. In this passage in particular, Adorno offers not only reflections from damaged life but also advice about how to live in it: make like the rabbits. It is true in this case that joy is to be snatched quite literally from the jaws of death, as a matter of survival. Still, this act of survival is only possible within an aesthetic mode: there is "still life" only in a realm that has been torn away from all utility and in which illusion defeats reality. That is to say, it is only by laughing and leaping up that one can live at all. The avowal of pleasure and the further insistence that pleasure is impossible without risk forges a link between Sedgwick and Adorno. Such claims only take on their full meaning when we understand their criticisms as erotic in the sense Sloterdijk intends: their utopianism consists in "keeping the senses sharpened"—in maintaining not only proximity to the object but also an erotic openness to it. This sustained sensitivity underwrites a shared method, what Sloterdijk refers to as a "micrology": "not an elevated, distanced critique that achieves grand overviews but a stance of extreme closeness" (xxxiii). Adorno and Sedgwick are both committed to maintaining such a stance as an ethical practice: this extreme commitment to proximity accounts for the dizzying

---

[6] Stefan Mueller-Doohm, Adorno's biographer, identifies this story as taken from the "song book illustrated by Ludwig von Zumbusch that had accompanied him through his childhood" (Mueller-Doohm 345).

turnabouts in their work. In following their example of an affective criticism committed to the cause of human flourishing, we may well ask whether the categories of pleasure and pain, or positive and negative affect, are up to the task of describing these exposures.

Works Cited

Adorno, Theodor. *Minima Moralia: Reflections from Damaged Life*. Translated by Edmund F. N. Jephcott, Verso, 1974 (1951).

Love, Heather. "Compulsory Happiness and Queer Existence," *New Formations*, vol. 63, Winter 2007/2008, pp. 52–111.

Mueller-Doohm, Stefan. *Adorno: A Biography*. Translated by Rodney Livingston, Polity Press, 2005 (2003).

Sedgwick, Eve Kosofsky. "Queer Performativity: Henry James's *The Art of the Novel*." *GLQ*, vol. 1, no. 1, 1993, pp. 1–16.

Sedgwick, Eve Kosofsky. "Paranoid Reading and Reparative Reading, or, You're So Paranoid, You Probably Think This Essay Is about You." *Touching Feeling: Affect, Pedagogy, Performativity*, Duke UP, 2002, pp. 123–151.

Sloterdijk, Peter. *The Critique of Cynical Reason*. Translated by Michael Eldred, U Minnesota P, 1987 (1983).

Wiegman, Robyn. "The Times We're In: Queer Feminist Criticism and the Reparative 'Turn.'" *Feminist Theory*, vol. 15, no. 1, 2014, pp. 4–25.

Index

For the benefit of digital users, indexed terms that span two pages (e.g., 52–53) may, on occasion, appear on only one of those pages.

Note: Figures boxes are indicated by *f* following the page number

abnormal psychology, 145–46
abuse, of children, 65
Aché (Lorde), 129
activism, 31, 32
Adams, William, xxi
Adeyemi, Kemi, 135
Adichie, Chimamanda Ngozi, 38–39
adolescents, 26–27
Adorno, Theodore, 20, 116, 213–18
aesthetics, 9, 14–15
affective relationships, 15–16
affect studies, 19–20, 207–18
Africa, 136
African American criticism, 11
Afro-pessimism, 123
Against Happiness (Wilson), 7–8
aging
    geropsychology and, 164–66, 174–80
    positive, 165–66
    in positive psychology, 18, 164n.1
    psychology of, 18
    wisdom and, 167–68
Ahmed, Sara, 7–8
Aidoo, Ama Ata, 7–8
Akbar, Arifa, 110n.5
amelioration, 207–18
ameliorative sentimentalism, 103–9
Americanah (Adichie), 38–39
American Psychological Association
    (APA), xix
Ammons, A. R., 18, 161, 175–78, 177n.12,
    179–80, 179n.15
Anderson, Amanda, 148n.8
Anderson, Hephzibah, 107–8
Angelou, Maya, 84–85
Annas, Julia, 4

antidepressants, 27–28
anxiety, 25, 27n.1, 202–3
APA. *See* American Psychological
    Association
Aristotle, 1–2, 4–5, 160
Arnold, Matthew, 9–10, 85–86
art. *See also specific topics*
    Arts Alive Wales, 109–10
    philosophy of, 81–82
    values from, xv–xvi
    visual arts, xvi–xvii
The Art of Growing Older (Booth), 175–76
assumptions, in higher education, xii
At Last, the Real Distinguished Thing
    (Woodward), 171–72, 173
"Aubade" (Ammons), 176–77
Austen, Jane, 5–7
Austin, J. L., 89
Australia, 36–37, 38–39
avant-garde music, 46–47
Axial Age, xx–xxi

Baldwin, James, 85
Ball, Jesse, 155–61
Baltes, Paul, 165, 167–68
The Banner of Light, 66–70
Barbados, 123
Barker, Emma, 104
Barnes, Elizabeth, 146–47
Barsby, Susan E., 99–101, 118–20
Bates, Catherine Young, 68–69
Bechdel, Alison, 154–55
Beckerman, Hannah, 100–1
beliefs, 14–15, 70–75, 70n.1, 77–78
Bennett, Jane, 75, 76–77
Berlant, Lauren, 203

Berthoud, Ella, 30–31
bestselling novels, 42–45, 44f–45f
The Better Angels of Our Nature
(Pinker), 25–26
Better Life Initiative (OECD), xviii–xix
bibliotherapy, 13, 107–8
big data, 39
Bion, Wilfred, 91
Black ecological optimism
with cancer, 126–29
flourishing and, 123–26
in hurricanes, 133–34
poetry and, 130–32
repetition of, 134–39
Black feminism, 129
Black feminist culture, 134–39
Blackmur, R. P., 84
Black Studies, 136–38
"Blackstudies" (Lorde), 136–38
The Bluest Eye (Morrison), 7–8
Blum, Beth, 32–33, 86, 108–9
Bode, Katherine, 38–39
A Body, Undone (Crosby), 114–15
Booth, Wayne, 175–76
Bosh and Flapdoodle (Ammons), 175–78,
177n.12, 179–80, 179n.15
Bourdieu, Pierre, 47–48
Brooks, Gwendolyn, 174–75, 175n.10
Burnett, Dean, 99–100
Butler, Judith, 1–2

cancer, 126–29
Cancer Journals (Lorde), 16–17, 126–29
Cannon, Joanna, 100–1, 102–3
Caribbean, 123–26, 134. *See also*
specific topics
Cavell, Stanley, 90
Celenza, Anna Harwell, xvi
censorship, 31
Census (Ball), 155–61
Chafer, Camilla, 58–59
Chandler, James, 104
Changing Lives Through Literature, 31
charisma, 32–33, 199–204
children, 31, 65
Christianity, 4–5, 31, 68–69
Cinema, Media, and Human Flourishing
(Corrigan), xvi
classical music, 46–47, 216–17

Clifford, William, 70–71
Clinton, Bill, 84–85
Cognitive-behavioral therapy, 186, 189–
92, 190f
cognitive frustration, 173–74
cognitive science, 25, 26, 36–37
Cohen, Adam, 151n.11
Cold War, 32, 202–3
collective reparation, 212
Collingwood, R. G., 91
community, xv–xvi
Conlan, Bridget, 68
Connolly, William, 75
"Contradictions" (Rich), 174–75
Coopersmith, Jonathan, xxiii
Corrigan, Timothy, xvi
cosmetic surgery, 29
COVID-19, xviii
Crane, Hart, 7–8
Craps, Stef, 111n.6
"The Crazy Woman" (Brooks), 175n.10
critical affect, 207–18
criticism
African American, 11
data on, 86
ecocriticism, 202
of literature, 9–12, 32–33, 81–83
New Criticism, 9–10
philosophy of, 210–13
psychology and, 84–87
by Ruskin, 91–95
scholarship on, 19–20
by Sedgwick, 19–20, 172–74, 217–18
of Up Lit, 116–20
by Woodward, 171–72, 173
The Critique of Cynical Reason Sloterdijk,
Peter, 214
Crosby, Christina, 114–15
Csikszentmihayli, Mihaly, 80,
164–65, 167. *See also* positive
psychology
culture
Black feminist, 134–39
cultural omnivores, 46–48
cultural studies, 10–11, 32
after Enlightenment, 5–7
feminism and, 171–72
geropsychology and, 171–74
of Greece, 185–87

in modernity, 83–85
of online reading, 48, 48n.19
scalability in, 88–89
social sciences and, xxii
sociology of, 46–47, 58–59
spiritualism in, 65–66
of US, 27
virtue in, xx–xxi

The Daily Stoic (Holiday), 188
Dancer, Thom, 200
data
   big, 39
   on criticism, 86
   from Goodreads, 40–46
   on literary reception, 36–40
   on modernity, 52n.23
   on reading, 56f
   from reviews, 40n.8, 54f
   scholarship and, 36–40
Davis, Jane, 32
deflection, 90–91
depression, 27–30
De Quincey, Thomas, 81–84, 88–89
The Descent of Winter (Williams, W. C.), 149–53
DH. *See* digital humanities
Diamond, Cora, 89–91
Dickinson, Emily, 165–66
Didion, Joan, 107
Differential Linguistic Analysis (DLA) toolkit, 42
digital humanities (DH), 38–39
digital technology, 48, 48n.19
disability
   disabled people, 17–18
   Down Syndrome, 149, 156–60
   eudaimonic turns with, 149–53
   hermeneutics of, 143–47, 143n.1, 144n.2, 145n.3, 146n.5, 149
   ID, 149–61, 149n.9
   in literature, 155–61
Disability Studies (DS), 144–47, 145n.3, 146n.5, 154–55
disaster, 125, 126–29, 133–34. *See also* hurricanes
disciplines
   in higher education, x–xii
   interdisciplines, 12–13

learning and, xxi
scholarship and, xx
discussions, in education, 17–18
disposition, in higher education, 19
Distinction (Bourdieu), 47–48
DLA toolkit. *See* Differential Linguistic Analysis toolkit
domain experts, 2–3
Dove, Rita, 7–8
Down Syndrome, 149, 156–60
"DRAB POT" (Ammons), 177–78
DS. *See* Disability Studies
Dubois, Paul, 192–93
Dyer, Richard, 10–11

eclecticism, 35, 46–60, 51f–55f
ecocriticism, 202
ecology. *See* Black ecological optimism
education. *See also* higher education
   community and, xv–xvi
   COVID-19 and, xviii
   cultural studies, 10–11
   discussions in, 17–18
   history of, xx–xxi
   of positive psychology, 2
   STEM, xxi
   in UK, 31
Ego Is the Enemy (Holiday), 189, 202–3
Elderkin, Susan, 30–31
elderly people. *See* aging; geropsychology
Eleanor Oliphant Is Completely Fine (Honeyman), 100–1
Eliot, George, 32, 85
Eliot, T. S., 8
Ellis, Albert, 189
EmoLex, 40–42, 41f, 41n.10
enchantment, 75
engagement, xxi, 15–16
English, James F., xiii–xiv
English as a Vocation (Hilliard), 10
Enlightenment, 5–7
Enselin, Astrid, 46n.17
Epictetus, 189, 194
Epicureanism, 4
epistemology, 12, 130–32
escapism, 112–13
ethics, 4–7
Ethics and Enjoyment in Late Medieval Poetry (Rosenfeld), 4–5

eudaimonia
  concepts of, 4
  in Greece, 5
  happiness and, 11–12
  Pawelski on, 148n.7, 165–66
  scholarship on, 117–18
  virtue and, 4
The Eudaimonic Turn (Pawelski and
    Moores), 165–66
eudaimonic turns
  with disability, 149–53
  in humanities, xxi
  in literature, 143–47, 143n.1, 144n.2,
    145n.3, 146n.5, 153–55
  in novels, 155–61
  in psychology, xix
  scholarship and, xxii–xxiii

faith-vetoers, 71
feeling, as epistemology, 130–32
Felski, Rita, 37–38, 186–87, 199, 200–1, 202
feminism
  Black, 129, 134–39
  culture and, 171–72
  to Lorde, 123–26
  philosophy of, 196–97
Ferenczi, Sandor, 89
fiction books. *See* novels
Figuring Age (Woodward), 171–72
film, 8
Fleissner, Jennifer, 194–95
flourishing
  Black ecological optimism and, 123–26
  concepts of, 65–66
  HHF Project, xxii, 38–39, 38n.4
  poetry and, 66–68, 165–66
  from positive psychology, 144
  psychology of, 118–19
  scholarship on, xii–xviii, 70–75, 70n.1
  spiritualism and, 67–70, 75–79
"Focal Lengths" (Ammons), 176
Fool (Welsford), 174–75, 174n.9
fool-literature, 174–80
Foucault, Michel, 185–86, 202
The Fountain of Age (Friedan), 171–72
Fow (Csikszentmihayli), 164–65, 167
"The Free Skater" (Barsby), 99–
    100, 118–20

Freud, Sigmund, 89, 211, 211n.3
Friedan, Betty, 171–72
Fries, Kenny, 154–55
The Fries Test, 154–55
Frude, Neil, 27–28
Fruit of the Lemon (Levy), 7–8

The Gates Ajar (Phelps), Phelps's 43
gender, 46n.17, 52–53nn.24–25, 53n.26
genre-intolerance, 35, 46–57
genres
  eclecticism and, 46–57
  of music, 46–47
  research on, 39–40, 51–52, 51–52n.21, 56f
geropsychology
  aging and, 164–66, 174–80
  culture and, 171–74
  literature and, 174–80
  positive, 165–66
  scholarship on, 167–71
Gestalt psychology, 186
Giddens, Anthony, 48
Gilroy, Paul, 10–11
Glück, Louise, 167
"God, Don't Let Me Lose My Mind"
    (Pushkin), 165–66
The Golden Notebook (Lessing), 195–98
Good Kings Bad Kings
    (Nussbaum), 153–55
Goodreads
  data from, 40–46
  research on, 14, 35, 57–60
  reviews on, 41f
  scholarship, 36–40
Greece
  culture of, 185–87
  Epicureanism and, 4
  eudaimonia in, 5
  Rome and, xx–xxi, 185
Grenada, 123
Grenfell Tower catastrophe, 16, 99–101
A Grief Observed (Lewis), 107
Guess, Raymond, 81

Hadot, Pierre, 201–2
Haig, Matt, 100–1, 106–7
Haiti, 78–79
Hall, G. Stanley, 165, 171–72

Hall, Radcliffe, 7–8
Hall, Stuart, 10–11
happiness. *See also specific topics*
  Aristotle on, 4
  epistemology of, 12
  eudaimonia and, 11–12
  history of, 4–8
  literature and, 210–13
  in modernity, 7
  philosophy of, 213–18
  from positive psychology, 3n.2
  race and, 16–17
  research on, 25–26, 41*f*
  scholarship on, 4–5, 7–8, 12–20
  science and, 2–3
  Seneca on, 194
  sources of, 93–94
  UN on, xviii–xix
"The Happiness Lab" (podcast),
  xviii–xix
The Happy Brain (Burnett), 99–100
Hell under God's Orders (Lorde), 133–34,
  135–36
hermeneutics
  in *Census*, 155–61
  of disability, 143–47, 143n.1, 144n.2,
    145n.3, 146n.5, 149
  in *Good Kings Bad Kings*, 153–55
  literature and, 147–61
Herring, Scott, 161
Heti, Sheila, 19, 186–87, 191–92, 193–
  94, 198
HHF Project. *See* Humanities and Human
  Flourishing Project
higher education
  assumptions in, xii
  in Australia, 38–39
  Black Studies in, 136–38
  disciplines in, x–xii
  disposition in, 19
  DS, 144–47, 145n.3, 146n.5, 154–55
  humanities in, 1–3
  idealism in, 9
  inequality in, 11–12
  professionalism in, xxi, 1–2
  reader studies, 13
  in UK, 11
  well-being studies, 2–3
  workshops in, 13
  after World War II, 9–10
Hill, Nathaniel, 69–70
Hilliard, Christopher, 10
Hilton, Tim, 91
History and Human Flourishing
  (McMahon), xiii
Hoggart, Richard, 10–11
Holiday, Ryan, 188–89, 202–3
Holland, Norman, 36–37
Holloway, John, 85
Holo, Selma, xvi–xvii
Honeyman, Gail, 100–1
How to Stop Time (Haig), 100–1
Hughes, Langston, 175
"Hugo I" (Lorde), 131–32, 132n.6
human flourishing. *See specific topics*
humanities
  cognitive science in, 26
  DH, 38–39
  eudaimonic turns in, xxi
  HHF Project, xxii, 38–39, 38n.4
  in higher education, 1–3
  history of, xx
  in modernity, xxi
  Pawelski on, xvii–xviii
  scholarship and, vii–xviii, xx–xxiii
  in science, 25
  social justice in, 16–17
  social sciences and, xiv–xx
The Humanities and Human Flourishing
  (Pawelski), xvii–xviii
Humanities and Human Flourishing (HHF)
  Project, xxii, 38–39, 38n.4
Hume, David, 103
Hunter, Ian, 9
hurricanes
  Hurricane Hugo, 16–17, 123, 124, 125,
    129, 131–32, 132n.6, 133–39
  Hurricane Katrina, 125–26
  Hurricane Maria, 125–26, 134,
    135–36
Hurston, Zora Neale, 124
"The Hurt Hare's Form" (Loncraine, R.), 115

ID. *See* intellectual disability
idealism, 9
identity, 58–60

ideology, 10–11
ideology critique, 81
"idiots," 149–53, 158n.15
incentives, 56f–58f, 57–59
inequality, in higher education, 11–12
information, in modernity, 87–89
In Search of Lost Time (Proust), 172–73
intellectual disability (ID), 149–61, 149n.9
interdisciplines, 12–13
Intimations (Smith, Z.), 187–88

Jaggar, Alison, 196–97
James, C. L. R., 78–79
James, David, 193
James, Henry, 5–7, 211–12
James, William, 14–15, 70–75, 70n.1, 77–78, 92n.3
Jaspers, Karl, xx–xxi
Johnson, Sally, 46n.17
Jonathan, Sophie, 110
Jones, Lisa Renee, 58–59
Joseph, Gloria, 133
joy, 217–18
Joyce, Rachel, 100–1
judgment, 50

Kafka, Franz, 7–8, 30, 155–56
Keats, John, 12
King, Martin Luther, Jr., 78–79
Kirkwood, Charlie, xxiii
Kirkwood, Ginny, xxiii
Kirkwood, John, xxiii
Klein, Melanie, 148n.8, 207–8
Knausgaard, Karl Ove, 19, 186–87, 198–99
know-it-all-ism, 173
knowledge, 82–83

Laam, Kevin, 5–7
"The Lamp of Power" (Ruskin), 85
Lanchester, John, 84–85
language
   of Christianity, 31
   gender and, 46n.17
   linguistic analysis, 40–42
   ordinary, 89
   stereotypes and, 17–18
   therapeutic redescription and, 191–99
   of Up Lit, 109–16

Lasch-Quinn, Elizabeth, 189
Latour, Bruno, 75, 76, 77, 87–88
learning, xxi, 4–8, 17–18
Leavis, F. R., 10
Lessing, Doris, 19, 186–87, 192, 195–99
"A Letter from St. Croix" (Lorde), 132, 138–39
Levy, Andrea, 7–8
Lewis. C. S., 107
Libraries Without Borders, 31
The Limits of Critique (Felski), 199
linguistic analysis, 40–42
Linguistic Inquiry and Word Count (LIWC) tool, 42n.11, 43f
Lip Glock (Scott), 58–59
literary pedagogy, 9
literary reception, 36–40
Literary Studies. *See specific topics*
Literary Studies and Human Flourishing (English), xiii–xiv
"Literary Studies and Well-Being" (workshop), 12–13
literature. *See also specific literature*
   activism and, 31
   Changing Lives Through Literature, 31
   criticism of, 9–12, 32–33, 81–83
   disability in, 155–61
   eudaimonic turns in, 143–47, 143n.1, 144n.2, 145n.3, 146n.5, 153–55
   fool-literature, 174–80
   The Fries Test for, 154–55
   geropsychology and, 174–80
   happiness and, 210–13
   hermeneutics and, 147–61
   learning from, 4–8
   literary sentimentalism, 101–2
   marginalization in, 45n.16
   in positive psychology, 1–2, 123
   psychology and, 13, 191–99
   reading, 14, 76
   reality and, 76–77, 80, 84–87, 91–95
   research on, 36–40
   reviews of, 41f–45f
   scholarship on, 2–3, 203
   self-help books and, 25
   Up Lit, 16
   utility of, 37–38, 87–91
Litvak, Joseph, 173–74

Liu, Alan, 38–39
LIWC tool. *See* Linguistic Inquiry and
    Word Count tool
Loewald, Hans, 89
Loncraine, Rebecca, 16, 105–6, 108–16
Loncraine, Trisha, 109–10
Long, Elizabeth, 37–38
longform reading, 26
Lorde, Audre, 16–17, 123–39
L'Ouverture, Toussaint, 78–79, 187–88
love, 159–60, 159n.17
Love, Heather, 186–87, 199–200
Luckhurst, Roger, 111n.6
Lynch, Deidre, 200–1

MacIntyre, Alasdair, 5–7
Marcus Aurelius, 185–87, 201–2
Marcuse, Herbert, 100
marginalization, in literature, 45n.16
Marx, Karl, 207–8
May, Teresa, 102–3
May, William F., 143n.1
MCA. *See* multiple correspondence
    analysis
McDaniel, Justin Thomas, xiv–xv
McFarland, Ella Augusta, 68
McKittrick, Katherine, 124, 124n.2
McMahon, Darrin M., xiii, 117–18
McRobbie, Angela, 10–11
Metcalfe, Anna, 116–17
methodological pluralism, 49n.20
Milner, Marion, 89
Milton, John, 5
Minima Moralia (Adorno), 20, 209–
    10, 213–18
modernity
    culture in, 83–85
    data on, 52n.23
    digital technology in, 48, 48n.19
    eclecticism in, 57–60
    happiness in, 7
    humanities in, xxi
    information in, 87–89
    novels in, 19
    Up Lit in, 100–1
Modern Painters 5 (Ruskin), 91–92
Mood Boosting Books, 29, 30
Moores, D. J., 105–6, 165–66

The Morality of Happiness (Annas), 4
Morrison, Toni, 1–2, 7–8
Moten, Fred, 138
Motherhood (Heti), 186–87, 191–
    92, 193–94
Mourning Happiness (Soni), 7
Mrs. Dalloway (Woolf), 7–8
multiple correspondence analysis
    (MCA), 47–48
Munro, Alice, 30
music, xvi, 27, 46–47, 216–17
Music and Human Flourishing
    (Celenza), xvi
My Struggle (Knausgaard), 186–87, 198

Nakamura, Lisa, 57–58
naturalistic study of reading (NSR), 38–39
Neugarten, Bernice, 165
neuroscience, 25–26, 36–37
New Criticism, 9–10
New Zealand, 113–14
NHS Wales Book Prescription
    program, 28–30
Nicomachean Ethics (Aristotle), 4–5
Nietzsche, Friedrich, 207–8, 213–14
Nilsson, Bo, 115
normativity, 13
Norton, Brian Michael, 5–7
novels
    bestsellers, 42–45, 44f–45f
    eudaimonic turns in, 155–61
    in modernity, 19
    in psychology, 29–30
    reading, 30
    reviews of, 44f–45f
    scholarship on, 5–8
    Stoicism in, 191–99
NSR. *See* naturalistic study of reading
Nussbaum, Susan, 153–56

Oatway, Charlie, 29–30
The Obstacle Is the Way (Holiday), 188
OECD. *See* Organization for Economic
    Co-operation and Development
"Of Generators and Survival" (Lorde),
    133–34, 135–36
Ohlin, Peter, xxiii
Ollivier, Michèle, 47–48

omnivore concept, 46–57
On Being Ill (Woolf), 111–12
online reading, 35, 48, 48n.19
oppression, 127–28, 130
ordinary language, 89
ordinary readers, 37–38
Organization for Economic Co-operation
    and Development (OECD), xviii–xix
*Oxford Handbook of the Positive
    Humanities*, xxii
Ozeki, Ruth, 107–8

Paradise Lost (Milton), 5
"Paranoid Reading and Reparative Reading"
    (Sedgwick), 207–12
Patterson, Orlando, 123
Pawelski, James O.
    on eudaimonia, 148n.7, 165–66
    on humanities, xvii–xviii
    on James, W., 73n.2, 92n.3
    reputation of, 146–47, 146n.5
    Up Lit and, 105–6
pedagogy, xxii–xxiii, 9, 17–18
performance, xv–xvi, 211–12
Perthes, Bill, xxiii
Peterson, Christopher, 168–71, 169f,
    170n.6, 173
Peterson, Richard, 46–48
Phelps, Elizabeth Stuart, Phelps's 43
phenomenon, 133–34
Phillips, Adam, 190–91
Phillips, Natalie, 36n.3
philosophy. *See also* hermeneutics
    of Adorno, 20
    of Aristotle, 4
    of art, 81–82
    concepts of, 12
    of criticism, 210–13
    of feminism, 196–97
    of happiness, 213–18
    history of, 1–2
    of Hume, 103
    ordinary language in, 89
    of positive psychology, xix–xx, 81
    of reading, 14–15
    scholarship and, xii–xiii, 201
    Stoicism, 4, 19, 185–89, 191–204
    values from, xii–xiii

Philosophy and Human Flourishing
    (Stuhr), xii–xiii
Philosophy as a Way of Life (Hadot), 201
Picador, Rebecca, 110
picture books, 29
Pinker, Steven, 25–26
Piper, Andrew, 38–39
Plato, 1–2
pleasure, 213–18
pleasure reading, 25–26
poetry. *See also specific poets and poetry*
    Black ecological optimism and, 130–32
    flourishing and, 66–68, 165–66
    learning from, 18
    of Lorde, 130–39
    of Rome, 4
"Poetry Is Not a Luxury" (Lorde), 130
politics, 10–11, 31, 135, 147–48, 151n.11
positive aesthetics, xxi
positive psychology
    Adorno and, 216
    aging in, 18, 164n.1
    in DS, 146–47
    education of, 2
    flourishing from, 144
    history of, 171
    literature in, 1–2, 123
    philosophy of, xix–xx, 81
    Positive Psychology Center, 36
    Positive Psychology Manifesto, 164–65
    reality in, 80–81
    scholarship on, xix–xx, 3n.2, 148n.8
    science of, 126–27
Post, Amy, 73
Post, Isaac, 73
Potkay, Adam, 5–7, 8
poverty, 69–70
power, 82–83
Price, Leah, 104
professionalism, xxi, 1–2
The Promise of Happiness (Ahmed), 7–8
Proust, Marcel, 19, 172–73, 186–87, 192–
    94, 211
Psychic Treatment of Nervous Disorders
    (Dubois), 192–93
psychology. *See also* geropsychology;
    positive psychology
    abnormal, 145–46

of aging, 18
of anxiety, 25
of beliefs, 14–15
Cognitive-behavioral therapy, 186,
    189–92, 190*f*
criticism and, 84–87
deflection, 90–91
eudaimonic turns in, xix
of flourishing, 118–19
Gestalt, 186
of incentives, 56*f*–58*f*, 57–59
of judgment, 50
literature and, 13, 191–99
novels in, 29–30
of Proust, 192–94
psychological disorders, 168–71,
    169*f*, 170n.6
reading and, 58*f*
reality in, 87–91
scholarship and, xviii–xix, 170
students of, xviii–xix
of therapeutic redescription, 199–204
"Psychology and the Good Life" (course),
    xviii–xix
Psychology of Abnormality (Peterson,
    C.), 170
Puerto Rico, 125–26
Pushkin, Alexander, 165–66

"Queer Performativity"
    (Sedgwick), 211–12
queer theory, 19–20

race, 16–17
radical pessimism, 74
Radway, Janice, 37–38
Ransom, Daniel, 67–68
reading
    activism for, 31
    critical affect and, 207–18
    data on, 56*f*
    depression and, 27–30
    eclecticism in, 49–57, 51*f*–55*f*
    gender and, 53n.25, 53n.26
    identity from, 58–60
    ideology critique and, 81
    literature, 14, 76
    longform, 26

music and, 27
in neuroscience, 25–26
novels, 30
NSR, 38–39
online, 35, 48, 48n.19
ordinary readers, 37–38
philosophy of, 14–15
pleasure, 25–26
psychology and, 58*f*
reader network map, 54–57, 55*f*
reader studies, 13
research on, 26–27, 36n.3
scholarship on, 40–46
self-help books, 30–31
taste profiles of, 47–48, 47n.18, 51*f*, 55*f*
television and, 58n.29
Up Lit, 99–103
reality
    literature and, 76–77, 80, 84–87, 91–95
    in positive psychology, 80–81
    in psychology, 87–91
    with scalability, 83–85
    therapeutic redescription and, 187–91
    Trilling on, 89
Reasons to Stay Alive (Haig), 106–7
redescription, 19
reflexive sentimentalism, 116–17
religion, xiv–xv, xx–xxi, 4–5, 31, 68–69
*Religious Studies, Theology, and Human
    Flourishing* (McDaniel), xiv–xv
reparation, 207–13
repetition, 134–39
research
    on adolescents, 26–27
    on antidepressants, 27–28
    on anxiety, 27n.1
    on children, 31
    on genres, 39–40, 51–52, 51–52n.21, 56*f*
    on Goodreads, 14, 35, 57–60
    on happiness, 25–26, 41*f*
    HHF Project and, xxii, 38–39, 38n.4
    on literature, 36–40
    methodology, 53–54n.28
    on online reading, 35
    on reading, 26–27, 36n.3
    scholarship and, xxi
    technology for, 51–52
    from UK, 53n.26

resilience, 36, 36n.2
reviews
    data from, 40n.8, 54*f*
    gender and, 52n.24
    on Goodreads, 41*f*
    of literature, 41*f*–45*f*
    of novels, 44*f*–45*f*
Rich, Adrienne, 174–75
Richard III (Shakespeare), 5–7
Ricoeur, Paul, 147–48
Robertson, Donald, 186
Rome, xx–xxi, 4, 9, 185
Rorty, Richard, 1–2, 192
Rosenfeld, Jessica, 4–5
Rowe, Hortense, 133
Rowell, Charles, 125
Ruddick, Lisa, 200–1
Ruskin, John, 15–16, 85–86, 91–95

sage writing, 85–86, 88–89, 91–95
Saint-Amour, Paul, 199
St. Croix, 123, 125, 134
Sandel, Michael, 143n.1
Santos, Laurie, xviii–xix
Sarton, May, 175
satire, 9
scalability, 83–85, 88–89
Schafer, Roy, 190–91
scholarship
    on bibliotherapy, 25–33, 27n.1
    charisma and, 32–33
    on criticism, 19–20
    data and, 36–40
    disciplines and, xx
    on eudaimonia, 117–18
    eudaimonic turns and, xxii–xxiii
    on film, 8
    on flourishing, xii–xviii, 70–75, 70n.1
    on geropsychology, 167–71
    Goodreads, 36–40
    on Grenfell Tower catastrophe, 16
    on happiness, 4–5, 7–8, 12–20
    humanities and, vii–xviii, xx–xxiii
    on literature, 2–3, 203
    on novels, 5–8
    philosophy and, xii–xiii, 201
    on positive psychology, xix–xx,
        3n.2, 148n.8

psychology and, xviii–xix, 170
    on reading, 40–46
    on reparation, 207–10
    research and, xvi
    satire in, 9
    on skepticism, 72
    surveys in, 36–37
    on therapy, 78
    on Up Lit, 16
    values in, 168–71, 169*f*, 170n.6
Schulman, Peter, xxiii
science
    cognitive, 25, 26, 36–37
    happiness and, 2–3
    humanities in, 25
    neuroscience, 25–26, 36–37
    of positive psychology, 126–27
    social sciences, xiv–xx, xxii
    of well-being studies, 59–60
Scott, D. D., 58–59
Sedgwick, Eve Kosofsky
    criticism by, 19–20, 172–74, 217–18
    on reparation, 207n.2, 207–8,
        210–13
    reputation of, 147–48, 148n.8, 200, 207–
        8, 215–16
self-help books, 25, 30–31
Seligman, Martin, xxiii, 80–81, 164–65.
    See also positive psychology
Seneca, 4, 190, 192–93, 194, 198–99
Senescence (Hall, G. S.), 171–72
sentimentalism, 101–2, 103–9, 116–
        17, 119–20
Seven Lamps of Architecture (Ruskin), 85
Sexton, Jared, 123
Shadow Land (Smith, E.), 77
Shakespeare, William, 5–7
Sharp, Christina, 124, 124n.2
Sheldon, Rebekah, 118
Shim, Yerin, xxii
Sidoti, Sarah, xxii
Signs (Lorde), 130
Sister Killjoy (Aidoo), 7–8
Sister Outsider (Lorde), 130
skepticism, 72
Skinner, B. F., 175
Skybound (Loncraine, R.), 16, 105–6, 108–16
Sloterdijk, Peter, 214–15

slurs, 153–55
Smith, Elizabeth Oakes, 77
Smith, Zadie, 187–88
social justice, 16–17
social sciences, xiv–xx, xxii
society, xxiii, 16
sociology, 46–47, 58–59
Solnit, Rebecca, 107–8
Solomon, Robert C., 105
Soni, Vivasvan, 7
Sontag, Susan, 85–86
spiritualism
    aesthetics and, 14–15
    Christianity and, 68–69
    in culture, 65–66
    flourishing and, 67–70, 75–79
    James, W., on, 70–75, 70n.1
Statistical Panic (Woodward), 171–72
STEM education, xxi
stereotypes, 17–18, 153–55, 158n.15
Sternberg, Robert J., 167, 179
Stewart, Chris, xxii
stigma, 13
Stilettos and Scoundrels (Turner), 58–59
Stoicism, 4, 19, 185–89, 191–204
Stones of Venice (Ruskin), 91
Straus, Madame, 192–93
students
    engagement of, xxi
    learning from, 17–18
    in pedagogy, xxii–xxiii
    positive aesthetics for, xxi
    of psychology, xviii–xix
Stuhr, John J., xii–xiii
Sukenick, Lynn, 196–97
Supreme Court, 147–48, 151n.11
surveys, in scholarship, 36–37
survival, 126–29, 133–34, 136–37. *See also*
    hurricanes

Tackling Life (Oatway), 29–30
taste profiles, of reading, 47–48, 47n.18,
    51*f*, 55*f*
Tay, Louis, xxii, 39
Taylor, Charles, 5–7
technology
    digital, 48, 48n.19
    of double-click communication, 87–88

for research, 51–52
for survival, 136–37
television, 58n.29
Templeton Religion Trust, xxii
Thayer, R., 66–68
theatre, xv–xvi
Theatre and Human Flourishing
    (Young), xv–xvi
Thelwall, Mike, 52–53
theology, xiv–xv. *See also* religion
therapy. *See also* psychology
    bibliotherapy, 13, 107–8
    Cognitive-behavioral, 186, 189–92, 190*f*
    scholarship on, 78
    therapeutic redescription, 185–204
Thomas, Dylan, 7–8
Three Things about Elsie (Cannon), 100–
    1, 102–3
Thug Guard (Chafer), 58–59
"Tom Fool" (Ammons), 176
Too Much Happiness (Munro), 30
Trilling, Lionel, 8, 85–86, 89–90
Troilus and Cressida (Shakespeare), 5–7
Trust Me, I'm Lying (Holiday), 188–89
Tsing, Anna Lowenhaupt, 83–84
Turner, Laina, 58–59
24 Stories of Hope (Barsby), 99–101
Tyler, Anne, 107–8

UK. *See* United Kingdom
UN. *See* United Nations
Underwood, Ted, 38–39
United Kingdom (UK)
    Australia and, 36–37
    education in, 31
    higher education in, 11
    research from, 53n.26
    society of, 16
    US and, 28, 45–46, 85
    Wales, 28–30, 109–10, 113
United Nations (UN), xviii–xix
United States (US)
    Africa and, 136
    African American criticism in, 11
    Caribbean and, 134
    Changing Lives Through
        Literature in, 31
    culture of, 27

United States (US) (*cont.*)
  disasters to, 125
  Haiti and, 78–79
  Libraries Without Borders in, 31
  New Criticism in, 9–10
  UK and, 28, 45–46, 85
University of Pennsylvania, xxii, 36
The Unlikely Pilgrimage of Harld Fry
  (Joyce), 100–1
"Untitled" (Thayer), 66–68
uplift, 105–6, 105n.2, 116–20
Up Lit
  ameliorative sentimentalism in, 103–9
  criticism of, 116–20
  James, D., on, 193
  language of, 109–16
  in modernity, 100–1
  Pawelski and, 105–6
  reading, 99–103
  scholarship on, 16
US. *See* United States
"The Uses of Anger" (Lorde), 129
Uses of Literature (Felski), 37–38
utility, of literature, 37–38, 87–91

Vaillant, George, 178
values
  from art, xv–xvi
  from history, xiii
  from literary studies, xiii–xiv
  from music, xvi
  from philosophy, xii–xiii
  from religion, xiv–xv
  in scholarship, 168–71, 169f, 170n.6
  in society, xxiii
  from visual arts, xvi–xvii
  wisdom and, 168, 169f
"The Values in Action Classification of
  Strengths" (Peterson, C.), 168–71,
  169f, 170n.6
Vaziri, Hoda, xxii
virtue, xx–xxi, 4, 5–7
visual arts, xvi–xvii
Visual Arts and Human Flourishing
  (Holo), xvi–xvii

Wales, 28–30, 109–10, 113
Walker, Alice, 124
Ward, Michaela, xxii
The Waste Land (Eliot, T. S.), 8
"weaponed woman" (Brooks), 174–75
well-being studies, 2–3, 12–13, 59–60
Well of Loneliness (Hall, R.), 7–8
Welsford, Enid, 174–75, 174n.9
West, Cornel, 1–2
"Wetter Beather" (Ammons), 176
Why Smart People Can Be So Stupid
  (Sternberg), 179
Wicked Werewolf Night (Jones), 58–59
Wilde, Oscar, 87
Williams, Raymond, 10–11, 81
Williams, William Carlos, 149–53, 155–
  56, 157
Williamson, Jennifer A., 101–2, 103–4
The Will to Believe (James, W.), 70–74
Wilson, Eric, 7–8
Winfrey, Oprah, 49–50
Winnicott, D. W., 89
Winter, Angela, 164n.1
wisdom, 166, 167–68, 169f, 170, 173
Wisdom (Sternberg), 167
The Wisdom of the Ego (Vaillant), 178
Wittgenstein, Ludwig, 89
women, 127–28, 129, 134–39. *See also*
  feminism
Woodward, Kathleen, 171–72, 173
Woolf, Virginia, 7–8, 111–12, 115, 116–17
Wordsworth, William, 165–66
"The Work of Iron" (Ruskin), 92–95
workshops, 12–13
World Happiness Report (UN), xviii–xix
World War II, 9–10
Wright, David, 48
writing, 15–16, 85–86, 88–89, 91–95. *See*
  also specific topics
Wynter, Sylvia, 124

The Year of Magical Thinking (Didion), 107
Young, Harvey, xv–xvi

Zhang, Dora, 186–87, 203–4

Printed in the USA/Agawam, MA
December 12, 2022

802793.069